Workgroup Computing

Workflow, Groupware, and Messaging

Alan R. Simon
and William Marion

McGraw-Hill
New York San Francisco Washington, D.C. Auckland Bogotá
Caracas Lisbon London Madrid Mexico City Milan
Montreal New Delhi San Juan Singapore
Sydney Tokyo Toronto

McGraw-Hill

*A Division of The **McGraw-Hill** Companies*

pbk 1 2 3 4 5 6 7 8 9 DOC/DOC 9 0 0 9 8 7 6

Library of Congress Cataloging-in-Publication Data

Simon, Alan R.

Workgroup computing : workflow, groupware, and messaging / by Alan R. Simon and William Marion.

p. cm.

Includes index.

ISBN 0-07-057628-9 (pbk.)

1. Work groups—Data processing. 2. Groupware (Computer software)

I. Marion, William. II. Title

HD66.2.S56 1996

658.4'02'0285—dc20 95-5918

CIP

McGraw-Hill books are available at special quantity discounts to use as premiums and sales promotions, or for use in corporate training programs. For more information, please write to the Director of Special Sales, McGraw-Hill, 11 West 19th Street, New York, NY 10011. Or contact your local bookstore.

Acquisitions editor: John Wyzalek

Editorial team: Laura J. Bader, Book Editor

Susan W. Kagey, Managing Editor

Lori Flaherty, Executive Editor

Production team: Katherine G. Brown, Director

Rhonda E. Baker, Desktop Operator

Lorie L. White, Proofreading

Jennifer M. Secula, Indexer

Design team: Jaclyn J. Boone, Designer

Katherine Lukaszewicz, Associate Designer

GEN1

0576289

Contents

Preface

The workgroup computing revolution continues on, and, no doubt about it, it's an ever-changing one.

From the time we began working on this book, many major events in this computing realm have occurred, each of which significantly changed the workgroup computing landscape. IBM purchased Lotus; the workflow imaging market has seen a number of mergers and acquisitions; the Internet and the World Wide Web—particularly when instantiated as "Intranet" technologies and architectures—are now considered viable alternatives in the workflow and groupware domains for organizations.

The list goes on and on. Despite significant changes in this market and with the technologies, our original purpose in writing this book has stood up very nicely. Specifically, we wanted to focus on the *business* and *general technology* side of workgroup computing, using specific product implementations as *examples* (in contrast with providing detailed documentation of the inner workings and user interfaces of products in the many realms of workgroup computing). Even in 1993, when we began our research, it was evident that many changes would come to every aspect of this area—not only the technologies and the products, but even the basic approaches to workgroup computing.

What remains constant, however, are the lessons we emphasize in the opening chapters of this book:

- Each area of workgroup computing—workflow-enabled applications, the many realms of groupware, etc.—is as much about *business process* and *organizational culture* as it is about technology. That is, the lessons learned in the information technology (IT) world, particularly in the last 10 to 15 years, indicate that we can't simply "throw technology at a problem and fix it," which is especially applicable to workgroup computing.

- Workgroup computing is as much about the underlying technologies—distributed computing architectures, middleware, etc.—as it is about the layers on top of the distributed computing infrastructure. The most robust, full-functioned, flexible architecture imaginable requires the supporting mechanisms beneath it, and a thorough understanding of every level of these areas is important.

Finally, we emphasize that workgroup computing is certainly an area to watch over the next few years. The changes will still be coming, have no doubt, but by building a thorough understanding of not only the technology, but also the organizational and process issues associated with this domain, you will be on your way to taking advantage of the workgroup computing revolution.

Alan Simon

Bill Marion

Part 1

Background

1

Introduction to workgroup computing

Workgroup computing . . . collaborative computing . . . whichever term you choose, this area will be among those having the greatest impact on computing environments through the rest of the 1990s and into the next millennium.

In this introductory chapter we will discuss the basics behind workgroup computing, our goal being to set the stage for the rest of the chapters in this book. Among other subjects, we'll look at

- The different types of workgroup computing, such as workflow-enabled applications and groupware
- The background and evolution of workgroup computing
- The benefits of workgroup computing to organizations that deploy these technologies

Definitions

Like many "movement" terms in the information technology realm (e.g., *open systems, enterprise computing,* etc.), workgroup computing lacks a consistent, formal definition. In many cases, its definition is often confused with that of its two major components (workflow and groupware). For purposes of the discussion throughout this book, we'll provide definitions for these terms and an introductory explanation.

Workgroup computing permits the sharing of information among (1) individual users, and (2) those that can be categorized as belonging to a "workgroup." A workgroup (Fig. 1-1) may be

- All members of the accounting department in the Seattle location of a multinational corporation
- All members of both the sales and marketing departments in all New England offices of a computer systems manufacturer
- All persons anywhere in the world who need data about their employer's new product offerings before the products come to market, regardless of their respective job functions, formal organizations, geographical locations, etc.

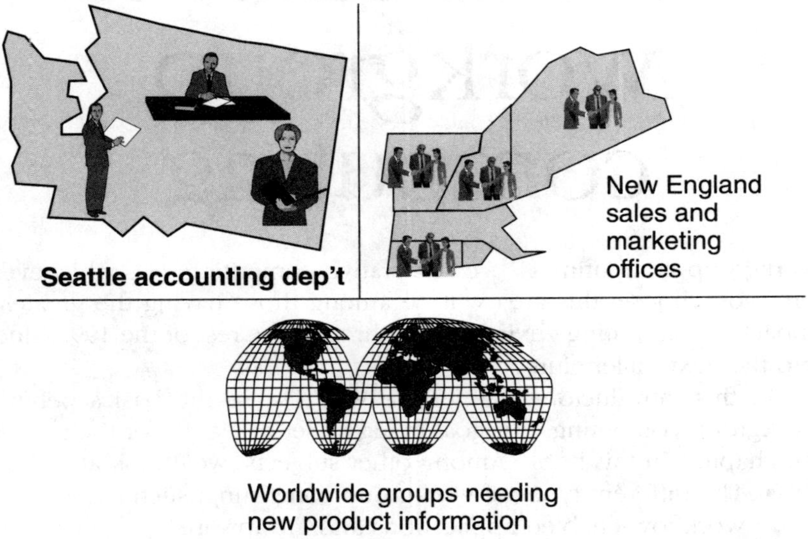

1-1 *Examples of workgroup computing.*

In general, then, a workgroup is little more than people who—by definition—need to work together to accomplish some task or for the regular performance of their jobs. Workgroup computing is simply a computing style that supports the workgroup paradigm in as efficient a manner as possible.

There should be little that is revolutionary, or even eyebrow-raising, about workgroup computing. For many years practitioners of all types—systems analysts, strategic planners, application and system architects, etc.—have preached the benefits of sharing information among users in an automated, timely manner. Anyone who has been in corporate or government life for any amount of time, however, is well aware of a simple fact of life: despite its conceptual simplicity and obvious benefits, workgroup computing has traditionally been extremely difficult to achieve, as we'll discuss in the next section.

Workflow technology is often confused with "workgroup computing" (or at least their commonly used definitions tend to overlap), most probably because both terms begin with the word *work*. While workgroup computing is more of an all-encompassing "let's all work together" feel-good category, workflow is a specific technology area in which information is routed among users and applications in a formalized manner according to established processes. As we'll discuss in Chapter 4, these processes may be predefined and never-varying, or they may be rule-based and subject to change. Ideally, the workflow control mechanisms are handled in the middleware component of the application and system architecture by formal workflow management engines rather than having the workflow rules coded into the application logic. In Chapter 3, we'll discuss middleware and emerging distributed system architectures as part of our coverage of enabling technologies. A simple workflow example is shown in Fig. 1-2.

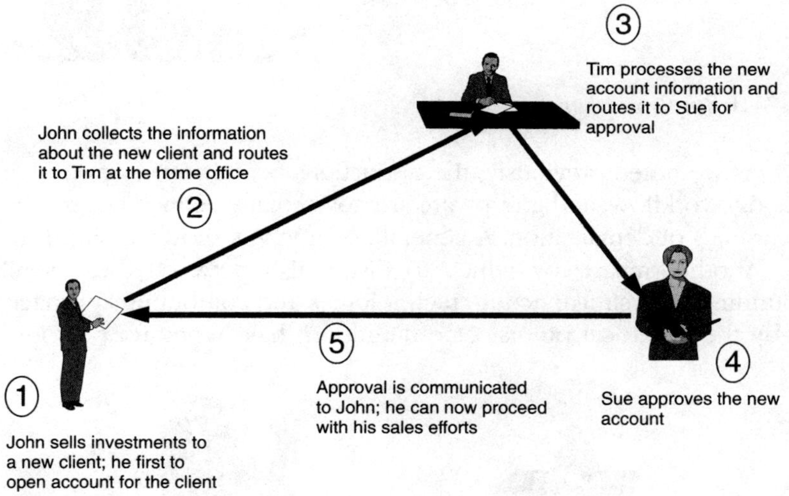

1-2 *A simple workflow example.*

Finally, groupware is a special category of software (and increasingly, hardware) that permits collaborative efforts such as

- Two or more people working together, simultaneously, on a single document even though they are located in different cities
- Real-time video-conferencing with real-time exchange of data through file transfers, faxes, and other means
- "Electronic brainstorming" systems in which anonymous discussions and conferences can be held using bulletin board and similar paradigms

and similar working-together paradigms. Figure 1-3 illustrates the groupware approach.

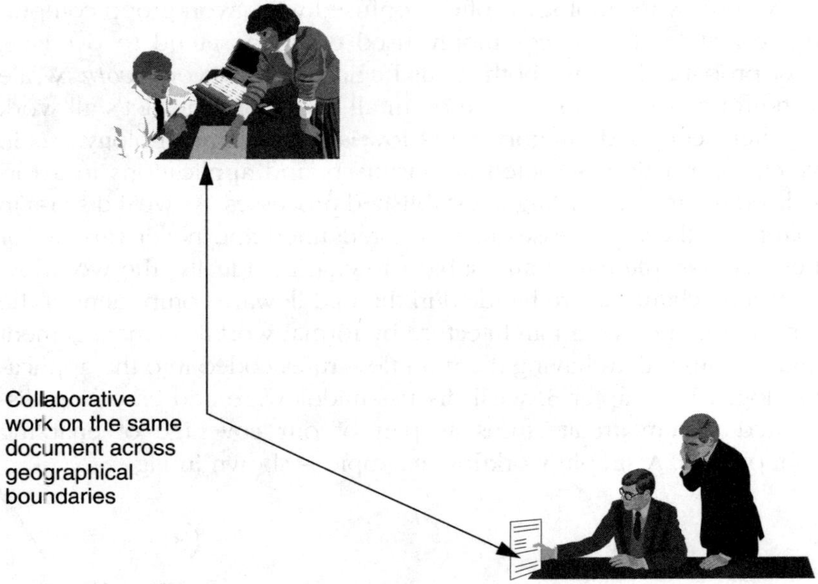

1-3 *A simple workgroup example.*

As we noted previously, the distinctions between workgroup computing, workflow, and groupware are not formally defined nor are there clear lines of demarcation. A general taxonomy is shown in Fig. 1-4.

Another means by which to distinguish between these similar sounding (and similar acting) technologies and computing approaches is by the key focal points. One definition[1] has "workgroup products

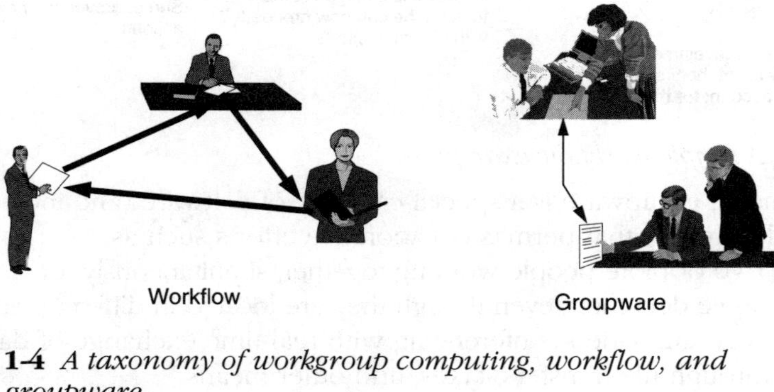

1-4 *A taxonomy of workgroup computing, workflow, and groupware.*

1 T. Koulopoulos, "The 'New Workflow Software,'" in "The CW Guide to Workflow," Computerworld, February 28, 1994, p. 100.

let[ting] workgroups or individuals transfer and share information with one another. The key ingredient is information." Alternatively, "in a workflow application, the process knowledge that applies to the information is also managed, transferred, and routed. The key ingredient is the process."

The challenge of workgroup computing

At first glance, the premise of workgroup computing seems relatively easy to implement. Since

- The benefits of workgroup computing are undeniable
- Distributed computing technology has come a long way in terms of usability to meet real-world application needs
- Workgroup computing products of all types are starting to appear, and in some cases, mature

then it stands to reason that nearly all applications being developed today (that is, the mid-1990s) should have some degree of a workgroup computing component to them. That degree may vary from simple electronic mail communications among group members and with members of other groups (or other companies), or it may be a full-blown workflow infrastructure based around middleware building blocks and the other facets that will be discussed throughout this book.

Why, then, is workgroup computing so difficult to implement correctly? There are a number of challenges facing those whose mission it is to introduce or grow workgroup computing technology within an organization. These challenges include

1 Resistance in the organizational culture: As we will discuss in Chapter 2, workgroup computing is about change. While the 1990s have certainly been the decade of change within corporate America (and, indeed, in the business communities around the world) with the emphasis on business process reengineering (BPR) and related efforts, there is hardly a uniform consent about the "goodness" of workgroup as an enabling technology of this change.

This resistance comes from all corporate ranks, top to bottom, though in different forms depending on various human factors. Both workflow technology and groupware go a long way toward enabling a collaborative workplace,[2] one that em-

2 As discussed in Chapter 2, the book Transforming the Way We Work: The Power of the Collaborative Workplace, E. M. Marshall, American Management Association, 1995, discusses the philosophy and techniques behind the collaborative workplace.

powers organizational workers at all levels to get the job done regardless of corporate cultures, autocratic authority lines, and similar constraining facets that often hamper organizational efficiency and effectiveness.

But can one really believe that the holders of corporate power, those who over the past 20 or 25 years (more in some cases, less in others) have clawed and fought their way to the top of their organizations, worked in (and in many cases, had their personal lives enveloped by) a given corporate power structure, will willingly abdicate power and knowledge to their subordinates? As we'll discuss in Chapter 2, cultural change among the top managerial ranks is often difficult despite pronouncements about "being receptive to change" and "understanding the need to reinvent ourselves." In that context, workgroup computing is often looked upon as a dangerous tool—an enabling technology that empowers workers to a degree uncomfortable to their superiors.

It's not only at the lower corporate echelons that workgroup computing meets cultural resistance. Many lower-ranking jobs are built around the (usually) efficient management of thousands, often millions, of documents and forms. Much of workgroup computing is designed not only to streamline processes and improve communications and cooperability among workers but also to reduce the amount of physical paper that is distributed and managed within an organization. Document management, electronic mail, automated workflow, all should cause a streamlining of the paper-pushing processes.

But how about those workers whose jobs exist solely to manage that mountain of perpetual paperwork? With half a decade worth of corporate cutbacks (actually, more like 15 years, dating back to the recession of the early 1980s), can one really expect those whose jobs may very well be eliminated by the introduction of workgroup computing to embrace such technology?

Consider this exchange (paraphrased) between Lt. Colonel Henry Blake and Corporal Radar O'Reilly on an old episode of M*A*S*H:

Col. Blake: "What am I signing now, Radar?"

Radar: "This is the form to indicate that we need the forms to order more forms, Sir."

Then think of all the TV comedy segments built around the paperwork shuffle to which most of us have been exposed at some point, whether in the context of our jobs or as a customer:

The pink copy goes to Purchasing but only after you take the yellow copy to Finance for a signature on line 31, and then you have to drop the yellow copy off in Accounting and pick up the green 5 × 7 card to accompany the pink copy to Purchasing. Then you take those copies, plus the light blue one—not the darker light blue one, but the lighter blue one—to . . ."

Who's on first, again?

The point is simply this—the inefficiencies in business processes may be incredibly obvious as to be the butt of jokes inside a company, but the age-old "the computer will take my job" worries seem to have found a final battleground in the workgroup computing area—all of which leads to incredible cultural resistance that has nothing to do with the underlying technology of workgroup computing.

2 Technology that is still maturing: With respect to the aforementioned workgroup computing technology, there quite simply is a long way to go for much of the technology required for many of the facets of workgroup computing to achieve their full potential. This is not only true in the arena that comprises the various workgroup computing services (i.e., workflow design and automation, real-time collaborative work sessions, etc.), but in much of the underlying base technology (as we will discuss in Chapter 3).

For example, the computer industry is still grappling with exactly what the phrase *open systems* means even as some industry analysts proclaim that the days of open systems are dwindling. Client/server computing, a model that took hold in the mid- to late 1980s with the desktop computing and local area network (LAN) boom, has recently been proclaimed (again by some industry analysts) to have been a "failure" in its first incarnations, and it's only now with new and improved three-tier architectures (we'll discuss these in Chapter 3) and middleware that the real client/server boom can begin. Which is fine; yet middleware technology in general is relatively young, some facets such as distributed transaction processing and directory services—not to mention the management of distributed systems and networks—are still going through growing pains. In short, then, the concepts of workgroup computing might be solidifying, but all the pieces aren't quite in place yet to the degree needed to make workgroup computing a "second nature effort."

3 Lack of consensus: Is workgroup computing necessary? How valuable is it? Do organizations really perform more efficiently and effectively when workflow processes are automated? Does electronic conferencing really enable discussions that are "personality neutral," that is, aren't overshadowed by one or two individuals using strong personalities (or sometimes bullying tactics) to bring others around to their way of thinking, whether or not they are correct?

The answers to the previous questions are in dispute, and the evidence is just now beginning to trickle in from the first generation of workgroup computing implementations. One could argue that workgroup computing technology should be a valuable asset to any organization. But as with many other areas of information technology and, in general, business practices, there is always a question as to whether the assumptions will be proven correct.

Given that the investment required to enable workgroup computing in an organization—the cost of the software, possibly additional hardware, training, support, and all of the other "hidden" costs—often cause budget-conscious managers to question the payback and return on investment from implementing the technology.

4 The need for an architectural basis: Finally, to correctly implement workgroup computing there must be an architectural foundation. That is, there must be an infrastructure of distributed computing services that enables the tying together of user's PCs and/or workstations, the organizational and departmental servers, possibly the data center mainframe and other computing assets, most or all of the applications software, and everything else that needs to be part of the workgroup computing environment. Workgroup computing must not be a haphazard jumble of interprocess communications—"put something in the database so it can be read later by somebody else"—or similar kludged-together interfaces. Such an environment, one without any architectural foundation, will quickly fail (if it is even implemented at all before being overcome and undone by its inefficiencies and problems).

Summary

In this chapter we've taken a brief, "setting the stage" look at the foundations of workgroup computing. As was discussed in the previous section, one of the most important issues isn't so much the technology involved but the answer to the question of "why should we care about this in the first place?" In Chapter 2, we'll answer that question in the context of examining corporate change toward a collaborative work model, and why workgroup computing should be an important part of both the change process and the end result.

2

The reason for workgroup computing

The collaborative workplace

Why workflow? Why groupware? What is the real value of these classes of workgroup computing technologies (or, more appropriately, is there any real value)?

The answer, in our opinion, to the previous "why" questions is simply this: all of the facets and individual technology areas of workgroup computing (i.e., workflow automation, electronic mail, document management, electronic conferencing, etc.) are oriented primarily toward corporate efficiency in a model that encourages a collaborative workplace. That is, there are two fundamental premises at work here:

1 The collaborative workplace is the "correct" model to which most businesses should be migrating, and

2 Workgroup computing is potentially the key set of technologies by which the collaborate workplace can be truly and permanently enabled.

We say "potentially" in the previous paragraph because, as noted in Chapter 1, there are often many corporate cultural barriers to the successful implementation of workgroup technologies. It is our view that the previous two points are actually part of an iterative, incremental movement away from organizational and corporate inefficiencies and ineffectiveness toward a model that can enable success and survival in the years to come. Cultural change doesn't happen overnight, nor does the infusion of technologies designed to facilitate that cultural change. Both take time, and the value of both facets needs to be embraced by those whose jobs and careers will be affected by the change.

In this chapter we'll look at the first of the above points—the collaborative workplace as the model toward which business change should evolve. Too often computer-related books (especially those dealing with emerging technologies) don't do an adequate job of examining the "whys," as in "why is this important, technological merits aside?" We will attempt in this book to not be caught up in this shortsightedness, and with that we present our discussion with respect to the collaborative workplace.

The material in this chapter is referenced from the book *Transforming the Way We Work: The Power of the Collaborative Workplace*[1] by Dr. Edward M. Marshall, and we strongly recommend this book (we also recommend it to anyone interested in the subject of corporate change).

Reengineering . . . but to what?

Most readers are aware of the "business process reengineering craze" that has taken hold throughout most of this decade. Coupled with the recession at the beginning of the 1990s, hardly a single corporation has not made some effort to "reengineer itself" and develop new—and, of course, better—business processes to that end.

The merits of business process reengineering (BPR) can be debated, though most would argue that a business that does not evolve and change as necessary will eventually face hard times. The successes, or lack thereof, of 1990s-era BPR will be debated for years to come. Advocates would argue that at worst, BPR exposes the inefficiencies in corporate processes, and even if the reengineering doesn't "take" immediately, the weaknesses are subject to subsequent action. In the best case though, inefficient processes are eliminated, workflows are altered to suit the new missions of the corporation, and costs are, in many cases, dramatically reduced.

Others claim that BPR has been little more than a boondoggle for management consultants, a means by which weak managers can use outside resources to do the job they themselves should be doing,

1 E. M. Marshall, *Transforming the Way We Work: The Power of the Collaborative Workplace* (New York: American Management Association, 1995).

and, in general, has had a spotty success/failure record across the board, at least in the initial attempts.

Our point is not to take either side but simply to echo the "change is necessary for survival" argument. Whether the techniques of BPR are correct or not, or whether or not they have (to date) been implemented correctly or not, is an argument we'll leave to the management and business school researchers.

More pertinent to the subject of this book is the answer to the question: If we accept that change is necessary and good, what is the target of that change? We believe, as Dr. Edward Marshall proposes in his book, that there is a fundamental shift from a hierarchy-based organizational culture toward a culture in which collaboration—new models of working together—will be

- A totally new manner in the way people will work together rather than simply a program or technique (or, as we would add, a fad)
- An entirely new work ethic; that is, a recognition that work is accomplished through people, that people want and need to be valued, and that change toward this model is highly desirable
- A common denominator for relationships, in that the collaborative nature of work processes fosters trust-based relationships that can only be beneficial to the organization
- A decision-making framework. As we noted in Chapter 1, one of the goals of workgroup computing is to reduce the likelihood of decisions being made on the basis of personalities and power, but there is still a question as to the effectiveness of the technology to enable that. In general, there is a much stronger likelihood of personalities and power being neutralized when the underlying culture supports collaborative efforts; in effect, the marriage of culture and technology is crucial to success in this area.
- A set of methods and tools that are designed to foster the alignment of the workforce toward achieving high performance in their work processes

Marshall argues that there are demonstrable, significant benefits from the implementation of collaborative work models, including

- A move toward internal collaboration with the goal of competing externally (we presume the focus on "competing externally" is in contrast to internal competition or, as most of us know it, the focus on succeeding at the corporate politics game rather than achieving anything of value); workforce energy is directed toward satisfying customers rather than engaging in internal conflicts and battles

- A faster, higher-quality, and customer-driven decision-making model
- Decision-making based on principle instead of power or personality, with the result being a higher degree of buy-in from those involved and a greater impact as a result of the decisions made
- A reduction in cycle time and elimination of nonvalue-adding work (one might recognize this as one of the stated goals of many BPR methodologies)
- A doubling of workforce productivity capacity
- Highly successful strategic alliances
- Greatly increased returns on investment
- Greatly increased spans of control (e.g., less overhead-laden supervision and management needed for the workforce)
- An infusion of responsibility and accountability into the workforce
- Reductions in conflict
- Collaborative mergers and alliances, resulting from common goals among the workforce population
- Change is viewed as "good" instead of ominously
- The organization becomes self-sufficient toward the goal of sustaining the ongoing development of the company

In short, the benefits of a properly implemented collaborative workplace can be dramatic, especially in an intensively competitive global marketplace.

Establishing a collaborative work ethic

Most readers have been involved to some degree in organizational and corporate politics—environments where the work at hand takes a back seat to climbing the managerial power structure, where input from the lower-ranking echelons is summarily ignored regardless of the merits, and, when the failure of efforts is finally heeded, the cleanup processes consist of a frenzied set of cover-your-butt (or a more colorful term) actions on the part of those culpable, including layoffs, hand-wringing, the forming of committees to make sure that the same mistakes don't happen again, and so on.

Our purpose is not to examine why certain organizational structures are prone to failure or, at best, mediocrity, but rather to emphasize the merits of collaborative models, including the establishment of a collaborative work ethic. It is arguable that the management of a company or organization can make all the pronouncements it wishes about establishing newly redesigned collaborative processes, how everyone in the organization can "make things happen," and so on, but without instituting an underlying work ethic that is firmly grounded in these attributes, the words tend to be little more than empty slogans. Additionally, the workgroup computing technology that should be enabling these collaborative models will become little more than a highly efficient means for the workforce to mock the goings-on at their company (e.g., e-mailing "Can you believe how idiotic management is?" messages across groups, posting "This just isn't the same company I joined five years ago; look how they've ruined it" messages in electronic conferences, etc.).

Dr. Marshall notes that there are six fundamental assumptions about workforce ethics and culture that are closely related to fundamental assumptions about human behavior, including (we've added our own commentary to these points)

1. The recognition that work is done through people, regardless of the simplicity of the work processes, the supporting technology, and similar facets.
2. The successful business values its people. The "expendable assets" or "interchangeable cogs" approach to employee relationships rarely works, nor does freezing out those members who are "in the trenches" from participating in critical business decisions.
3. The workforce owns successful change. The workforce are the people who are affected by change and to exclude them from the change process or to dictate changes to them only serves to invite sabotage and eventual failure.
4. It is essential that there be a shared perception of reality. Instituting change or facilitating collaborative processes does little when "they're not all on the same page of the playbook."
5. There is a bottom-line value to an organizational culture. The phrase "organizational culture" (or "corporate culture") is not just some remnant from a Management 301 or Organizational Behavior 502 course you (or your boss) attended in college, but a real thing. A great deal of the intangible strategic assets that an organization possesses begin with the culture, the adherence to certain norms of behavior, and an enthusiasm and passion for the work at hand. Absent this, "It's not an adventure, it's just a job" (our apologies to the U.S. Navy!).
6. Integrity begins at the top. Most of us have been in settings where the words coming down from top management have

> little bearing on the realities of what's going on, or there is an incredible arrogance with respect to their views about the general workforce population and the business as a whole. How can people be expected to give their all, to cooperatively work for the benefit of the organization, if there is a disguised scorn toward them on the part of those who control their professional destinies? Answer: they probably can't.

Quite possibly at this point, some readers might be digesting the discussion so far in this chapter with a high degree of skepticism. "Sounds like utopian, socialist, mumbo-jumbo" might be the thought of someone who has been firmly grounded in autocratic managerial and leadership principles. We can only point to the evidence coming forth from all corners of American and, increasingly, global business over the past decade: organizations that flaunt autocratic cultures and are openly scornful of their workforce population tend to have a much harder time getting over the inevitable bumps and challenges confronting them. The company that

- Annually announces massive layoffs
- Faces dwindling market share and continuous product introduction delays
- Has a high failure rate in the deployment of new information management technologies
- Repeatedly reorganizes to the tune of "we think we've got it right this time"

and, in general, seems to be having tremendous difficulty adapting to change is very likely to be failing miserably at effectively utilizing the assets of its workforce.

Leadership in the collaborative workplace

Both of the authors of this book are former U.S. Air Force officers [in fact, we attended college together at Arizona State University in the late 1970s and were in the Reserve Officer Training Corps (ROTC) program at the same time]. The fundamental principles that we came away with from our particular ROTC leadership and management training are that leadership is something that rotates among qualified individuals according to the needs of the moment, often has little to do with formal lines of authority, and, in general, is something that is dynamic. Unlike the autocratic, hierarchical work culture to which most of us have been exposed at one time or another, the focus during our time in college was increasing levels of responsibility being granted to individuals as their experience levels and knowledge increase (but that the mantles of leadership would rotate frequently).

Those familiar with the military structure of ranks and "absolute authority" might view the above statement with skepticism, and indeed the "real-world" military is usually grounded in a rigid, hierarchical structure with single-point leadership within an organization. Paradoxically, though, our training—both during the normal school year and during the four-week formal training we attended the summer before our junior year—was firmly grounded in a model of rotational, situational leadership.

For example, the four-week encampment we attended at an Air Force base featured a model where leadership roles rotated every three or four days, where individuals were encouraged to step to the forefront in ways totally undefined by any temporary formal rank hierarchy, and all of our efforts were focused on team success (e.g., that of our "flight" of 20 or so members) rather than individual glorification. For one three- or four-day period an individual might be the Group Commander, or the chief cadet among the entire encampment, responsible for the actions and successes (or failures) of hundreds of other individuals. Yet, at the end of that brief period, he or she was back to being a "plain old cadet," waiting in the wings for the next position to which he or she would be assigned. In effect, we learned that leadership was a temporary situation and that decisions should be made carefully, for we would have to live with the consequences once we were returned to the rank and file.

We were each able to carry this model with us into our various roles as Air Force officers and later into civilian life, and indeed we both have been fortunate to have been involved in settings where collaborative practices and collaborative leadership have been followed.

In the context of the collaborative workplace, then, what exactly is "collaborative leadership?" Dr. Marshall notes that in the collaborative workplace leadership is dynamic and multifaceted, including

- The strategic leadership team (SLT), or the entity that provides overall strategic direction and guidance for a company, department, or unit
- The functional team, or a standing group that has a designated functional responsibility in the context of the SLT; these tend to be clustered by geography or task into manageable units

- The project team, or a temporary grouping that may last from several days to a year or longer
- The cross-functional team, which may be a temporary or permanent team of people that comes together across boundaries to focus on areas of concern to the organization as a whole

In Marshall's collaborative workplace model, the leader isn't so much a "boss" as

- A sponsor, or someone who "makes sure the resources are there" and the processes are put in place so the job can be done by the team members
- A facilitator, or someone who makes sure that all meetings, team dynamics, and interpersonal relationships function effectively and who guards the integrity of the team process
- A coach, or someone in a supporting role to provide guidance to the team members
- A change agent (or catalyst), or someone who is charged with holding individuals responsible for their actions, to make "unpopular" observations, and to enable breakthroughs wherever possible
- A healer, or someone to mediate disputes and put things back in order
- A member, or someone who doesn't stand aloof above the other members of the team but who actively participates, who has his or her own responsibilities, and who abides by the rules he or she sets for others
- A manager or administrator, someone who takes care of the necessary administrative tasks

In short, the leader in a collaborative environment functions very differently (and—hopefully—more effectively) than one from an autocratic setting. In some instances, he or she will be filling one or more roles, while at the same time it is likely that he or she will be a "regular old team member" in other settings. In short, "The Boss" as the model of leadership is an ineffective, ill-advised model to follow.

Jumping once again back into the workgroup computing area, it is important that the leaders in such a setting recognize the facets of leadership, the differences in leadership in an autocratic setting, and so on. Leaders should encourage—not tolerate—the use of conferencing systems for honest, thought-provoking discussions about the merits (or lack thereof) of the direction of the organization. E-mail should be used for rapid-fire notification of problems that one encounters. Automated workflow processes should be welcomed as a means to ensure that things don't fall through the cracks, rather than looking on workflow automation as a means of others intruding into one's territorial "kingdom."

The strategic business alignment

Dr. Marshall devotes a chapter to the subject of mobilizing the workforce to build value, refocus the company's direction, and break the crisis cycle, all through a process he terms the "Strategic Alignment Method." We won't delve into this process in detail, but rather will make several observations of note:

1. Much of the strategic alignment method deals with items similar to both the BPR and information architecture worlds. Specifically, there is a need to articulate an organizational vision [where we are today, where we want to go and at what points, what our mission(s) should be, etc.].
2. With respect to observation 1, one of the steps Dr. Marshall recommends is that the mission statement be drafted by the team members "more or less off the top of their heads. They use a blank-sheet process to take a first crack at defining what the company is all about." We would point out that such a process, together with the accompanying discussion, challenging of ideas, etc., is a perfect area to which workgroup computing technologies (specifically, electronic conferencing, exchanging of strategic planning documents for comment and markup, etc.) can be adapted.
3. Dr. Marshall notes that the action plan—the steps that have to be taken by all organizations involved (e.g., product development, sales, marketing, finance, etc.)—must be called out. We again note that workgroup technology is ideally suited to facilitating and adding value and efficiency to this cross-organizational process and the required consensus building within a collaborative organization.

Collaborative teams

Earlier we discussed the different types of teams that a collaborative workplace model would have (in the context of discussing the different faces of leadership under such a model). Dr. Marshall points out that a collaborative team "will generate a number of governance documents during its life span," and that those documents "represent the identity of the team and provide a reminder as to what was agreed." Specifically, documents will be developed that deal with the people and the organizational culture, the business and its customers, and the business process.

We would contend that the document management facet of workgroup computing, together with electronic conferencing through which concepts and ideas can be challenged and reexamined as necessary, are ideally suited to supporting such a model. By making such documents readily available to all appropriate personnel and encouraging feedback as necessary, the collaborative process can become institutionalized, rather than being yet another area that is explored and eventually discarded in favor of the status quo.

Change

Dr. Marshall argues that change—via the collaborative method—is guided by a number of key assumptions, including

- Workforce involvement. Change is implemented by the workforce, not the leaders, and therefore the workforce must be involved in all aspects from strategic alignment to the actual implementation.
- Modeling the process after a circle, rather than a pyramid. Marshall makes observations about the relative "structural" merits of a circle versus a pyramid (equality and common purpose, distribution of pressure against one side, geometric "strength"), but his point is well taken that "circular" collaboration—as contrasted with hierarchical mandates—tend to be a far more effective model for implementing change.
- Change must be comprehensive. All aspects—the customers, the culture, the work relationships, the business strategy, and so on—must be considered when facilitating and implementing change.
- Using behavioral change (e.g., the executives really participating in collaborative decision-making) to validate that the cultural change has occurred.
- Having a results-driven plan of action to validate that "things are working right."
- Doing "real work in real time," to ensure that ongoing work and customer relations don't falter during the change process.

Dr. Marshall describes the collaborative method, so we won't go into detail here other than to note once again that most of the facets, from completing the team formation process to creating and sustaining realistic expectations to announcing the detailed change process, can be greatly aided by workgroup computing tools and technology.

The limitations of workgroup computing technology

We make a final observation with respect to the limitations of workgroup computing technology in the context of the collaborative business organization. Dr. Marshall notes that "it is not advisable to use either E-mail or voice-mail to resolve an interpersonal dispute," and he cites an anecdote of participants in a video conferencing situation hitting the mute button because they felt excluded from the mainstream conversation. As we noted in Chapter 1, workgroup computing—both workflow technology and those sets of services classified under "groupware"—are not an answer in themselves, but rather are productivity tools through which "correct" business models can be enhanced and more productively deployed than without such facilities. Workgroup computing facilities should not be viewed, as pointed out in a recent *Forbes* ASAP article, as "The Field of Dreams:" something that once built will be openly embraced by all organizational participants.[2] The author of the article cites an example at a large oil company where "collaborative tools like [Lotus] Notes depend on maximum penetration . . . at least 30 different small-business units have Notes licenses, but [the manager of end-user computing tools] cannot mandate its use. "The problem, he explains, is that "we're buried in a hierarchy," and that he doesn't have the authority to tell the business units what to do and even if he did, "it wouldn't work anyway."

Later in the same article another anecdote is related of a $15 million groupware rollout at a $100 billion Canadian bank, where "resistance fighters tried to derail the project in the bank's Chicago offices." In this case, the "resistance fighters" were primarily from the secretarial and clerical ranks, those whose jobs depended on managing large volumes of paper and documents (recall our discussion in Chapter 1 with respect to this type of situation).

Finally, we note that in the same Chicago-based situation, the following observation was made: "Access to information was a major source of power. . . . Groupware is knocking down a tremendous number of barriers to information. People perceive that as a loss of power."

With that, it should be obvious that workgroup computing technology by itself is little more than another set of software, processes, and technologies systems managers need to be concerned about supporting. As we noted at the outset of this chapter, the potential is there for groupware and workflow technology to have a tremendous impact on organizations that are serious about transforming them-

2 G. Rifkin, "A Skeptic's Guide to Groupware," *Forbes*, June 1995, p. 76.

selves into a collaborative-type structure, both during the transformation process itself and following the successful transitioning. Without both sides of the equation—the business structure and processes, and the supporting technology—the whole exercise falls short.

Summary

It is our contention that workgroup computing and the underlying corporate and organization processes it supports should be aligned. That is, implementation of workgroup technology in a highly autocratic, hierarchical environment will likely have little benefit other than to provide the workforce with a set of tools such as e-mail and conferencing through which marginal productivity gains can be achieved, but nothing approaching radical business process transformation.

The final word in this chapter with respect to the previous paragraph is that Dr. Marshall cautions that collaborative approaches are "not for everyone," that there appears to be a common denominator in environments where senior management simply doesn't accept that collaboration is the way in which they want their organization to evolve[3] (refer back to our discussion in Chapter 1 with respect to cultural resistance to workflow computing). The lack of senior-level commitment with respect to change in this direction is, in our opinion, likely to overshadow any grass-roots effort at instituting either the collaborative processes and infrastructure or the technology (specifically, workgroup computing) needed to support and institutionalize it.

Thus we once again emphasize the need to understand the relationship between the business models for which workgroup computing will work best and the technology itself. Too often complaints are heard that "we installed e-mail for the entire company yet all the workforce uses it for is to send around nonwork material that they download from the Internet." If, indeed, that is the case, it is hardly the fault of the workgroup computing technologies, but rather the corporate culture into which those technologies have been introduced. If there is a realization among the workforce that extensive use of collaborative workgroup technologies may very well end up "squashed" by an autocratic manager then a "why the heck bother?" attitude will likely reign, regardless of the tools they've been given.

3 Marshall, *Transforming the Way We Work*, pp. 6–7.

3

Enabling technologies

In the larger scope, workflow and groupware technologies might be viewed simply as a set of services through which certain functions and roles (specifically, those dealing with workgroups) are implemented. In later chapters we'll discuss each of these sets of technologies in more detail.

Before that point, however, it's important to understand the underlying technologies that, in effect, enable those workgroup computing services to be realized. In this chapter we briefly discuss these enabling technologies, including

- Distributed computing principles and standards
- Networking and communications
- Client/server technology, including emerging models
- Middleware
- Data management and data warehousing
- Transaction processing

Each of the above subjects is discussed briefly, and references are provided for further information.

Distributed computing

In general, there is little about workgroup computing that is inherently distributed, that is, it must be implemented on distributed platforms. Indeed, the earliest versions of groupware computing products (e-mail and single-machine conferencing systems) were centralized in nature. Rather, distributed computing (or, more appropriately, distributed heterogeneous computing) has become a "fact of life" by way of the 1980s-era growth in personal computers, LANs, UNIX-based systems, and, in effect, a transition away from single-vendor solutions.

As a result, effective workflow and groupware services must take this distributed, heterogeneous nature into account and be able to

- Operate on multiple hardware and systems software platforms
- Function in complex client/server architectures (discussed next)
- Adhere to standards whenever possible

In general, all distributed computing environments can be described as consisting of multiple hardware platforms that are connected together via network services. This is, however, a gross overgeneralization. Departmental computing environments—those systems that support an organization such as corporate finance or, even more narrowly, a specific set of applications within the finance department (but not others)—will be built around radically different networking architectures than, say, those distributed computing services that must support a national or international user base that crosses many different organizational boundaries (and, increasingly, outside the organization, or interenterprise).

The fact remains that regardless of how the user community is comprised, regardless of the specific software applications (custom and/or commercial) found within the realm of a computing environment, distributed computing is a fact of life. Therefore, workgroup computing services must not only take this into account, but must exploit the inherent services to the greatest extent possible. For example, in Chapter 4 we'll discuss workflow technology in greater detail. Consider the application environment illustrated in Fig. 3-1, in which an IBM mainframe is connected via a network to a number of UNIX servers and Microsoft Windows-based client PCs.

In this particular environment, certain departmental applications run on the various UNIX servers, while other applications run on the IBM mainframe. The workflow models that have been designed require that support be present for all of these platforms, including the client PCs. Therefore, the workflow infrastructure for this environment must be (1) distributed in nature (i.e., capable of sending messages across the network among machines and processes), and (2) heterogeneous (e.g., not constrained by the diverse hardware and system software base).

With respect to distributed computing, most readers are likely to be aware of the many different standards efforts that are perpetually underway within the information systems world. The primary purpose of most standards efforts is to facilitate distributed computing regardless of the underlying platforms, so, for example, messages can be exchanged between IBM mainframes, UNIX servers, and PC clients in a manner that is universally understood by all.

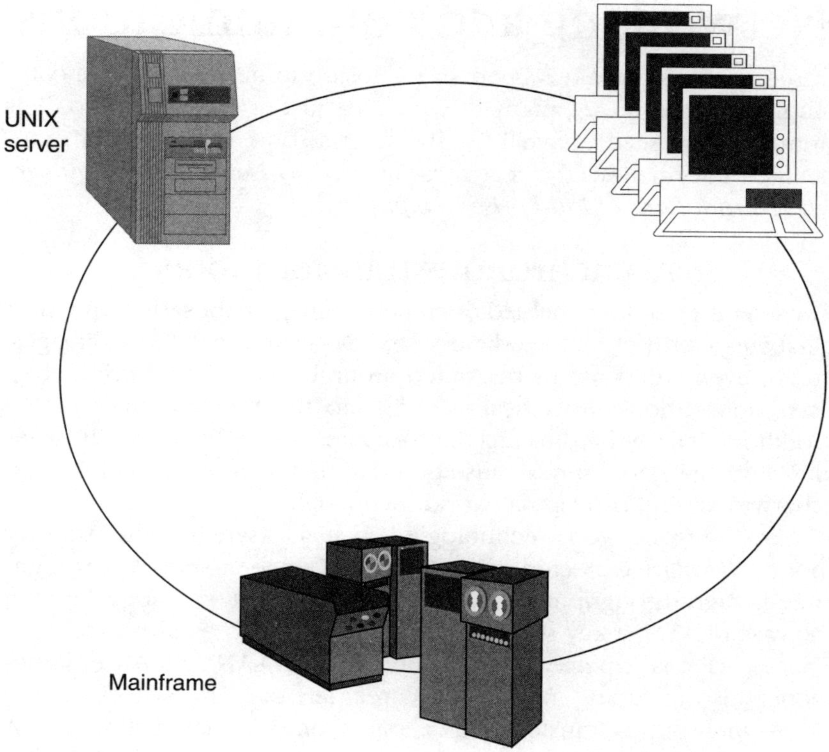

3-1 *Sample distributed computing environment.*

Tracking standards efforts can by itself be a full-time job, as the pace of such activity has tremendously increased in the past decade. Today, it isn't only the formal standards bodies such as the American National Standards Institute (ANSI) or the International Organization for Standardization (ISO) that are involved in such activities, but also consortia [the Open Software Foundation (OSF), for example] and industry-specific efforts (e.g., those dealing with open systems for the petroleum or health care industry). Standards, unfortunately, come and go, many never get past the working draft stage, and there's always the danger that the "design by committee" approach results in standards that are too cumbersome to implement and eventually fade away.

It is important, then, to track not only trends and developments in the base distributed computing technology itself, but also in the standards designed to facilitate that technology.

Networking and communications

In recent years there has been an explosion in networking and communications advances, many of which are just now coming into their prime. In this section, we'll briefly discuss some of these. For more detailed information, the reader is directed to *Network Re-Engineering: Foundations of Enterprise Computing.*[1]

Asynchronous transfer mode

Consider a workflow-enabled document management system in which gigabytes worth of multimedia documents—text annotated by images, audio, even video—must be routed around a global network among users and various processes according to the business rules of the workflow. It's not hard to imagine that capacity and bandwidth issues and problems could surely cause problems in the implementation of an otherwise-sound conceptual workflow model.

Emerging network technologies such as asynchronous transfer mode (ATM) are expected to be one of the key enablers of very high-speed, high-throughput, wide-area networking technology and, in the case of ATM, a key solution to the LAN/WAN integration problem. That is, ATM is expected to be scaleable from LAN to WAN environments (also including metropolitan area networks, or MANs).

Asynchronous transfer mode is based on cell relay technology. A cell is a fixed-size group of data (53 octets in the case of ATM, with five octets used for the header and 48 octets allocated for information).[2] The fixed-size nature of the cell facilitates extremely high-speed switching—millions of cells per second. Also, the 48-octet data size was selected as a compromise for the multimedia requirements expected to boom throughout the rest of the decade, in that voice communications operate better with smaller cells with a short latency while data communications prefer a larger cell (i.e., a higher ratio of user data to overhead). Given the trend toward multimedia data that has taken shape—and the incorporation of that multimedia data into workgroup computing models that aren't constrained by geography—ATM is expected to be a boon to handling large volumes of such data.

Asynchronous transfer mode cell-switching speeds operate from 1.544 megabits per second to 1.2 gigabits per second, with several specified interim speeds.[3] Since the cell sizes are fixed, network de-

1 A. Simon, *Network Re-Engineering: Foundations of Enterprise Computing* (Cambridge, Massachusetts: Academic Press Professional, 1994).

2 C. Lamb, "Speeding to the ATM," *UNIX Review*, October 1992, p. 31.

3 P. Schnaidt, "ATM Tutorial," *LAN Magazine*, October 1992, pp. 21–22.

lays can be predicted and real-time information (such as WAN video) can be supported over ATM environments. Therefore, real-time video conferencing as a groupware service can be greatly enhanced by the use of ATM technology.

Other advanced WAN technologies

Asynchronous transfer mode has implications and applicability at all levels of an enterprise and applications (including workgroup computing) from LAN to WAN. There are, however, other technologies that are specific to WAN environments and improving performance and throughput in that domain. These include

- Frame relay. Frame relay is conceptually similar to today's common X.25 packet-switching networks (e.g., variable length packets routed from a source address to some destination over a complex network), with the exception of greatly enhanced speeds. Frame relay is primarily a data service and is based on T1 services.
- Switched multimegabit data service (SMDS). Another technology is SMDS that is applicable to data, voice, and video and requires T3 for widespread deployment.[4] SMDS employs fixed-length cells like ATM does, and features a 53-octet cell structure with five bytes of overhead just as ATM does.

The importance of networking technologies to workgroup computing

Workgroup computing is about productivity. In Chapters 1 and 2 we discussed the cultural resistance toward workgroup computing that many organizations encounter. Given this, it is a serious mistake to implement, say, collaborative document composition systems (e.g., two or more staff members working on the same document in real-time) or video conferencing systems without having the underlying networking and communications infrastructure capable of supporting the required response time, throughput, availability, and other inherent attributes of the environment. Ideally, the coupling of the workgroup computing technology with substantiated change toward a collaborative culture (Chapter 2) will go a long way toward blunting most resistance. But it's naive to assume that all parties within an organization will embrace workgroup computing (or any other new technology, for that matter). Giving the "disgruntled few" ammunition such as "the response time stinks" or "my document takes forever to deliver over the network" can only lead to problems.

4 T1 and T3 are discussed in A. Simon, *Network Re-Engineering*.

Typically there is a network planning organization within the company that is responsible for long-range migration to new technologies and infrastructure components. It is essential that the requirements of the workgroup computing services be communicated to these planners to ensure that adequate services and capacities are deployed, thus ensuring that the workgroup imperatives aren't thwarted because of insufficient underlying infrastructure.

Client/server technology[5]

Client/server technology is no doubt familiar to most readers in terms of being one of the most promising—yet at the same time most aggravating—set of information systems methods. Originally conceived in the mid-1980s because of the advent of desktop computing (PCs and workstations) and the growth of LAN technology, it became obvious that tremendous benefits could be obtained by partitioning functions onto different classes of platforms within a given environment. The classical approach in the early days of client/server technology was to separate some application back-end functions, specifically those dealing with information management (e.g., the database), from the other functions in the application. Let's look at this in more detail.

In nearly every case, an application has three major components:

- Presentation (the portion with which the user interacts)
- Business logic (the "thinking portion" of the application)
- Data management (the storage and retrieval of data, ideally done in the most expedient manner and always in conjunction with data integrity rules)

All three of these areas communicate with one another—that is, they share data and control information—as shown in Fig. 3-2.

Note that, for example, the presentation portion must communicate with the business logic portion (example: some logic must determine what screen to present to the user under what circumstances), the business logic portion must communicate with the data management area (retrieving data as requested by the user from a screen or in conjunction with precoded logic), and so on.

In reality, the conceptual picture of Fig. 3-2 is more complex in that each of the three areas is usually made up of a number of subcomponents. That is, a number of modules might exist within the business logic area, and these modules communicate with each other

5 Portions of this section are adapted from A. Simon and T. Wheeler, *Open Client/Server Computing and Middleware* (Cambridge, Massachusetts: Academic Press Professional, 1995), chap. 2. The reader is also directed to W. Marion, *Client/Server Strategies* (New York: McGraw-Hill, 1994).

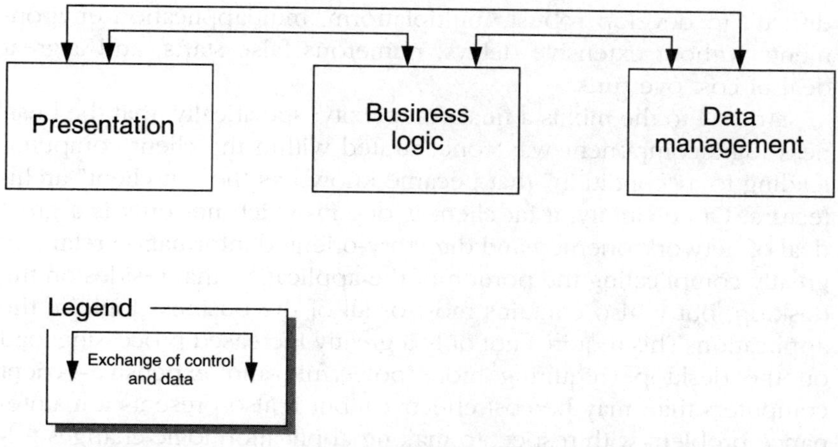

3-2 *Communications among the three major application components: a conceptual view.*

(example: one module activating another because of some data condition or in response to the processing logic for a user command), not only within each area but with modules of another area. A more detailed—but still conceptual—illustration of the required communications is shown in Fig. 3-3.

It is arguable that the first generation of client/server computing was, at best, only a moderate success. Outside of relatively simple departmental applications with homogeneous environments (i.e., all Unix or all Windows clients with a NetWare server), it was extremely

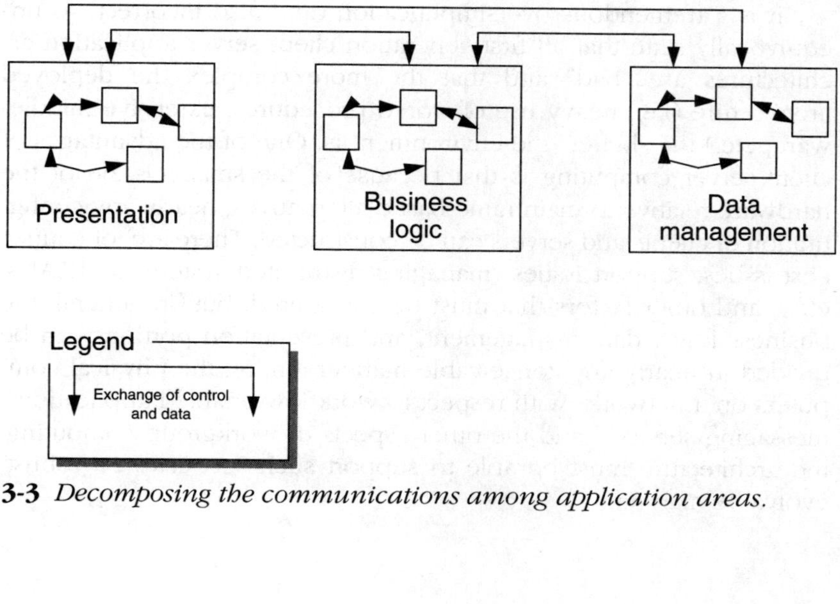

3-3 *Decomposing the communications among application areas.*

difficult to develop robust, multiplatform, multiapplication environments without extensive delays, numerous false starts, and a great deal of cost overruns.

Adding to the mix is a final complexity; specifically, that the business logic component was concentrated within the client computer, leading to a "condition" that became known as the "fat client" architecture. Quite simply, a fat client is one in which not only is a great deal of network-oriented and directory-oriented information retained, greatly complicating the portion of the application that resides on the desktop, but it also contains most or all of the business logic of the application. This requires not only a greatly increased processing load on the desktop (requiring more powerful—and expensive—client computers than may be cost effective), but it also presents a maintenance problem with respect to making application logic changes following initial deployment.

In large workgroups, it is likely that hundreds or thousands of desktop computers are part of the environment, meaning that if, for example, processing logic that ideally should be stored and managed within the database server is instead put on the client, then all updates need to be propagated to each client system. The same is true for directory information and all other items that involve information about the locations of services that are accessible. Or, more to the point of this book, so too would this be true for workflow and other groupware services. As we'll discuss in Chapter 4, the mode of automating the flow of information and control among physically separate clients and servers becomes so complex that it is almost unimplementable under a first-generation client/server architecture.

It is a tremendous oversimplification (and also incorrect) to unequivocally state that all first-generation client/server application architectures are "bad" and that the more complex the deployed architecture (i.e., heavy use of stored procedures, extensive middleware, etc.) the "better" the environment is. One of the advantages of client/server computing is that because of the smaller scale of the hardware relative to mainframe-based alternatives, nearly any configuration of clients and servers can be constructed. There are, of course, cost issues, support issues (managing distributed systems and LANs, etc.), and other factors that must be considered, but, in general, the business logic, data management, and presentation portions can be divided in nearly any conceivable manner among the physical computers on a network. With respect to workflow-enabled applications, messaging services, and the other aspects of workgroup computing, the architecture must be able to support such services in a robust, evolvable manner.

Second-generation client/server architectures began with the inclusion of stored procedures, or "database server logic," within database management system (DBMS) server products. Using stored procedures, a great deal of the required logic could be pushed out of the client domain into the servers.

This, however, does not solve the architectural deficiency issue in most cases, but merely shifts the focus away from the client to the server. A more general model is shown in Fig. 3-4, in which different categories of distribution architectures are created and can be adapted to the specific needs of a given environment.

Note that the middle model in Fig. 3-4—distributed logic—is, in general, the most flexible in that business logic can, in effect, exist on any class of physical machine in the networked environment.

What ties it all together? The answer is middleware, as we'll discuss in the next section. For our purposes here, though, it is important to recognize the importance of an architecturally sound client/server environment in the context of workgroup computing. Hard-coding workflow destination addresses into client applications across the enterprise, for example, as would be required under a first-generation approach, is a nearly certain way to lead to maintenance problems down the road, among other problems.

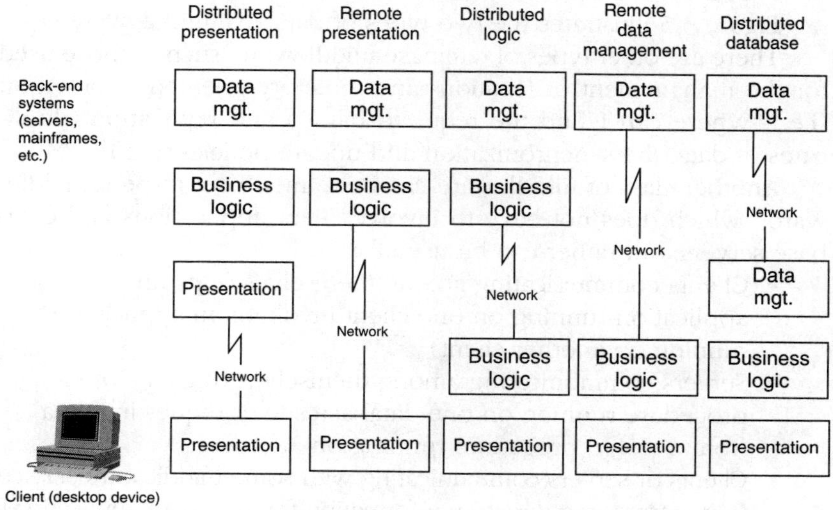

3-4 *Five different client/server architectural alternatives.*[6]

6 Adapted from a Gartner Group-provided figure in S. Rabin, "Critical Technical Issues When Building Enterprise Client-Server Applications," *American Programmer*, November 1994, p. 18.

Middleware technology[7]

As is often the case with emerging computing technologies, there is rarely a clear, distinct categorization of middleware. That is, there are several different classifications that may be used to divide different middleware technologies into separate groups, and these classifications overlap one another.

As with client/server computing in general, the first area in which middleware became widely used was in the area of database management. Within database management, the first functions of middleware were to provide some degree of abstraction from underlying local data managers to client applications, for two purposes:

1. Gateways to other DBMS products. Gateway-oriented middleware is used to permit an application that "normally" would run against, for example, a Sybase database to access data that is contained under the management of another DBMS product (e.g., Oracle or DB2).
2. Multiple-DBMS access. Expanding on gateway-oriented middleware, this class of database middleware provides standardized access to multiple underlying DBMS products, handling the various mappings and other interface functions in this layer rather than forcing the client application to do so.

Figure 3-5 illustrates the two types of database middleware.

There are other types of database middleware, such as those used for the management of location- and directory-oriented information (i.e., "Where can I find the required data?") and replication (duplicates of data, the synchronization and update policies, etc.).

Another class of middleware can be termed peer-to-peer middleware,[8] which does not have to involve client applications and database servers, but rather can be used for

- Clients communicating among themselves (e.g., an application running on one client invoking an application running on another client)
- Servers communicating among themselves (e.g., a stored procedure running on one database server requesting data from a stored procedure running on another)
- Clients or servers communicating with some middleware service (e.g., requesting directory information for an e-mail application)

7 Portions of this section are adapted from A. Simon and T. Wheeler, *Open Client/Server Computing*, chap. 3.

8 This term is used in P. Korzeniowski, "With C/S Apps, Middle Can Become Bottom Line," *Software Magazine*, July 1994, pp. 59–60, to refer to both remote procedure call (RPC) and messaging middleware.

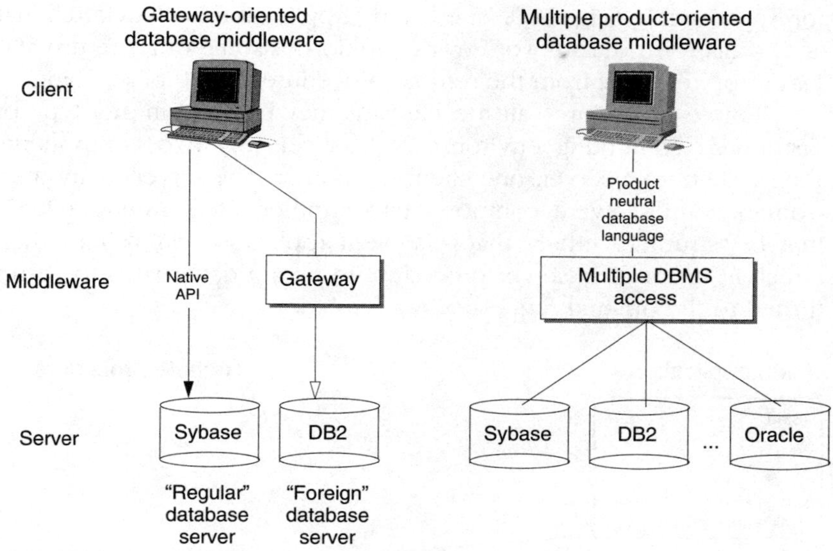

3-5 *Two types of database middleware.*

These types of interactions can be handled in one of several ways. The distinguishing characteristics of database middleware is that (1) the functions don't necessarily have to be database oriented, and (2) the interaction does not necessarily have to involve a client application and a database server.

As application architectures become increasingly complex, the need for middleware has expanded beyond that of the database-oriented mechanisms described previously. Specifically, the concept of application partitioning, in which formerly singular applications are decomposed and placed on multiple platforms, requires that the components be able to invoke one another and share control information and data as necessary (as was discussed earlier).

While cross-platform application communication is complex enough in homogeneous (e.g., only one variety of hardware and operating system) environments, it becomes more difficult when heterogeneity is added to the picture. One early mechanism that is still widely used is that of remote procedure calls (RPCs). As implied by the name, the RPC mechanism uses a procedure call paradigm as would be found within a single-platform program structure, but extends it into the network realm, enabling procedure calls to be made from one computer to another.

Traditionally RPC facilities have been synchronous, that is, one procedure calls another and waits for the response to come back before proceeding (Fig. 3-6). The calling application is "blocked," that is, it waits for the result (or error condition or some other return status) to be returned from the remote procedure before proceeding.

Remote procedure call mechanisms may be used in any type of distributed computing environment between any two components (i.e., a client to a server, one client to another, one server to another, from one middleware component to another, etc.). Multiple RPCs may be "strung together," that is, a client application can call another, which in turn calls a server procedure to obtain data that is to be returned to the original requester.

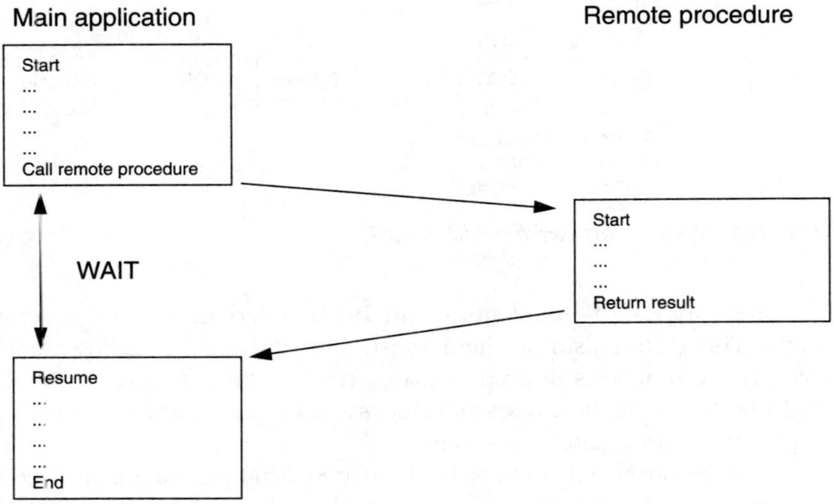

3-6 *RPC synchronization operation.*

One of the purported shortcomings of RPC models is that the synchronous nature can cause bottlenecks and performance problems in environments other than relatively small LANs with one or two servers and a homogeneous network and systems software infrastructure (i.e., all Unix and TCP/IP).[9] To overcome these claimed deficiencies, a new class of middleware has evolved in recent years and appears to be passing RPC models in terms of usage in complex heterogeneous client/server environments. This middleware class—messaging—is discussed next.

Unlike RPC technology, messaging middleware is inherently asynchronous. Built around the passing of messages, each component of

9 C. Amaru, "Building Distributed Applications with MOM (Message Oriented Middleware)," *Client/Server Today*, November 1994, p. 85.

an application (client, server, middleware services) can make its own determination as to whether or not processing should continue while waiting for a response to its message, and if so, what exactly should be done.

Conceptually, message-oriented middleware (MOM) is relatively simple to understand and, in fact, is very much like building applications around e-mail. Applications send messages to other applications (or components thereof) by placing messages into one or more queues, typically organized around the types of services needed. A local queue manager then determines if the request can be satisfied locally or if a remote service needs to be used and the message passed to that remote service.[10] Meanwhile, the requesting application can pursue other processing (determined by the application logic) until a response comes back via the queue manager.

As with the other topics in this chapter, messaging can be handled in a point-to-point manner (i.e., from one client application directly to another, from a client application to a server, etc.), or a middleware component can be added to the architecture. In effect, once the local queue manager determines that it is necessary to pass the message to an outside service, the message can be given to middleware for determination as to the destination instead of hard-coding the distributed message control within the application itself. This model is very similar to that of an object broker, a technology used in object-oriented middleware (discussed next). The message middleware acts as a "broker," determining for any given message and its particular attributes what the most appropriate destination of that message should be.

The asynchronous nature of MOM arguably gives this paradigm an edge over RPC technology in complex, large-scale environments, particularly those that are heterogeneous. To support the complexity and heterogeneity, in 1994 the Message-Oriented Middleware Association (MOMA) was formed, a consortium of vendors with the charter to "promote MOM technology and educate potential customers about the technology's benefits through seminars, developer conferences, and other marketing activities."[11] The goal of MOMA, at least at the time of this writing, is not to become another standards organization, but rather to promote interoperability across vendors' product lines and to develop standard terminology.[12] Many efforts by MOMA ven-

10 R. Whiting, "Getting on the Middleware Express," *Client/Server Today*, November 1994, p. 74.

11 Ibid.

12 Ibid.

dors are dedicated to closing the gap between RPC and MOM technologies and practices, in effect bringing about a coexistence of these two middleware approaches and alleviating the either/or nature that is faced by systems architects today.

Middleware and workgroup computing

Very simply, the arguments presented earlier for second-generation client/server architectures as appropriate for workgroup computing are the same ones applicable to why middleware technology and products are important. Consider workflow management, as we'll discuss in Chapter 4. Workflow should ideally be implemented in a middleware domain; for example, there should be a set of services that are platform-neutral, inherently distributed, and not within either the client or server domain that allow the routing of data and control according to the workflow rules. These workflow services may very well use other middleware services (e.g., directory management, database replication, etc.) to perform their required functions.

Data management and data warehousing

For much of the 1980s, the DBMS vendor market—and the leading forces within the user community, particularly large aerospace companies and defense contractors—pursued the elusive distributed database management system (DDBMS). Even before desktop computing became widespread it was recognized that heterogeneity and distribution among multiplatform environments were dribbling into reality, particularly because of the increase in the number of minicomputers that began in the 1970s. As data began to become distributed in nature, the inefficiencies and problems of that distribution became readily apparent. Inconsistencies and outright errors across the multiple platforms, the inability to "ask questions" whose answers required access to multiple databases, and many other problems called out for a solution. Vendors and researchers proposed that DDBMSs provide an "umbrella" that would initially accompany homogeneously distributed environments (e.g., multiple platforms of the same hardware and systems software composition) and, eventually, move into heterogeneous realms (multiple platforms, multiple DBMS products and models, etc.).

Unfortunately, the DDBMS approach has proved to be less than satisfactory in solving the distributed data problem, to the point where only a hearty few are still pursuing this technology. The reasons are numerous and beyond the scope of our discussion here,[13] but the end result has been that database implementations built around client/server technology (including stored procedure implementations in the database server domain) and middleware (to handle the replication—or "controlled duplication"—of data, gateway access across heterogeneous environments, and directory services) have become the favored approaches to handling heterogeneous data management. While not as technically elegant as the DDBMS approach and, in general, a less than optimal solution, the need to get a handle on widely distributed data management today has caused the user community, for the most part, to forego DDBMS technology.

At the same time, much of the DDBMS approach has found its way into the area that has become known as data warehousing. In effect, a separate informational database—as contrasted with a transactional or operational one—is created into which data from many different operational database environments can be placed, either in its "raw" form or, more commonly, in some type of summarized or "rolled up" form. The data warehouse is a physically separate instance from the operational database and serves the user community that must perform "what if?," "why did this happen?," and similar functions, the area that has become known as on-line analytical processing.

Finally, the area of object-oriented databases (ODBs) that began in the 1980s has, in recent years, taken two different branches. One branch—the "pure ODB"—is basically an implementation that has no ties to relational DBMS technology. The other branch, which is commonly called the "extended relational approach," in effect adds object-oriented capabilities to a relational framework.[14]

So taken together—middleware and client/server databases in lieu of DDBMS technology, data warehousing, and different flavors of ODBs—what is the relationship to workgroup computing technology? The answer depends on the different areas of workgroup computing and, of course, different product implementations, but, in general, the leading products make as great a use as possible of emerging data management technologies such as those discussed previously.

For example, document management products should be capable of handling multimedia data, and multimedia data is particularly suited to object-oriented implementations, yet at the same time there is a need to maintain control information in a relational format for use by

13 The reader is directed to A. Simon, *Strategic Database Technology: Management for the Year 2000* (San Francisco: Morgan Kaufmann, 1995), chaps. 2–7.

14 These subjects are discussed in detail in A. Simon, *Strategic Database Technology*, chaps. 8–10.

the document management engine and other applications with which this data must be shared and routed. Therefore, it is arguable that as extended relational databases (e.g., relational DBMSs with object-oriented capabilities) become more commonplace, the underlying data management services will likely be supplied by DBMS server engines that fit the extended relational model.

Similarly, workflow services must often cross heterogeneous system boundaries and exchange data between different DBMSs. The use of database gateway technology (as contrasted with a DDBMS approach) is a technique that for the most part is compliant with the modes used by multiplatform applications in general.

Finally, as on-line analytical processing (OLAP) applications running against data warehouses become more commonplace, this will be a natural place for collaborative groupware services to be implemented. For example, user 1 may "dig around the warehouse" and uncover something of interest (a pattern that indicates a business opportunity, an anomaly that may bear further investigation, etc.). By using groupware services user 1 may enter into a collaborative workgroup mode with other appropriate staff members and collectively analyze the situation, partition a set of steps for further investigation, collect the results, route the results to the appropriate manager (depending on the critical nature of the situation), and so on, all using workgroup computing services that are integrated with emerging data management technologies.

Transaction processing

Finally, with respect to the data management technologies discussed above, the second-generation client/server models, and other emerging distributed technologies, it is evident that the traditional means by which transaction processing has been accomplished are no longer sufficient, and these issues have a great impact on the workgroup computing arena.

Transaction processing is the general area in which the principles of data integrity and "correctness" are handled; that is, services provide assurance that situations don't occur where two of three database tables are updated correctly, but because problems occur with the other, that part of the transaction is "lost" and the database is at an incorrect state.[15]

15 Actually, transaction processing is somewhat more complex, but the simplified explanation in this chapter is sufficient for our purposes. For further discussions the reader is directed to A. Simon, *Strategic Database Technology*, chap. 20, or to the many reference sources available that deal exclusively with transaction processing.

Traditionally, transaction processing models have been "flat" in nature. For example, they do some sequence of operations within the context of a transaction, and if everything completes successfully the transaction as a whole is committed (i.e., "made official"), if not, everything is backed out and no inconsistent states occur. This flat transaction model has worked very well in centralized, high-throughput database environments where the typical transaction involves one or more database tables (or, in older database models, records or segments) that are physically located on the same machine, and where the typical duration of each operation is relatively short (i.e., simply updating a row in a table, possibly inserting a new one or doing a deletion, etc.).

The distributed nature of today's and tomorrow's computing environments, however, has caused a number of inefficiencies and problems to enter into the transaction processing domain. Rather than go into a long discussion, we will simply state that "flat transactions do not work well in environments where complex, lengthy processing—such as workflow and groupware services—is an integral part of the processing infrastructure."[16]

Consider the simple workflow example shown in Fig. 3-7. A client process, by virtue of the rules of the workflow, must route various portions of a document to three other users for their comments and additions to the work done to date.

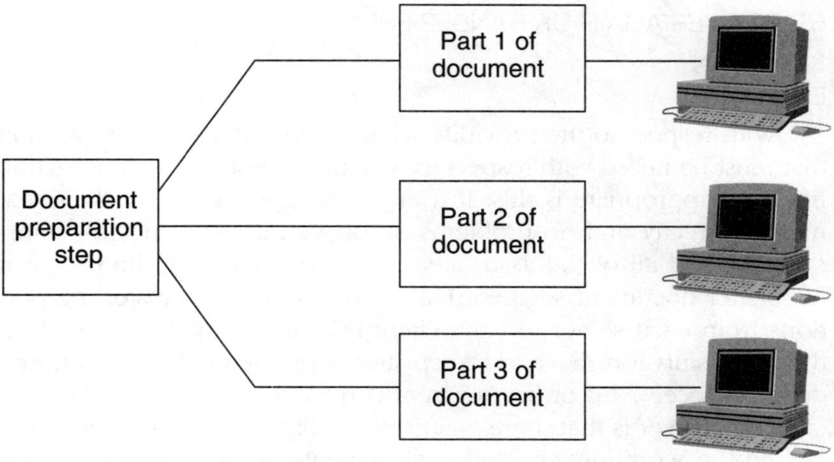

3-7 *The transaction semantics behind simplified workflow.*

16 For detailed examples, the reader is directed to A. Simon, *Strategic Database Technology*, chap. 2–7, 20.

Several items are noted with respect to the example in Fig. 3-7. First, all of the users involved with the workflow belong to different workgroups, all are physically distributed around the country at different sites, and all are working on different LAN-based computing environments that are connected via the company's enterprise-wide WAN. Next, each of the subcomponents of the document are large, say several hundred megabytes worth of multimedia data in each section, including video segments.

The traditional flat transaction approach to this particular sequence of events would, at a conceptual level (ignoring the underlying physical implementations, because they aren't important for purposes of this discussion) would be as follows:

```
START TRANSACTION
SEND SEGMENT 1 TO SYSTEM FOR USER 1
SEND SEGMENT 2 TO SYSTEM FOR USER 2
SEND SEGMENT 3 TO SYSTEM FOR USER 3
WAIT FOR "SUCCESS" NOTIFICATION
RECEIVED FROM EACH USER'S SYSTEM
IF ALL THREE = "SUCCESS"
COMMIT TRANSACTION AND
END
ELSE
ROLL BACK TRANSACTION
START OVER AGAIN OR HANDLE ERROR
SITUATION
END IF
```

With respect to the previous scenario, the fundamental question that must be raised with respect to whether or not this flat transaction model is appropriate is this: If users 1 and 2 each receive their segments correctly and no problems occur with those respective transmissions and all of the associated overhead (notifying the user that his or her document segment has arrived, possibly transferring portions from each server to each client PC, etc.), why should each of those transmissions have to be repeated if problems occur and user 3 does not receive his or her segment correctly?

The answer is that there is no reason that this should have to occur, and in workflow-enabled environments in which large volumes of multimedia data are being transferred, this is a tremendously inefficient transaction model.

A better solution—and this is the direction in which distributed transaction processing is heading—is to classify each of the three distinct transmissions as "subtransactions," each with their own rules of semantics (e.g., determining the success or failure of each, etc.), and in the event of the failure of one subtransaction, others that have successfully completed do not need to be repeated.

There are, of course, complications to this decomposed transaction approach, and distributed transaction managers need to be sophisticated enough to support the concept of subtransactions, tracking each one and ensuring that the transaction as a whole is managed along with each individual transaction. Increasingly, distributed transaction management is (1) being decoupled from the DBMS engines, and (2) being hosted in the middleware domain, for example, in a place where services can be provided to many different clients and servers with respect to transaction management.[17]

With respect to workflow and groupware, then, the important thing to note is that transaction processing is becoming increasing more complicated to the point where the complexities of distributed workgroup computing can be supported by emerging transaction models, products, and architectures.

Summary

Obviously, trying to sum up the past half-decade's advances in distributed computing—and related trends—into a single chapter is an impossibility, but our purpose has been to emphasize that workgroup computing is dependent on a number of distributed computing services that provide the foundations for much of what we'll discuss in later chapters. It is imperative that anyone involved in implementing or planning for workgroup computing technology track the advances and trends in these (and other) areas discussed in this chapter, because the workflow and groupware products you'll use will no doubt be dependent on these technologies and need to integrate with them under the architectural foundations of your organization (and, increasingly, other organizations with which you will share workflow- and groupware-enabled transfer of information).

17 Transaction processing trends are discussed in A. Simon, *Strategic Database Technology.*

Part 2

Workgroup Technologies

4

Workflow technology

The classic example that is usually presented when explaining workflow technology is based around the routing of forms and/or documents, as in the example shown in Fig. 4-1. Purchase authorization forms, expense reports, specifications, or any of hundreds of other types of forms or documents are

1 Created by a given user
2 Sent to the next user who is the reviewing authority
3 Sent to two different approving authorities who can do the approval in parallel, and then
4 Sent to the final approving authority, before being
5 Sent to the department that handles the execution of whatever that form or document is designed to do

Workflow technology, the argument goes, will improve processes like that illustrated and described above, reduce (or, ideally, eliminate) lost paperwork, reduce delays caused by various personnel being absent, and so on. In reality, workflow technology can—and should—be a great deal more involved than that illustrated above. In this chapter, we'll discuss this area in detail, focusing on both sides of the workflow subject: the technology and the processes.

Roots of workflow

Conceptually, there is little that is new in the area of workflow-based computing. Progressive organizations have for years been designing centralized (mainframe- or minicomputer-based) applications—even cross-application environments—in which a rudimentary form of automated workflow assistance has been part of the environment. For example, as shown in Fig. 4-2—an environment based around a

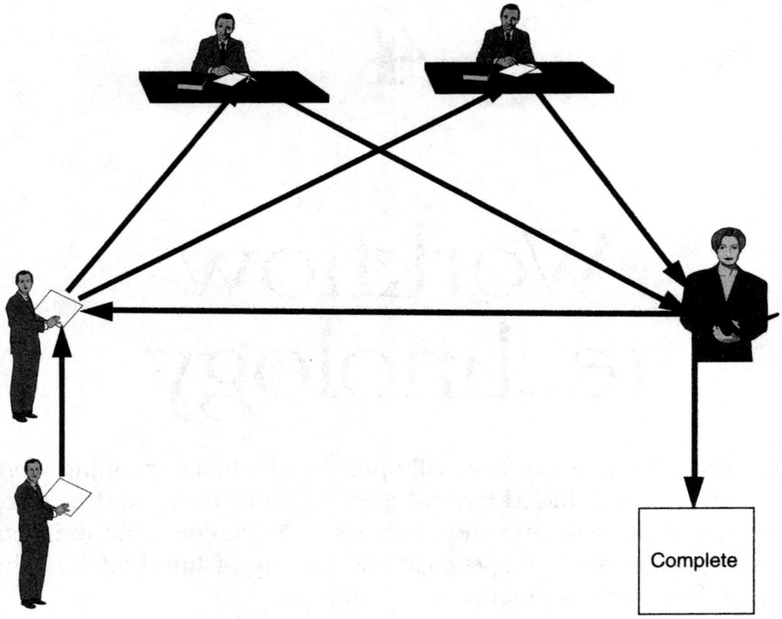

4-1 *Forms routing as an example of workflow.*

shared database—"flags" (semaphores), status variables, processes to check the flags and associated data, and similar constructs can be built in which

1 A user of an application (or application segment) can create some data—for example, the data required for a purchase requisition form, and

2 That data can be placed in the shared database, the "need first-line approval" flag set, and then

3 A process notes that the flag is set and the next time the user who is the first-line approving authority logs on, his or her startup script is notified by the process (or can even check the flag directly) and the first thing he or she must do is handle that particular item, and

4 The sequence will continue through all of the other approving authorities or recipients of documents or document segments.

In effect, the concept of automated workflow is nothing new, and the lack of widespread implementation has been more a result of political and organizational matters than insufficient technology; as described previously, flags, shared database information, and conditional notification of "events" is nothing new.

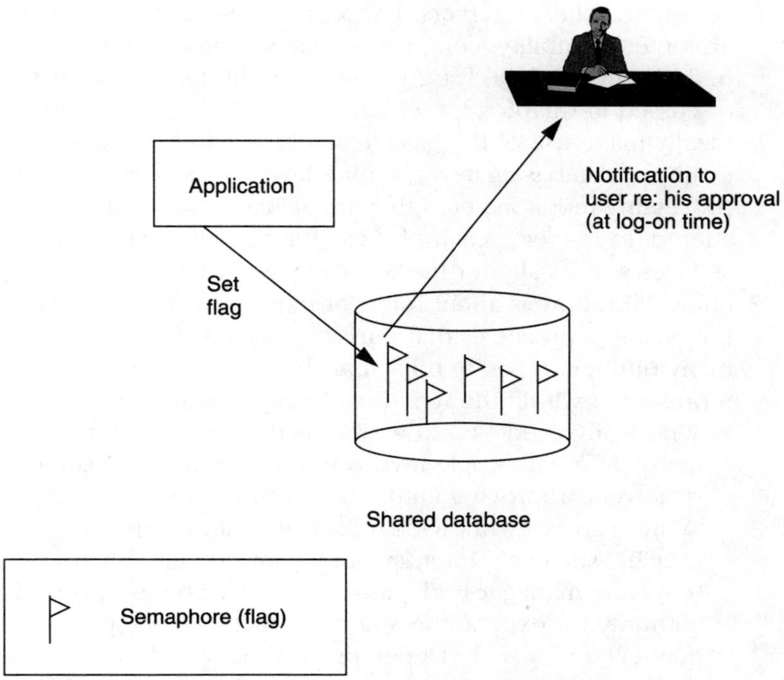

4-2 *The roots of workflow in centralized environments.*

The advent of distributed computing, however, brought a halt to attempts to enhance the area of centralized workflow-enabled computing. As we discussed in Chapter 3, neither the distributed computing architectures or, in many cases, the base technologies have been present to carry the concepts of cross-user notification, conditional routing of data, and other facets into the distributed arena.

In that spirit, a fresh look at workflow technology began occurring in the early 1990s, and by 1993 there was a generally accepted set of principles about what a workflow-enabled environment should be able to do. These items are discussed next.

Characteristics of a workflow-enabled environment

Today's and tomorrow's workflow-enabled environment should possess the following characteristics:

1 Support for distributed computing. As discussed in Chapter 3, distributed computing is here to stay, and any workflow environment must be able to support the concept of desktop computing clients, servers, LANs, cross-LAN communications and interoperability, complex transaction processing, middleware, and the list goes on. Note though that, as was discussed in Chapter 3, the workflow architecture should ideally make use of the base technologies and services (for example: database gateways, middleware-based transaction processing monitors, etc.) that are available rather than attempt to re-create each of these fundamental classes of services specifically for the workflow environment.

2 Rules. Workflow is about rules, or more precisely, the rules of the business processes that must be supported. There are many different types of rules that should ideally be represented within the workflow engine, including
   - Who is involved—for any process there are likely to be many different people involved (creators of information, reviewers, approving authorities, troubleshooters, etc.). "Who" can be by individual user (e.g., an enterprise-wide user ID, such as asimon@writing.com), by job function (e.g., any manager in department XYZ who has approval authority for expenditures of more than $10,000 per quarter), or by both. Depending on the specifics of any given flow, routing might have to be done to a specific individual. It may possibly be structured to flow to a preferred individual, but in his or her absence it may go to either someone designated as an official substitute or anyone else of a certain managerial rank, and so on.
   - When—every business process or subprocess has some dimension of time associated with it, even if that time is "it doesn't matter." The time element should be encoded as part of the rules and managed by the workflow engine. There are typically multiple time elements, such as
     ~No later than starting time
     ~No earlier than starting time
     ~Preferred completion time (or duration)
     ~No later than completion time
     ~Really no later than completion time
     ~Time to elevate the matter to someone for intervention or troubleshooting
   - Dependencies—very often, business processes require data or control information from other processes in order to move ahead. These dependencies should be captured, tracked, and managed by the workflow infrastructure, with appropriate incorporation of the "who" and "when" elements as described.

- Substitutions—not only in the "who" area, as described previously, but also in terms of alternate routes that may not be optimal but could work under certain circumstances (e.g., conditional approval of something, pending final approval at some later time).
- Evolution—as with any facet of computing, the management and evolution of something that is created is as important as the initial deployment. The rules of the workflow must be modifiable according to changing business requirements.
- Privileged information—the workflow infrastructure must be capable of supporting concepts of privacy and data security, ensuring that information is not routed to anyone inside or outside of an organization (or company) who is not allowed to see that information. In general, this aspect of workflow must work in cooperation with the overall distributed information security program (i.e., it doesn't stand alone).[1]

With respect to the previous items, the following should be emphasized:

1 Workflow technology is not simply a case of sending e-mail reminders across a network to someone responsible for accomplishing one or more steps in a chain or process, though e-mail can play an important role in workflow technology in terms of being a primary messaging/human alerting mechanism (e.g., notifying a user that there is a problem with a specific instance in a workflow environment).

2 Workflow is intended to ensure that things will be done, that they will be done in the correct order, and that problems aren't hidden or neglected.

3 Workflow engines can have varying capabilities (which will, over time, be increasing in commercial products and in custom-tailored environments), but in general the engine itself should have a means by which all of the items discussed so far (users, processes, timing constraints, alternatives, etc.) can be represented and easily managed.

4 An important part of the workflow environment is the alerting/troubleshooting environment, that is, involving the appropriate people (managers, for example) in time to resolve problems. For example, if a particular capital acquisition request keeps getting rejected by the approving authorities under the workflow environment and the

1 For further information about end-to-end, multifaceted security, the reader is directed to S. Shaffer and A. Simon, *Network Security* (San Diego: Academic Press Professional, 1993), and S. Shaffer and A. Simon, *Security for Open Systems* (San Francisco: Morgan Kaufmann, 1996).

equipment is needed ASAP for a crucial project, at some point the cycle must be broken and someone at the appropriate level brought in to resolve the problem. The workflow environment should be able to support this concept of elevation and resolution.

5 At various stages of the workflow-enabled environment, many different types of tools may be used. For example, an environment that is oriented around document production, approval, and storage would use
- Document composition tools early in the process
- Markup tools during the approval process
- Object-enabled database storage managers during the storage and access phase
- Directory services throughout so components can be located anywhere in the enterprise (if that is the scope of the workflow)
- E-mail to handle notifications and private communications
- Groupware (conferencing, etc.) to hold open discussions about key issues
- Other tools that are appropriate

Though the examples discussed involve workflow among users, there does not necessarily have to be a human element in all aspects of workflow. Increasingly, a goal of process improvement/reengineering is to automate as many of the processes as possible without human intervention (e.g., "lights out operations"). In this case the recipients of data, workflow-enabled control, and other facets might very well be applications or components of applications in the enterprise that do not require human involvement; all the business rules are encoded and humans may only have to be brought in at the resolution stage (as discussed previously).

Different classifications of workflow

While workflow-enabled applications and environments share (or should share) the characteristics described earlier, there are several different classes of workflow environments that are emerging. These are[2]

2 D. Black, "The Squeaky Wheel," *LAN Magazine*, January 1993, pp. 61–66. This article cites original research work done by Scott McCready of IDC/Avante in the course of conducting "one of the first major studies on workflow software" (according to the article). The descriptions that come from this article are augmented with observations by the authors of this book.

1 Administrative. Routing of regular reports, as described in the example at the beginning of this chapter, is an example of administrative workflow. Most of the processing is forms-based—occasionally including images, but usually not high-resolution, high-volume images—and tends to be outside the mainstream of the "mission-critical applications." In general, there may be efficiencies and cost savings that can be gained from process improvement and automation, but these tend to be small in terms of the overall business.
2 Production. These workflow-enabled processes tend to be in the mainstream of the business (or at least a major functional area of the business), such as claims processing in an insurance company. The phrase "white collar factory" is applicable to these environments, since characteristics include high-volume flows, rigidly enforced processing rules, and timing constraints. Production workflow systems are often integrated with a document management system (increasingly, one capable of supporting multimedia documents, including imaging and video). Repetitive tasks can be scripted, but exception handling and out-of-the-ordinary situations can also be handled by the workflow engine. In general (and in contrast to administrative workflow) a great deal of planning, analysis, and integration with other systems and software environments must occur, and increasingly there is a tight coupling between production workflow and business reengineering.
3 Ad-hoc. Ad-hoc workflows are of the type that aren't predictable and tend to be project-oriented (and therefore may only last for some finite period of time as compared with production workflow). Preparation of a business proposal, participation in a systems or software development project (as described in one of the examples at the end of this chapter), and similar functions can benefit from ad-hoc workflow environments. Rules tend to be dynamically created, and the workflow automation is more for ensuring that things aren't left out or that the best solutions are found rather than long-term critical business process improvement (as with production workflow) or squeezing out additional efficiencies (as is the case with administrative workflow).

All three classes of workflow are valuable, and should be investigated by any organization pursuing workgroup computing efforts. The tools will likely vary, different products being more suitable to one environment than another and different degrees of tangible benefits obtained under different circumstances, but in general, nothing but benefits can come from process improvement and automated support in each of the three different situations.

It should be cautioned, however, that in the spirit of our discussion in Chapter 2 with respect to moving toward collaborative processes—and the possibility of resistance—each of the three areas described is susceptible to such resistance. The technologies themselves must be carefully coupled with leadership and management transition toward an environment in which workflow is not tolerated, but is actively and vigorously supported by the organization's leaders. The automated routing of data, for example, to a given user based on his or her job function should not be viewed as "dumping work on me," but rather as "I'm a critical component of the business processes here, and I need to be involved in (whatever)." The fact that the workflow engine and infrastructure is equipped with deadline management capabilities and automatic notification to others if deadlines are missed can be a worrisome facet of the technology to many workers, who see those capabilities as little more than a means by which management can be alerted when the employee falls short. Conveying to the workforce that such capabilities are beneficial is tricky, but necessary (example: "If you continually miss deadlines in working on Form XYZ, then there are probably problems with the form's structure, or maybe you don't have all of the information you need in time to meet your deadlines, so we need to look at the processes involved and see how to tune them to help you out").

Clearly, cultural issues come into play here that are just as important as the underlying technology. The workforce—professionals, administrative staff, everyone—must be made to realize that when workflows are set up to include them at given steps (or, for that matter, to exclude them from other steps), it is for both the good of the overall organization and to their own benefit in terms of doing their respective jobs the best they can.

The workflow market and characteristics

As with other areas of technology, estimates about the marketplace for workflow technology vary from one analysis/estimate to another. In general, though, the trend is up. For example, Delphi Consulting estimated that the 1993 workflow market of $381 million would nearly double by 1995 to $750 million.[3] Interestingly, though, another

3 C. Frye, "Move to Workflow Provides Business Process Scrutiny," *Software Magazine*, April 1994, p. 79.

Delphi Consulting study (from 1994) noted that there is a vast distinction between "real workflow market growth" and "repositioned growth," the latter being imaging and document management companies with workflow capabilities repositioning themselves as workflow providers. When cast in this light, the 168 percent increase in the workflow market in 1993 became 35 percent in terms of "real" workflow vendors.[4]

With respect to the repositioned aspect of the marketplace, a study by BIS Strategic Decisions forecasts $700 million in total workflow software sales by 1997, with the majority coming in the "production imaging" category (around $350 million), another $150 million or so in "desktop imaging," and the balance in the "nonimaging" area.[5]

The size of workflow-enabled projects can vary dramatically, depending on the scale of the particular operation (e.g., departmental, enterprise-wide, etc.). Another Delphi Consulting study (early 1994) notes the following size breakdown:[6]

- Fewer than 25 users: 19 percent
- 25 to 49 users: 19 percent
- 50 to 100 users: 31 percent
- More than 100 users: 31 percent

Integration of workflow with other workgroup computing technologies

Workflow technology can, as indicated in some of the earlier examples, function in a manner in which it is integrated with other software and systems areas, but not necessarily anything else from the workgroup computing arena. The workflow engine may be geared solely to making sure that the right data gets to the right users or processes in time to do what must be done, that nothing is overlooked, but little else.

More sophisticated environments, though, will find workflow capabilities increasingly integrated with other workgroup services. Some, like document management, are fairly obvious. Others, such as those systems with workflow capabilities integrated with electronic conferencing, tend to be constructed on more of a situational basis according to the needs of a given organization.

4 E. Leinfuss, "Suppliers Reposition to Go With the Flow," *Software Magazine*, February 1995, p. 69.

5 "Go With the Flow," Client-Server Report, *Information Week*, March 28, 1994, p. 45.

6 Ibid., p. 42.

For example, an electronic conferencing groupware environment may have hooks by which a user can, upon finding information on various topics of interest to his or her group, automatically route downloaded copies of topics to other group members who need that information (or who would find it valuable). Carrying this approach a bit further, an organization working on a proposal might download technical reports, results from benchmarking studies, or information from electronic conferencing systems and route that information to the person responsible for that specific area of the proposal (no matter if the team is geographically dispersed), and the information would be automatically imported into the document management system for inclusion in the proposal. The information might also be stored in the database for future reference, automatically routed to other users who have "registered" their interest in the subject, and so on.

The point is that workflow technology, like other "infrastructure-oriented" technologies (database management, for example) will continue to evolve to a point where it is primarily a set of services that performs the functions discussed earlier in this chapter (routing to the appropriate party, ensuring completion, notification of problems, etc.). Incorporating workflow technology into workgroup-oriented, collaborative environments is conceptually identical to putting workflow technology under traditional computing services and applications, and when planning for future directions this should be considered.

Managing workflow-enabled systems

One of the important aspects of workflow-enabled environments is the ability to adequately manage them. Functions such as gathering statistics regarding the number of process steps that were or weren't completed on time, potential process flow bottlenecks based on historical results, and similar management-oriented tasks need to be incorporated. It's probably too early to predict that the job function of "workflow administrator" will take its place alongside network administrator, database administrator, systems administrator, security administrator, and others, but it isn't an inconceivable prospect. Just as each of the other areas mentioned previously have enough sophistication to them to require specialists to manage their operations, so too does workflow technology. At the very least, the workflow administration function is one that no organization can afford to overlook when implementing workflow-enabled processes.

Example #1: The budgeting process

We'll conclude this chapter by presenting several examples in which workflow technology is an integral part of the environment. The first example is for the annual budgeting process within a division of a large corporation. Any reader who has ever worked in a large corporation (or, for that matter, a government organization) is aware of the tremendous amount of time the budgeting process takes. It isn't only the "regular" functions (specifically, figuring out how much money is needed in the various categories) but things like

- Repeatedly having to adjust submissions, based on shifting priorities
- Corporate-level cutbacks that then have to be folded back into the budget process
- External events (e.g., a corporate merger or joint venture) that affect the budget

In companies where the principal participants in the budgeting process travel a great deal, there are also situations where "the numbers just aren't available; maybe they can fax them to me and I can work on them on the plane from Dallas to Cincinnati . . . no, make that Cincinnati to Memphis . . . anyway, I'll be late with my group, but I'll try, I'll really try, to get them in as soon as I can . . ."

The business processes for budgeting will vary from one organization to another, but in general they all involve more or less the same tasks:

- Gathering information about ongoing, in-progress projects from previous budgeting cycles and possibly making adjustments
- Looking at strategic plans and the projects that will be initiated during the next period, and factoring those costs in
- Getting "the numbers" that come out of the executive committee or the senior managerial ranks that apply to the organization (the previous two process components are bottom-up in nature—that is, they look at the things that need to be done and figure out how much money they will require; this step is top-down—that is, a specific number, or possibly a range, is provided against which the bottom-up plans will be allocated)
- Multiple passes will occur, managers will fight for their respective projects, trade-offs will be made, and so on

- Eventually, budgets will be created at the appropriate levels and passed upward
- Usually, multiple iterations will need to be made as external events, cutbacks, and other factors come into play in the cycle

Following the steps listed, a workflow-enabled budgeting system might look as shown in Fig. 4-3.

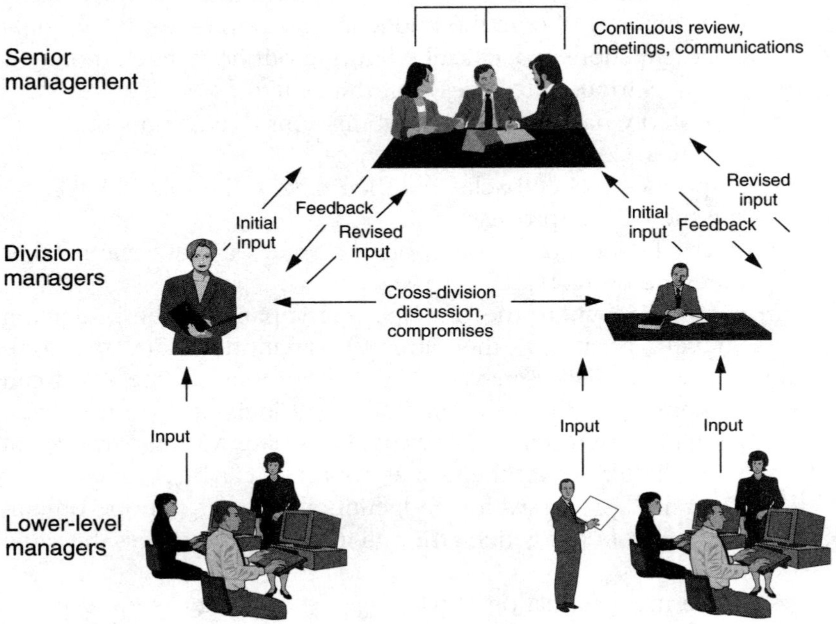

4-3 *A conceptual model of budgeting workflow.*

The workflow infrastructure should handle events such as

1 Initiating the budgeting process. At the beginning of each cycle there should be a "tuning" period in which any organizational and personnel changes since the last cycle, occurrences that will affect the budget (e.g., a crash project that wasn't part of the previous cycle, or the acceleration of an ongoing project), and other factors are brought into synchronization with the state of the organization. Following the principles of collaborative work models (Chapter 2), the hands-on managers and leaders (project managers and others) should be part of the cycle, and they should be included as workflow-enabled participants.

2 First cuts. Although many organizations do budgeting in a manner that is more top-down (e.g., the senior managers meet, fight over their respective pots of money, then pass the figures down to their ranks with "give me your budgets based on these figures" edicts), it is suggested that the budgeting process be more bottom-up, as was described earlier, with the top-down edicts being more supportive (e.g., looking at the first cuts that come up to the senior ranks and seeing if they are or aren't feasible, then passing amended totals down for adjustment). The purpose of this discussion isn't to discuss the merits of various approaches to budgeting, but merely to suggest that in a collaborative organization, the workflow will likely operate better in the former, bottom-up manner, and the technology should support this. That is,

- The initiation process should trigger each participant who must submit numbers, informing them of exactly what is needed, by when, and in what form, and pointing them to groupware conferences where they can discuss various items with their peers.

  For example, software development managers in an organization may be pointed to a conference where a discussion of reuse technology is ongoing, and the various project managers can see what the status of the organization-wide code reuse program is and whether or not they will be able to tap into that during the next year. If so, there are certain implications (e.g., additional training will be needed, but there will likely be cost savings in development).

  Likewise, the purchase of a new mainframe and the institution of a cross-organization help desk may have their costs allocated to multiple departments, and those managers will need to tap into the conference and associated databases to get the numbers being assigned to their organization. More importantly, the managers can make sure that their assumptions—and the resulting budget numbers—are in concert with one another with respect to the state of the organization.
- After the initial passes, they will receive the maximum numbers from their managers (these numbers may pass through multiple levels, each with its own workflow and associated deadlines, etc.).

3 Revisions. Based on the collection of information, revisions will likely need to be made, and the deadlines, associated constraints, approving authorities, additional participants, and other components of the workflow can be brought into the process.

4 Final approval. Once all the iterations have been completed, the final results will be communicated to each individual manager with financial responsibility, then their respective project and organizational plans can be adjusted in accordance with how the process has turned out.

This discussion is a condensed simplification of the budgeting process, but the main point—how workflow technology would be used to aid effectiveness and efficiency—should come across clearly. In this case, budgeting is tied into business plans for organizations and projects and other "real-world" data by the workflow engine, and by ensuring that (1) collaborative processes are used and (2) collaborative technology supports those processes, chances are many of the problems with organizational budgeting—lack of adequate information, overlap, having politics overwhelm merits and facts, and so on—may be significantly reduced making the process far more efficient than without using workgroup technology.

Example #2: Software development

As we discussed earlier, workflow technology doesn't only apply to "pure business processes" such as budgeting, but to any area in which collaborative efforts take place. Most professionals who have been involved in a large software development project have firsthand knowledge of process-oriented problems: modules that weren't adequately tested because they were forgotten, configuration management problems throughout the life cycle, software rollout issues, and so on.

By using workflow (and groupware) as part of the development process a number of benefits can and are likely to occur. Most of these will be because a methodology—hopefully, a good one—will now be formalized and enforced by the underlying workflow technology. This will make it difficult, if not impossible, for modules to be passed to integration testing without adequate unit testing (e.g., the "sign off" procedures won't be able to be ignored); requests for user community participation won't be able to be ignored, because unheeded requests will automatically go to the appropriate managerial level for resolution of the problem (the opposite is true, too; repeated user requests for certain features won't be able to be ignored, either); and so on.

Just as any business process must be sound before workflow support can be applied to it, so too must the software and systems development processes—the methodology—be sound. Applying workgroup computing support to software development if the methodology in place is poor (or, more likely, there isn't one) will have little or no benefit, other than possibly to bring attention to problems at an earlier point in the life cycle than if the processes were highly manual.

In general, though, our point is that workflow technology can be an aid to the development of computer and information systems, not just to the business processes that those systems are being created to support. Again, it all ties back to the discussion in Chapter 2—workgroup computing technology of any type (workflow, groupware) must be applied in concert with business processes that are designed to encourage participatory, collaborative efforts on the part of all involved. Even in the software development arena, application of workflow support will be viewed by the developers and others as intrusive if there is not complete agreement as to the processes that the workflow will support.

Summary

In this chapter we have looked at workflow technology as our first example of workgroup computing. In the next chapters, we'll turn our attention to different classes of groupware.

Again, as we noted in Chapter 1, it is important that the reader not be caught up in the terminology. "Workflow" to one person is "groupware" to another, and little agreement exists as to formal definitions—let alone characteristics—of these relatively new disciplines. Even as this book is being completed, the Workflow Management Coalition (WMC)—an organization comprised of workflow vendors and consultants—is "developing standards for terminology, interfaces, task parameters, and application programming interfaces" and "some standards [will be] developed by the end of the year [1995] or early next year.[7]

As a reader interested in workflow, you need to have an idea of what you want and need workflow software to do for you and your organization's processes and to develop plans along those lines. Products can be evaluated in accordance with your target features and capabilities and you can influence vendors' products so they will incorporate the things you have determined are important.

7 T. Ouellette, "Confusion Slows Down Workflow Software," *Computerworld*, May 29, 1995, p. 48.

Part 3

Workgroup Products

5

Categories of groupware

While groupware includes a number of different types of products, most can be classified into one of six basic categories based on functionality. These categories are useful when looking for a specific type of product to satisfy a specific business need. Some products may fit into more than one category since they incorporate the functionality of multiple products. These categories also represent the evolution of groupware products from simple e-mail to full-featured business process reengineering systems. In this chapter, we will define six basic categories of groupware and examine the functionality provided by each category of product. In the succeeding chapters, a category-by-category review of major groupware products will be presented.

Groupware categories

The term groupware encompasses a wide range of products. Given the high degree of interest in groupware and workgroup computing, more and more products are entering the market and many existing products are being remarketed as groupware. The earlier chapters of this text go into great detail on what groupware is and what it does. Based on our earlier definition of workgroup computing, we can define six distinct categories of workgroup software. These categories are

- E-mail and scheduling
- Electronic forms routing
- Image processing
- Document management
- Business process automation
- Business process analysis

Let us now examine each of these in more detail.

E-mail and scheduling

E-mail has been around for quite some time. Most of the early mainframe-based mail systems were little more than simple text editors with the ability to route messages or files to a designated user. As the mainframe computing environment matured, so did e-mail systems. Editing and routing features became more sophisticated and incorporated word processing software and predefined distribution lists. Some notable mainframe products include IBM's Professional Office System (PROFS) and the more recent OfficeVision. Both provide e-mail, individual and group scheduling features, and can even incorporate document imaging.

While e-mail may have had its beginnings on the mainframe, it really came of age with the introduction of the local area network (LAN). A LAN provides the connectivity necessary for e-mail to flourish. As with mainframe systems, LAN-based e-mail evolved from simple messaging to full-featured word processing, with the ability to attach word processing documents, spreadsheets, and other PC files. Several software vendors such as WordPerfect, Microsoft, and Lotus have integrated their e-mail products into other PC applications such as word processing, database, and spreadsheet applications. This provided the beginnings for some of the more advanced workgroup products described later in the text.

While connectivity in a LAN was valuable, as more and more LANs became interconnected, e-mail became an even more valuable tool. As wide-area networking (WAN) became more common, e-mail was perhaps one of the first applications to exploit this new type of connectivity. In many cases, e-mail has replaced hard copy distribution of memos, files, and other documents. This results in savings not only in distribution costs, but also in staff hours. Time spent preparing and mailing material is greatly reduced. Transit time is reduced, even when compared to overnight mail.

Faster distribution of information provides a competitive advantage in today's business environment. Given a large organization with many physically separate locations, it is easy to see the value of a means by which to quickly and economically distribute information.

The Internet is another example of the growth and popularity of e-mail as a means of communication. As the cost of PC hardware, WAN, and data communications drops, corporate e-mail systems can be expected to proliferate.

Figure 5-1 shows a typical corporate e-mail system. In addition to the network file server, often a dedicated mail server is utilized. This is particularly true in situations where a number of LANs are inter-

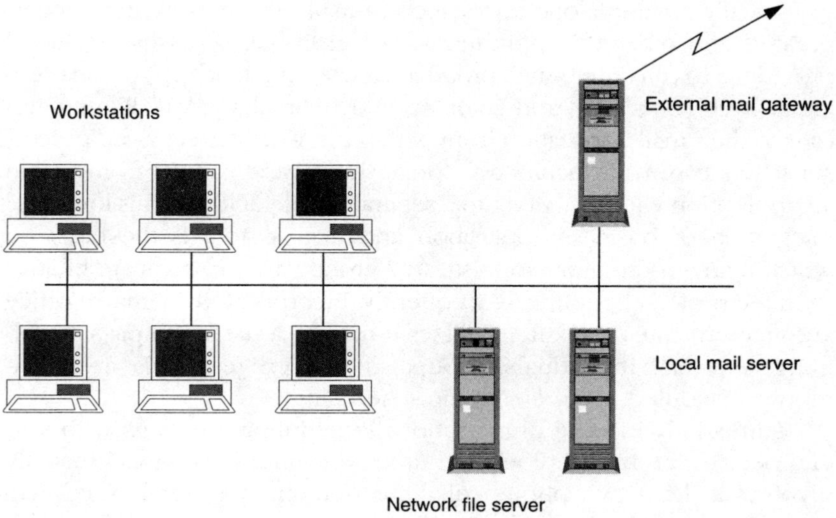

5-1 *Typical e-mail configuration.*

connected. The mail server acts as a central mail distribution and routing facility. The mail server can also function as a central mail directory, containing name and e-mail address information for all users.

When several different mail systems are in use, or when connectivity to an outside mail service such as the Internet is desired, a mail gateway is used. This gateway provides address and mail message translation to allow disparate mail systems to communicate. As the number and type of different systems grows, so does the complexity of the mail gateway.

Most e-mail vendors provide gateways to other mail systems and standardized formats such as Novell's Message Handling System (MHS) or the CCITT (International Consultative Committee for Telephone and Telegraph) X.400 and X.500 standards. The X.400 standard deals with the format and content of e-mail, while the X.500 standard addresses directory services. These standards are intended to provide e-mail connectivity between heterogeneous mail systems.

More complex multivendor, multiplatform, multiprotocol interconnections may require the use of products such as SoftSwitch, which is billed as an "anything to anything" mail gateway. Many e-mail vendors provide specialized gateways such as FAX gateways to allow FAXs to be sent through the e-mail system via a shared FAX server. This provides FAX capabilities to all users of the mail system at a much lower cost than providing individual FAX modems or shared FAX machines.

Initially a stand-alone application, e-mail now is commonly incorporated into other PC applications. For example, Lotus has included provisions to call their e-mail product from within their applications programs such Lotus 1-2-3 and Lotus Approach. Similarly, WordPerfect has calls to their mail application from within the WordPerfect word processor. Users can mail documents, spreadsheets, and reports from within an application without exiting to a separate mail package. This low-level integration of business application and mail system is the basis on which many of the more sophisticated groupware products are built.

Electronic scheduling is frequently incorporated in many office automation suites and often utilizes e-mail as a means to pass scheduling requests. Individuals, groups, and even resources are commonly scheduled using electronic scheduling.

Particularly in large organizations, scheduling meetings with several people can be a tedious and time-consuming exercise. It usually involves at least two phone calls and potentially several voice mail exchanges in order to resolve a meeting time acceptable to all parties. Next comes the task of locating a suitable conference room and the necessary resources such as audiovisual equipment. Electronic scheduling greatly simplifies this task by comparing the schedules of all members of the group, the schedule of available meeting rooms, and any other required resources.

When the meeting time and location has been resolved, all members are notified by e-mail message and an appropriate entry placed in their schedules. This serves as a reminder to the individual and prevents them from being scheduled for other events in the same time frame.

Several scheduling packages, such as WordPerfect, include a user-definable alarm that sounds at a preset time before an event such as a meeting to remind the attendee. Scheduling packages are generally viewed as a means for individuals to manage their personal calendars, but the real value in these products is their ability to share information and facilitate the scheduling of groups of individuals.

Characteristics

E-mail and scheduling provide the beginnings of a group computing environment in which individuals can exchange messages and documents and schedule meetings and other activities. In general, e-mail and scheduling applications possess the following characteristics when considered in the context of workgroup computing:

Replaces current manual methods/systems

In most instances, e-mail and messaging simply replace existing manual means of communication. Analysis and reengineering of the business process is not performed, the existing manual process is simply expedited. Rather than type, print, and mail a document for review, it is e-mailed from creator to reviewer to approver and beyond. While this may be a great improvement and result in time savings, the underlying process does not change. Groups of people are not able to collectively compose, review, and approve a document. The existing serial flow of information remains.

No imbedded business logic

E-mail and scheduling does not incorporate business logic or rules that pertain to the process. For example, a purchase request may have a specific routing based on a dollar amount—requests under $1000 may only require one departmental approval, while those over $1000 may require two. Basic e-mail systems cannot differentiate between the two requests. Using this example, if the purchase request required the approval of any one of three division managers, basic e-mail generally could not notify all three, accept approval from the first manager to deal with the request, and then forward the approved request for further processing.

User-controlled rules and routing

Since the mail system has no imbedded logic or routing, the user must apply the corrected rules and route the document appropriately. As in the previous example, the user must understand the underlying rules of the business process and route the document appropriately. The decision on what approvals were required based on dollar amount would be made by the user and the request would be routed by the user to the appropriate person for approval.

Little to no control or management

Most e-mail systems provide little information on the status of a message other than when it was received and perhaps when it was opened by the recipient. Information on where a document is in the overall process is usually not available. Each person in the process may know that the document was received and read by the next person in the process, but the status of the document in the overall process is not tracked. Generally, statistics on how long a document was in process are not provided and overall management of the process is limited.

Low level of applications integration

Other than the applications integration mentioned previously, there is little integration between the business application and the e-mail system. The e-mail system is simply replacing a manual means of distributing information; rather than placing documents in an envelope for distribution, they are mailed electronically.

Electronic forms routing

Electronic forms routing is in many ways an outgrowth of e-mail. Rather than a free-form text message, electronic forms provide a structure for data capture and entry. As electronic form systems have evolved, they have incorporated routing and other business logic into basic data collection. Based on certain criteria, the form can be routed to the next appropriate step in the approval or processing flow. This is an advance over the simple e-mail system previously described.

Some forms packages such as JetForm are follow-on products to hard copy form printing packages. It was a natural evolution to route a form via an e-mail system after producing it electronically. This basically replicates the manual flow of a paper document, but adds the benefit of producing and distributing it electronically. This provides, in most situations, some time and cost savings over a manual system.

Most forms packages utilize an e-mail system or a database to enter and route forms. In the case of an e-mail system, the form is simply a specialized type of mail message that is formatted for a specific purpose. It may have imbedded logic that edits and validates fields, as well as some type of routing logic that determines the next recipient of the form. The e-mail system is then used to distribute the form.

With a database system, an entry is made in the database for each new form. The same type of editing and validation that are used in an e-mail system can occur. Once the entry is made in the database, the next recipient of the form is notified by a mail message or when they access the forms application. Often this is in the form of an in basket or a queue of pending work.

The major difference between these two types of systems is the storage and routing of the forms. With an e-mail-based system, the forms are not stored centrally and are passed as mail messages. In a database system, the forms are centrally stored and managed. Both systems have advantages and disadvantages.

A forms system based on e-mail allows more flexibility in terms of the overall use of the mail system and does not restrict the distribution of forms and other documents to a specific application. For example, a help desk application that utilizes a database would be limited to only those forms that directly relate to that application. Another forms application or mail system would be required for administrative and general mail functions. An e-mail-based application would support the help desk application and other electronic forms routing applications as well as general e-mail.

A database system, on the other hand, provides a way to manage and monitor the processing of forms. This is a concern mentioned previously in the discussion of e-mail systems. A database-type system can report on the status of forms for management and statistical purposes. Most database forms systems are designed for specific applications.

While there are some mainframe and midrange electronic forms applications, most forms packages are targeted toward LANs. The combination of a LAN and a PC workstation provides a graphical interface for the forms package and a communications infrastructure to distribute the form. The relatively low cost of the LAN/PC combination offers an attractive solution for vendors of turnkey applications.

Several "shrink wrapped" forms packages, such as WordPerfect Informs, make electronic forms routing a viable solution for most small businesses and organizations. Figure 5-2 illustrates a typical electronic forms system. In this system an e-mail system is utilized to pass forms from one step to the next in a process. Figure 5-3 shows the same type of system utilizing a database to store forms.

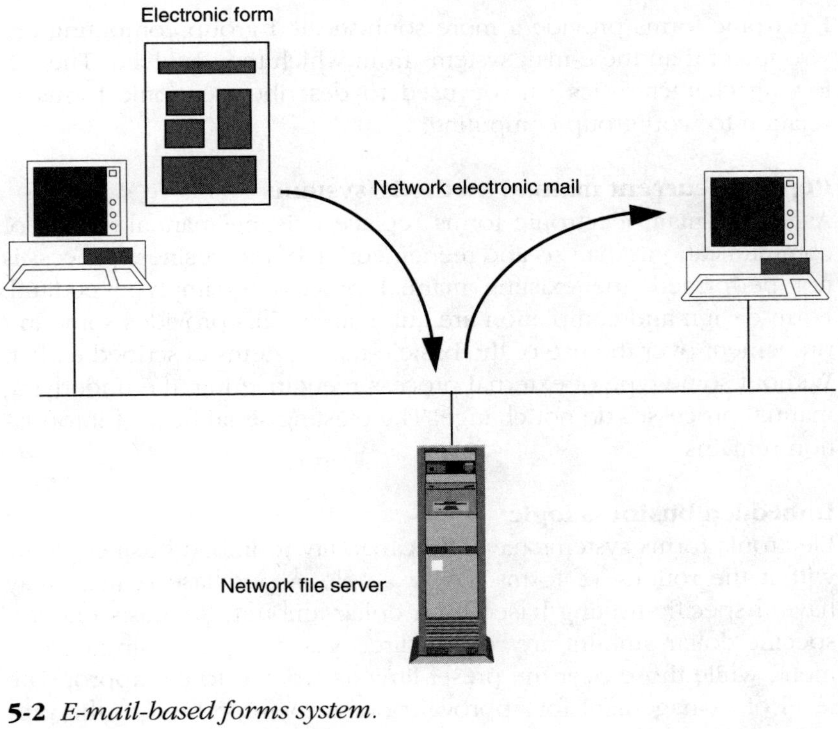

5-2 *E-mail-based forms system.*

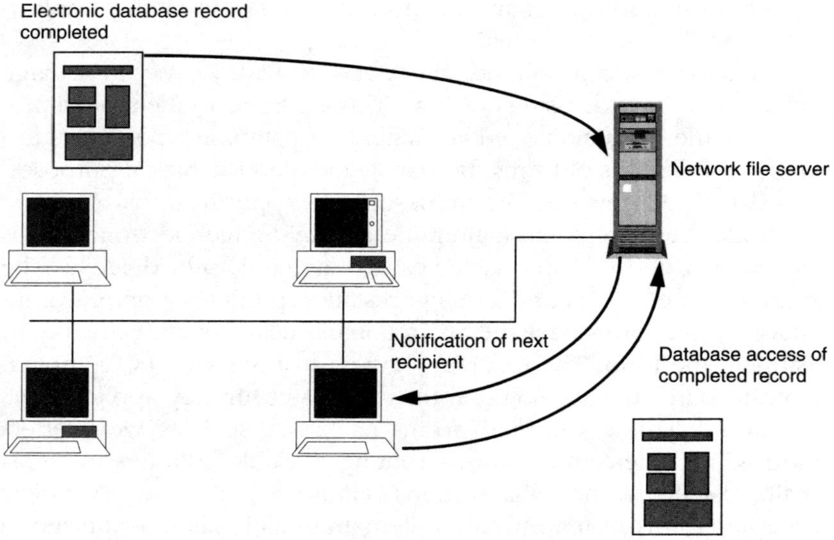

5-3 *Database forms system.*

Characteristics

Electronic forms provide a more sophisticated group computing environment than the e-mail systems from which they evolved. The following characteristics can be used to describe electronic forms in relation to workgroup computing:

Replaces current manual methods/systems

As with e-mail, electronic forms replace existing manual means of communication. Analysis and reengineering of the business process is not performed, the existing manual process is simply expedited. Form design and completion are automated. This provides some improvement over the use of the basic e-mail systems described earlier. Without some type of external process reengineering, the underlying manual processes do not change. The existing serial flow of information remains.

Imbedded business logic

Electronic forms systems have the capability to imbed business logic within the routing of forms. For example, a purchase request may have a specific routing based on a dollar amount. Requests under a specific dollar amount are routed directly to the purchasing department, while those over the preset limit are routed to the appropriate level of management for approval prior to being routed to the purchasing department. This is a significant improvement over basic e-mail. The users of the system are not required to apply the requisite business rules to transactions as they enter the information into the forms system. The level of sophistication of the business logic varies from product to product. Some specify only a simple routing flow, while others apply more complex routing algorithms.

Little to no control or management

As with e-mail systems, most forms packages provide little information on the status of forms once they have been created. If the forms package is based on an e-mail system, the e-mail system must be used as a means to track the distribution of the forms. Overall management of forms is usually not possible. Forms packages that utilize databases as repositories for forms can provide more information on the status of a form as it is processed.

Low level of applications integration

Generally the electronic forms system is the application and it is not integrated with other business applications. For example, an electronic forms system may be used to gather data for a loan application. The completed form may then be routed to the appropriate individual for review and processing. The actual processing of the loan application may involve other business applications that are not integrated with the forms application. Separate applications that check credit history, verify existing balances, and calculate maximum loan amount may not be integrated with the forms application. Forms packages that utilize databases may offer a higher degree of integration, in that other applications can be developed that access the database for information entered through the forms application.

Generally LAN based

Most electronic forms packages are designed to operate on LANs. The connectivity that LANs provide makes them an attractive platform for group computing applications such as electronic forms. In some cases, this may complicate the overall processing flow, particularly in situations where business applications are spread over multiple platforms.

Image processing

The use of electronic imaging in a group computing environment grew out of the initial use of imaging as a means to automate the filing and retrieval of hard copy documents. These early imaging systems were designed to reduce the amount of physical space required to store documents and to simplify the process of retrieving documents. Many organizations found that the storage of hard copy documents was costly and time-consuming. Documents had to be categorized in some fashion and then filed according to some preestablished structure. The retrieval of the document usually involved the search of some type of index and then the physical access of the original hard copy document.

The process is similar to the filing of a book in a library according to the Dewey decimal system. The book is categorized by title, author, and subject, given the appropriate coding, an entry is made to the card catalog, and the book is placed in the proper location. The retrieval of the book follows the same process. All of these activities are costly and time-consuming, particularly when dealing with large volumes of information.

In addition to the cost of storing physical documents, there are also concerns about security and data integrity. Physical security must be maintained for sensitive documents and all information must be protected from other hazards such as fire, water damage, and physical deterioration.

Image processing provided a solution to these many concerns. Banking, insurance, and government are some of the organizations that utilize document imaging as a means to deal with the storage and retrieval of large volumes of documents. As computer hardware prices and the cost of data storage have dropped, imaging has become an even more attractive solution.

Imaging technology has advanced in the past few years and is now within reach of most small businesses. Many vendors of business application software have "image-enabled" their products to deal with the demand for image processing. Most database systems now support the storage of images in addition to other types of data.

The use of imaging in workgroup computing grew out of early imaging storage systems much the same way electronic forms evolved from e-mail systems. Image processing systems function in much the same way as electronic forms systems. The major difference with imaging is that an electronic image of an original document is passed for processing rather than an electronically completed form.

There are many reasons for passing an image rather than entering data on an electronic form. One major reason is that the original forms were completed in hard copy external to the system. An example of this would be the imaging of packing slips and other shipping documents in an accounts payable system. The documents involved are prepared external to the system in formats that are not standardized, but contain information that is required to complete the receipt of goods and the payment of a vendor. By imaging the original documents, information on who signed for goods, when and where goods were received, and other detailed receiving information can be electronically attached to a vendor's request for payment. This allows the accounts payable function to review the appropriate documents when processing the payment request, as well as providing quick access to information when resolving problems or responding to inquiries.

Another reason for imaging documents is legal requirements. This is particularly true in government, banking, and the insurance industry. Many government entities are using imaging for documents processing as well as document storage. While the legalities of an electronic image versus an original hard copy document are still being questioned, the trend seems to be toward the acceptance of electronic images. The fear of alteration of images is reduced by the use of write once read many (WORM) optical storage systems.

Image processing systems are usually comprised of a number of components. Figure 5-4 shows a typical image processing configuration. This type of configuration would support an image storage system as well as an imaging group computing application.

The first step in the process is to scan the original document into the imaging system. This might be accomplished at a centralized location or at distributed sites. As the image is scanned, it is indexed in some fashion. This can be done via optical character recognition (OCR) software or data entry. In the case of OCR software, a specific area in the scanned image is used to obtain a reference or index number. For example, an invoice number or a claim number. The refer-

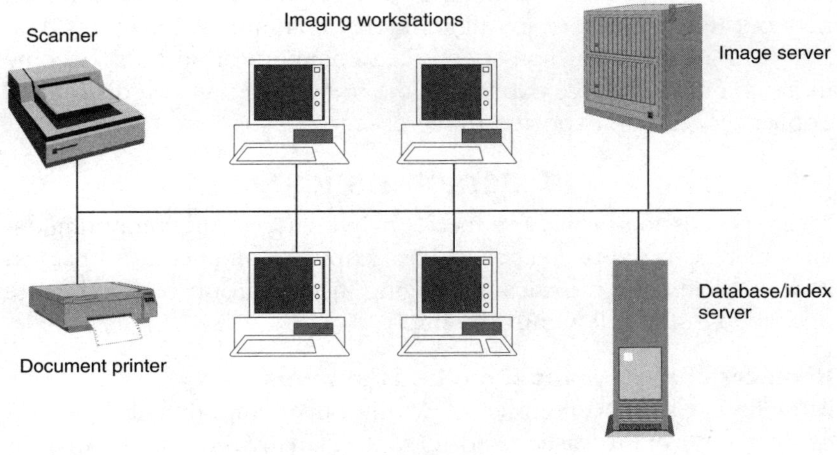

5-4 *Typical image processing configuration.*

ence or index is used to store the data and is used again to retrieve the document when requested.

Many imaging systems use both an image server and a database server. The database server contains index information, while the image server contains the actual images. The application program accesses the index database and uses that information to retrieve the desired image from the image server. In order to display the image, a specialized image workstation is normally required. These workstations typically have large high-resolution monitors and graphic cards designed to deal with images. An additional component of the system is an image printer to produce hard copies of stored images.

The primary difference between an image storage system and a workgroup imaging system is that workgroup systems typically incorporate images into the overall business process, while an image storage system is simply a means to store and retrieve images. In a storage system, all processing of the document occurs in other manual or automated systems and the image is not integrated into the process. In workgroup imaging systems, the image is incorporated into the business process. For example, the image of an invoice initiates the accounts payable process. As the process continues, images of the shipping and receiving documents and finally the check sent to the vendor are attached to the transaction. The overall business process is image-enabled.

A major concern with imaging is bandwidth requirements. Generally images require large amounts of bandwidth, and the passing of images over a WAN can quickly utilize all available bandwidth. Most imaging installations either restrict imaging to a local area, imaging at remote locations and transmitting to a central location at nonpeak network usage times, or install additional communications links dedicated to imaging. As high-speed data communication links become more common and less expensive, the use of imaging as a distributed application can be expected to increase.

Characteristics

Image processing provides a means by which a group computing environment can utilize images of hard copy documents in a business process. The characteristics of imaging in workgroup computing are described in the following paragraphs.

Replaces current manual methods/systems

As with the other categories of workgroup computing, image processing is in many cases used to replace manual systems. Analysis and reengineering of the business process may not necessarily be performed. The existing manual process is expedited, however; the process for handling, filing, and retrieving information is redesigned by virtue of the technology used to manage the images. These handling, filing, and retrieval processes may comprise a large share of overall resources. Significant savings may be realized even without altering the underlying business process.

Imbedded business logic

Business logic may not be imbedded in the images themselves but rather in the applications that utilize the images. Based on data contained in the images or entered manually, forms can be routed for processing and approval. Applications can be designed to base the routing and approval of transactions on the attachment of images as well. For example, an image of an invoice that does not have images of required receiving documents would be routed for further investigation, while an invoice image with images of the appropriate receiving documents would be routed for payment.

Process control and management

Since the images and the image index are centrally stored and managed, there is usually a high degree of control and management in image-enabled workgroup applications. The status of an individual document in the system can be determined and the functioning of the overall process can be measured and managed. Useful information, such as total workload and average process completion times, can be gathered for management reporting and process reengineering efforts.

High level of applications integration

Image processing is generally based on an existing business application. As previously mentioned, the exception to this is image storage, which does not integrate imaging with an application but instead functions as an independent storage and retrieval system. The image is often the core of the application and initiates the business process. An image-enabled insurance claim processing application is an example of a highly integrated imaging application. In this example, the image of the claim form completed by the policyholder initiates claim processing, with the end result being a settlement with the policyholder. At each step in the process the image of the claim form is the source document that is utilized in processing. Other images such as photographs of damages, quotes for repairs, and accident reports may become part of the overall electronic file for the claim. The images relating to the claim are integrated within the application and the overall claim process.

High resource requirements

Image-enabled applications have high resource requirements. This includes imaging hardware and network communications. Imaging hardware includes scanners, imaging workstations, optical servers, and image printers. As hardware prices continue to decline, the cost of this type of hardware is reduced but is still significant. As was mentioned earlier, network communications requirements are also a factor in imaging. In addition to hardware there may also be high support requirements for system administration and maintenance.

Document management

Document management deals with the management and coordination of documents and other automated products. This includes such products as engineering plans, designs, word processing documents, and computer software. In this type of group computing environment, individual members of the group can work on different pieces of a more complex project that is centrally stored and managed. Central storage is a definite convenience, but the real value in products such as this is the central management and coordination of work on individual pieces of the overall project. Members of the group "check out" their particular work assignments and then replace them after work has been completed. Other members of the group can access the completed work for review and for use when working on their own assignments. The status of the overall project and its component pieces can be easily managed.

Figure 5-5 shows a typical document management application. In this example, a group of writers are collaborating on a workgroup computing book. Each of the three writers has the task of contributing to the introductory chapter, as well as writing several chapters on specific topics. As each writer adds his or her section to the introductory chapter, the updated document is available for review and comment by the others in the group. As specific chapters are completed, they become available for the other members of the group to review and to refer to as they complete their assignments.

The editor can monitor the progress of the overall book project and send the completed sections for copyediting as they are completed. Compared to the manual process of sending hard copy documents to each writer on the project, the document management system offers a much more efficient means of sharing information and creating a group computing environment.

Many producers of application development software are including some type of document management capabilities with their soft-

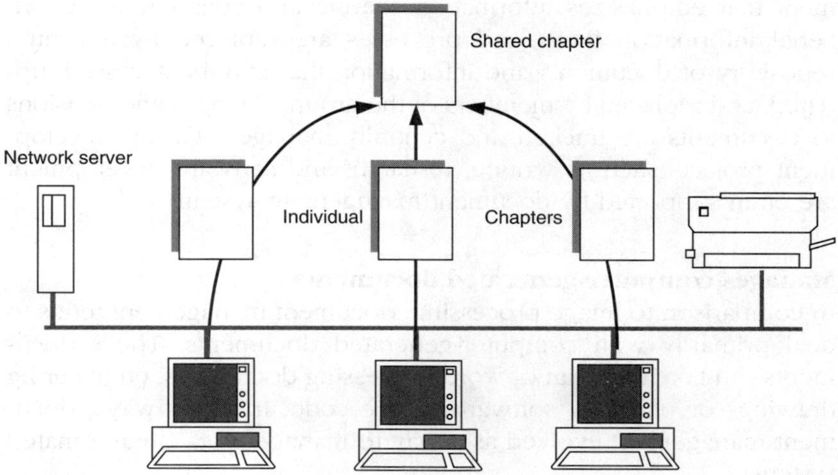

5-5 *Writers' workgroup document management.*

ware suites. This allows a number of programmers to work together on a single application. This greatly reduces application development time and facilitates the flow of information and completed application code between members of the group. An example of this is ObjectView, a client server application development package. The enterprise version of the software allows programmers to "check out" various modules of applications code and then reassembles the various modules into a completed application.

The software development environment introduces the added dimension of version control. As changes and modifications to programs during and after completion of the application occur, these changes need to be documented and tracked. Many application development packages, as well as third-party control software, provide this capability.

Characteristics

Document management systems provide a true group computing environment, in that the activities of a group of people are centrally coordinated and managed. These types of systems support collaborative efforts rather than automating existing manual processes or systems. The characteristics of document management are described in the following paragraphs.

Creates a "true" group computing environment

Document management systems often do more than simply replace existing manual systems. They create a group computing environment that emphasizes information sharing and collaborative effort. Serial information flows and processes are replaced by a central repository of documents and information that may be accessed, updated, and replaced by members of the group. Changes and revisions to documents are tracked and centrally managed. Group development projects such as writing, research, and software development are often supported by document management systems.

Manages computer-generated documents

In comparison to image processing, document management tends to deal primarily with computer-generated documents. These documents can take the form of word processing documents, engineering drawings or plans, or software source code. In many ways, document management evolved as a way to manage work on automated systems.

Document control and management

Centrally storing and managing documents provides a high degree of overall control and management. Most document management systems support change and version control, check-in/check-out, access control, and document search and retrieval. Change and version control provides a history of all changes to a particular document. This is particularly useful in managing software and engineering projects. The check-in/check-out process tracks which member of the group currently has control of a document and provides file- and record-locking functions similar to those found in database management systems. This prevents two members of the group from simultaneously changing documents and overwriting each other's changes. Access control provides a way to manage who can retrieve, change, and replace documents. Certain members of the group may only be allowed to view documents, while others may be allowed to alter and replace documents. Document search and retrieval can be useful when searching large volumes of documents for a specific reference. For example, search all marketing documents for the product name "XYZ" or search all source code for the routine "get_user_id." Once retrieved, the documents can be changed as needed.

Project-oriented rather than process-oriented

Document management systems are generally used to support development-type projects rather than ongoing business processes. The focus of document management systems is the document. Other categories of groupware are oriented more toward business processes.

Business process automation

Business process automation software is fundamentally different from the previous categories of groupware, in that it focuses on business processes rather than data. This forces an analysis of business processes and provides opportunities for process reengineering. The other categories of groupware products mentioned to this point focus on the management of data such as e-mail, forms, images, or documents. While process automation products do eventually deal with data, the first step is to deal with the underlying process and then design systems to deal with the data needs of the process.

The growing interest in total quality management (TQM) has sparked a great deal of interest in business process reengineering. Business process automation software provides an automated means to implement reengineering initiatives. The lure of high returns on investment and reduction in process costs have generated a growing demand for business process automation products. A recent study reported an average return on investment of over 100 percent and a median payback period of just over 2 years for one software package.

Often process analysis tools are used to document and analyze existing business processes. From this analysis reengineering of the process can occur. The analysis tools often feed other types of process automation design tools which actually create the automated process. To differentiate between the two types of products—process analysis and process automation tools—we will consider each separately. This section will cover process automation products and the next section will deal with process analysis and design tools.

Process automation software is similar to computer-aided software engineering (CASE) software in that it develops application code based on some type of higher-level design process. Generally the design process is graphical in nature and may relate to or be based on business processes modeled by process analysis tools. The application software generated is usually for a specific database such as Microsoft's SQL server or for a workgroup package such as Lotus Notes.

Database applications developed through process automation software can often be linked to user interfaces developed in other languages such C++ or Visual Basic that can call Windows dynamic linked libraries (DLLs). This allows for the development of user interfaces independent of the process automation software and the database.

Characteristics

Business process automation software is the tool by which workgroup computing applications are developed. Generally they are used to produce application software for a database management system or a workgroup environment. The following characteristics describe business process automation software:

Creates a "true" group computing environment
By generating an application based on the business process, a group computing environment is created. Flows of information between and among members of the group are established. Members of the group collaborate on the completion of a task through some business process that is facilitated by the application.

Process centered rather than data centered
The categories of products previously mentioned dealt primarily with data, while process automation software focuses on the underlying business process. These types of products force the organization to document, analyze, and potentially reengineer business processes. Existing processes are often discarded and replaced by new processes that are either more efficient, less costly, or provide some sort of competitive advantage.

Short application development time
Often these products utilize a graphical application design environment that can drastically reduce the amount of time required to develop an application. The skill set required for application development also changes and development may shift from information systems/information technologies (IS/IT) to the process owners. Processes are graphically modeled making them more understandable and more easily analyzed. Changes and modifications to applications are made more easily in a graphical environment.

Interface independent
Generally these products support the development of an application independent of the user interface. Interfaces can be developed using a number of tools and then linked to the process application.

Business process analysis

Business process analysis software is used to analyze and potentially reengineer business processes. This step is generally a precursor to the use of business process automation software. These tools facilitate the analysis and reengineering process and either directly or indirectly feed the process automation software. Tools can range from simple flowcharting packages to more complex process modeling and simulation packages.

Most advanced process analysis tools are based on some type of process methodology. This methodology defines how steps in processes are interrelated and how they contribute to completion of the overall process. Current processes are modeled and then analyzed using the methodology. Certain quantitative measurements may need to be taken and entered into the tool. This provides a way to measure the impact of changes in the process as various reengineering initiatives are applied to the model of the existing process. Often these quantitative measurements are in the form of time or dollars. The goal is to design a process that is either less costly in terms of dollars or more efficient in terms of time.

Manufacturing is an example of an area in which lower cost would be a goal, while a help desk or customer service organization would be an example of a process where a shorter response time would be a desirable goal. The two goals of lower cost and reduction in total process time may be at odds with each other in some situations. The purpose of process analysis is to point out these types of situations.

For example, in order to reduce the amount of time it takes to answer customer inquiries, it may be necessary to add additional customer service representatives. This may not be the lowest-cost alternative, but it would meet the shorter response time goal. A business decision would need to be made based on the results of the process analysis.

Characteristics

Business process analysis software is utilized in the analysis and reengineering of business processes. The following characteristics describe business process analysis software:

Process model tool rather than applications development tool

These tools are only for the analysis and reengineering of business processes. Other software is required for process automation.

Functions independently or in conjunction with process automation software

Most vendors of process automation software also market an analysis tool. The advantage of a single vendor solution is that the design from the analysis tool can feed the process automation package, expediting the application development process. The analysis tool can be used later to modify or change the application. Analysis tools can function independent of a process automation tool.

Graphical process modeling

Generally process analysis tools model business processes graphically. This facilitates process owner involvement and may reduce user training time.

Quantitative in nature

The analysis tool may require that certain quantitative measures be taken in the existing process and entered into the process model. These measures are used to determine the effect of reengineering on the overall process. Generally these measures reflect the current costs of steps in the process in terms of dollars or time.

May include simulation and modeling capabilities

More advanced tools include process simulation and modeling capabilities. This allows for "what if" scenarios in which variables in the process can be changed and the impact on the process studied. These capabilities can range from simple economic models to more advanced statistical modeling.

Summary

The categories listed previously are representative of the types of products that might be found in the workgroup computing market. Some products may fit into more than one category. A single workgroup computing solution might utilize products from several categories. For example, a process analysis tool might be used to reengineer a process that is then fed into a process automation package. The package may then be used to develop an application that utilizes e-mail and document imaging. These categories are by no means mutually exclusive and serve only as a means to categorize products.

In terms of complexity and potential return, it is generally true that the higher-end products, while requiring a larger investment, can provide a greater return. Figure 5-6 illustrates the relationships of the various categories of products and their potential return. This is not to say that relatively simple workgroup products such as e-mail cannot have a significant impact on an organization. Indeed, simple products can have a great potential impact. However, as applications become more integrated with the business process and that process becomes the subject of analysis and reengineering, the potential rewards can become much greater.

Later chapters discuss representative products in each of the categories described here. This is not a complete listing of all products, but a sample of the products and functionality available with various

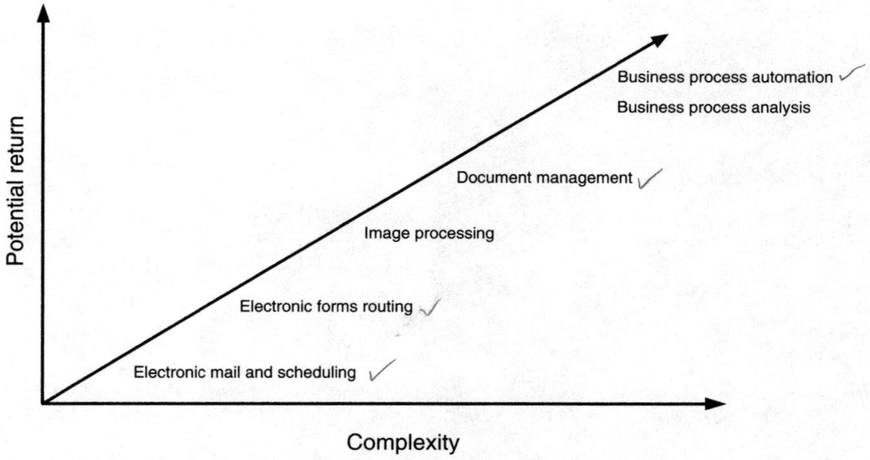

5-6 *Complexity versus potential return.*

workgroup computing solutions. While the authors have endeavored to provide the most accurate information available at the time of printing, it is suggested you contact the individual vendors for the most up-to-date product information. See the appendices for vendor listings and contact information. Specific products and manufacturers are mentioned for informational purposes only and no endorsement or recommendation of any product or vendor is made or implied.

6

E-mail and scheduling

Two major concerns with e-mail and scheduling products are interoperability and integration. Interoperability deals with the ability to interconnect mail systems regardless of the hardware environment and the mail system. This is of particular concern in large organizations with heterogeneous systems.

The computing environment that exists in most enterprises is a mixture of hardware and software acquired to meet specific business needs with little or no concern for interoperability. While this may not impact individual business applications, it will have a great impact on efforts to implement an enterprise-wide e-mail system. For example, it would be much more difficult to interconnect the e-mail systems on a DEC VAX, an IBM AS400, and an HP3000 than it would be to interconnect three like systems.

This difficulty in interoperability exists not only in terms of hardware, but also in terms of software. The way that mail systems address and format mail messages differs from vendor to vendor. There are two basic approaches to overcoming interoperability issues: proprietary gateways and messaging standards.

Proprietary gateways generally consist of software and/or hardware that link one proprietary e-mail system to another proprietary system. For example, Novell GroupWise offers a gateway to IBM OfficeVision/VM.[1] A concern with this approach is the availability of gateways from vendors that link specific mail products. If an organization has two proprietary mail systems, they would require a gateway that specifically dealt with those two mail systems. Proprietary

1 Technology Overview, GroupWise 4.1—Electronic Messaging Architecture (Provo, Utah: Novell, Inc.), September 10, 1994, p. 4.

gateways do not provide an all-to-all solution. Ongoing support as versions of software change should also be a consideration.

Messaging standards, on the other hand, provide a means to interconnect mail systems by conforming to a standard for message formatting. This allows any two systems that conform to the standard to exchange mail. The product previously mentioned, Novell GroupWise, also has gateways to X.400 and Simple Mail Transfer Protocol (SMTP).[2] These are two mail standards that a number of e-mail vendors support.

The X.400 standards are propagated by the International Consultative Committee for Telephone and Telegraphs (CCITT) and specify standards for the format and content of electronic messages. The SMTP is a part of the TCP/IP protocol suite that specifies a standard format for sending mail between platforms.[3] Other de facto mail standards include Novell Netware's Message Handling Services (MHS) and the recently released Global MHS. A number of third-party products and proprietary mail systems support MHS.

The second major concern is integration. The goal of integration is to combine the business application and mail system into a single application. With an integrated application, the users does not need to exit an application and then use a separate e-mail system to send work on to the next step in the processing flow. The business application becomes e-mail enabled. This integration can occur at many different levels.

At the lowest and least complex level, the mail system can be called from within a business application such as a word processor or spreadsheet program. Higher levels of integration remove the user from direct interaction with the mail system, and instead use application programming interfaces (APIs) to link the business application directly to the mail system. Microsoft's Mail Application Programming Interface (MAPI) is an example of this type of interface. Windows-based applications can use MAPI as a means to access different messaging systems for mail-enabled workgroup computing solutions.

E-mail and scheduling products

In this chapter we present several representative e-mail and scheduling products. This is not intended to be a complete review of all products nor a comparison of products. Specific products are used to illustrate

2 Ibid.

3 Douglas E. Comer, *Internetworking with TCP/IP*, 2nd ed. (Englewood Cliffs, New Jersey: Prentice Hall), 1991, p. 399.

the features of this category of groupware. Several e-mail products incorporate or include scheduling products as part of a complete workgroup computing package. A general description of the product is presented followed by a discussion of underlying process methodologies. Operating systems and hardware platforms supported are listed along with particular features of each product. To get the most recent information on specific products, please contact the vendors.

BeyondMail Version 2.0—Banyan Systems, Inc.

BeyondMail is a full-featured, LAN-based e-mail system. In addition to basic mail functionality it provides other workflow tools such as electronic scheduling and a rule language to automate the receipt and handling of mail messages. It utilizes Novell MHS, Global MHS, and Banyan Intelligent Messaging for VINES message transport systems.[4] This provides functionality with Novell, Banyan, and other MHS-compliant network operating systems. Figure 6-1 shows the main screen of BeyondMail.

From this screen, the various features and functions of BeyondMail are accessed. Navigation within the application is accomplished

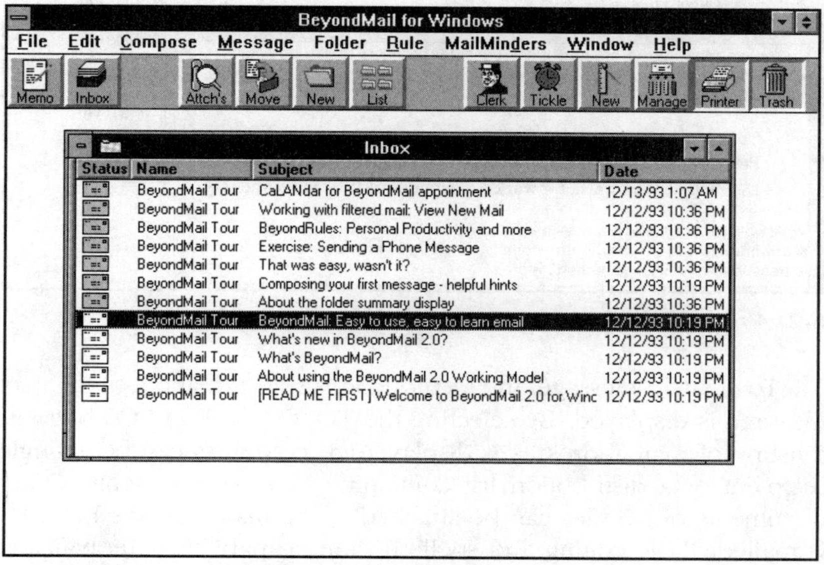

6-1 *Main screen of BeyondMail.*

4 BeyondMail Release 2.0, Product Overview (Westboro, Massachusetts: Banyan Systems, Inc.), 1994.

by either selecting a menu item or by using the icon bar. For example, messages can be deleted either by a menu selection or by dropping them on the Trash icon. The same is true for other functions such as printing.

The in-box contains mail messages that have been received and are awaiting disposition. Various folders can be set up to manage mail messages. Using a folder is similar to using subdirectories as a means to store related files. As folders are selected their contents are displayed. Users can define folders as needed. As individual messages are selected from the in-box or from a folder they are displayed. Figure 6-2 shows a typical mail message. By using the icon bar, the message can be replied to, forwarded, moved to a folder, printed, or deleted.

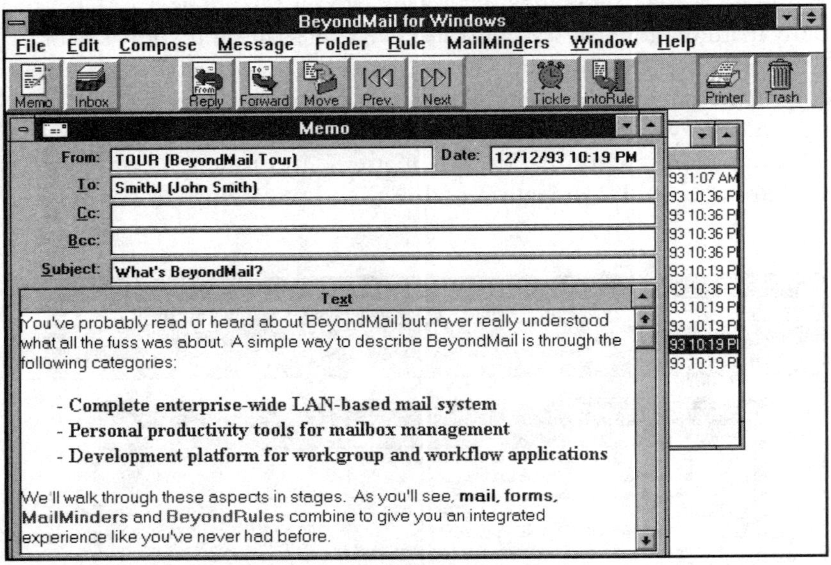

6-2 *A typical mail message in BeyondMail.*

To create a message, the Memo icon is selected and a blank mail message is displayed. By selecting the TO, CC, or Blind CC buttons, a listing of mail addresses is displayed. The address can be a single recipient or a distribution list containing multiple recipients. Other documents or PC files can be attached to the mail message before it is mailed. Basic editing and spell checking capabilities are available through the icon bar. Message priorities can be selected from the Options icon or from the priority box at the bottom of the message form. When the message is completed, it can be sent by clicking on the Send icon. Figure 6-3 shows a completed outbound mail message.

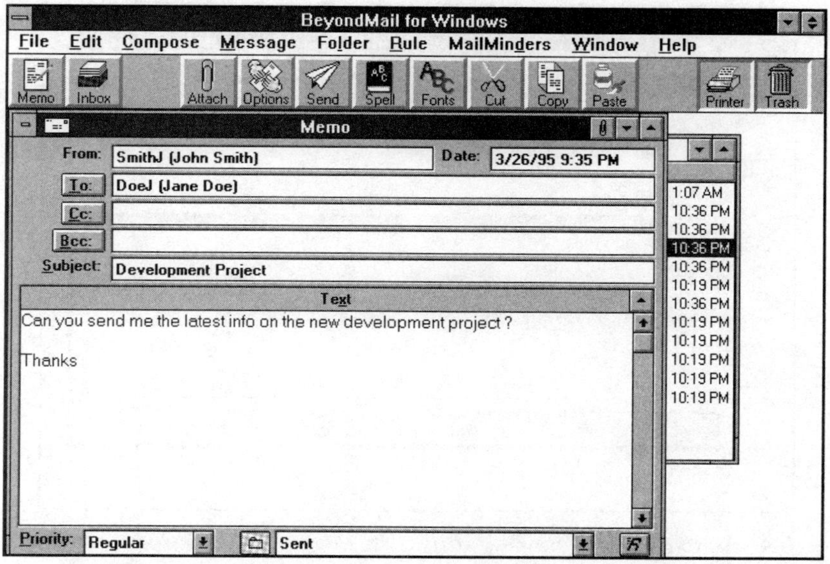

6-3 *A completed outbound mail message in BeyondMail.*

Two interesting features of BeyondMail are the MailMinder and BeyondRules. The MailMinder allows the automation of e-mail functions. Messages can be automatically filed, forwarded, or replied to. For example, during specific periods of time, such as during a business trip, mail messages can be automatically forwarded or replied to. The autoforward function can be turned on and off as desired. The Message Clerk automatically files new messages in specific folders when the feature is selected. Figure 6-4 shows an example of the Message Clerk function. In this example, any phone messages received are filed in the Phone folder and any Calendar messages received are filed in the Calendar folder.

BeyondRules is a scripting language that allows more complex rules to be applied to mail messages. These messages can be standard mail messages or other applications such as forms that utilize the mail system. Figure 6-5 shows an example of a simple rule. In this case, a mail message with a priority of "urgent" generates a beep at the users workstation and then is automatically filed in a folder labeled "Priority." More complex rules can be used to sort, file, and route mail messages. The case study at the end of this chapter cites an example of the use of BeyondRules in a complex workflow automation application.

Two versions of BeyondMail are available. The professional edition provides full e-mail functionality and includes the full rule lan-

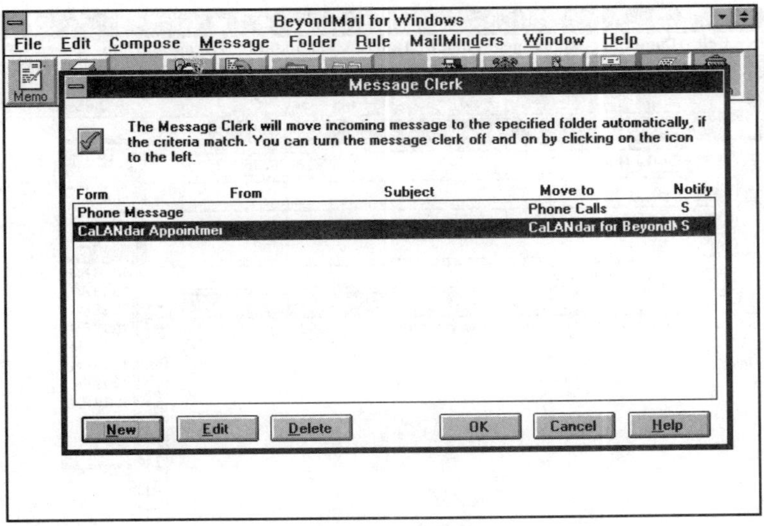

6-4 *An example of BeyondMail's Message Clerk function.*

guage. The standard edition is the base e-mail product without the full rule language.

Process methodology

BeyondMail is a client e-mail package that is designed to interact with several different mail transport systems. Figure 6-6 shows the layered

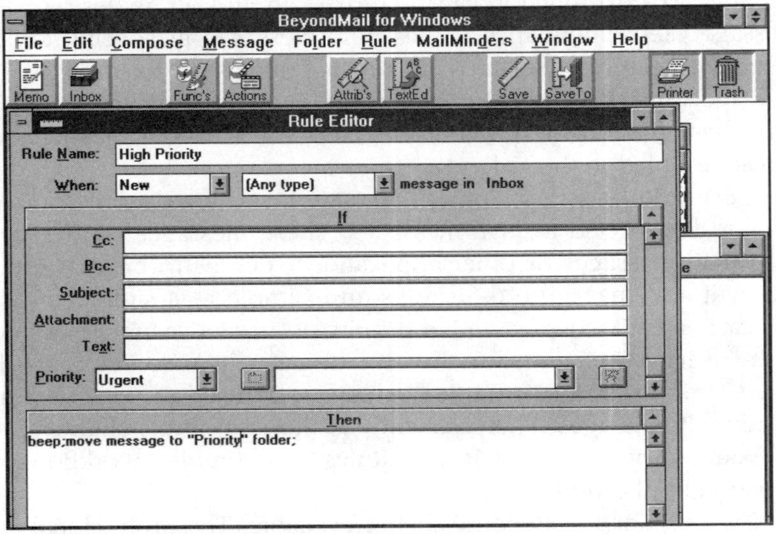

6-5 *An example of a simple rule in BeyondMail.*

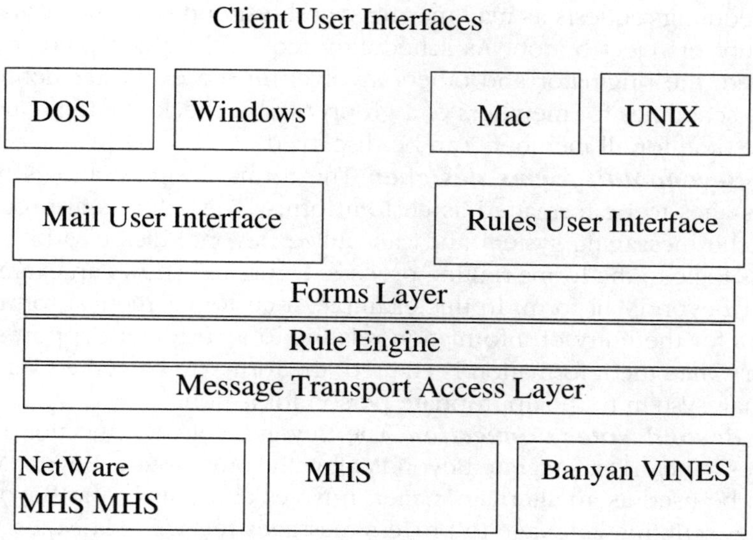

6-6 *Client-user interfaces.*

architecture of this product. The various user interfaces communicate with the mail interface and the rules interface. These two interfaces are built upon the forms layer, a rule engine, and a message transport access layer. The message transport access layer deals with the three mail transport systems. The GMHS and MHS transport systems are designed for Novell NetWare LANs. The MHS for non-NetWare LANs is designed for other LAN operating systems that conform to the MHS standard. The Banyan Intelligent Messaging for Vines transport system is also a supported transport system. This provides compatibility with existing BeyondMail 1.0 for Vines.

Operating systems and hardware platforms

BeyondMail currently operates on DOS and Windows clients connected to a PC-based LAN. Macintosh and UNIX client support is planned.

Features

In addition to the basic mail functions described previously, BeyondMail offers the following features:

BeyondMail CaLANdar BeyondMail CaLANdar, a companion product to BeyondMail, is an enterprise-wide scheduling tool for people and resources. It supports individual and group scheduling, appointment and meeting coordination, and task management. The calendar function utilizes the same messaging system as the mail product and offers the same cross-platform capabilities. Users receive scheduling requests as mail messages and respond to requests via an accept or reject button. As scheduling requests are accepted or rejected, the originator and others involved in the event are notified. The schedules for members of a group can be checked and an available time for all members can be displayed.

BeyondMail forms designer The forms designer allows mail messages to be formatted as custom forms. These forms are routed via the messaging system and can utilize BeyondRules to add business logic to the forms routing process. Figure 6-7 shows an example of a BeyondMail form. In this example, a customer request form allows for the entry of information relating to a customer support system. Once the information is entered, the form can be routed via the e-mail system to the appropriate person for action.

Beyond Notes Connection The Beyond Notes Connection provides a means to integrate BeyondMail with Lotus Notes.[5] BeyondMail can be used as an alternate mailer in Notes and utilizes the BeyondRules scripting language to process messages received via Notes.

Collabra Share Collabra Share creates an electronic forum for the exchange of information between members of a workgroup. Members of the group can exchange data in the form of text, numbers,

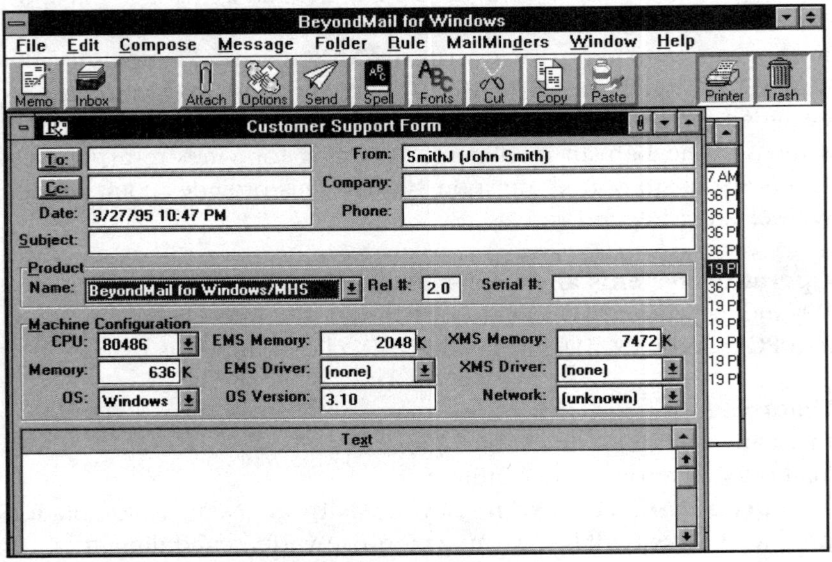

6-7 *An example of a BeyondMail form.*

5 BeyondMail and Lotus Notes, Product Overview (Westboro, Massachusetts: Banyan Systems, Inc.), 1994.

graphics, audio, and video. The Collabra Share product supports a number of messaging standards including BeyondMail and Banyan Intelligent Messaging.

cc:Mail—Lotus Development Corp.

cc:Mail is a LAN-based e-mail package that supports the transfer of messages, documents, graphics, and other PC files between connected workstations. Once mail messages are created, they can be sent to an individual, multiple individuals, or to a predefined distribution list. Carbon copies and blind copies are supported by cc:Mail. Recipients are notified of the receipt of new mail and the sender can also be notified that the recipient has received their mail. As with other mail systems, messages can be prioritized and incoming messages can be organized in user defined folders. The mail system can be password protected and messages encrypted to ensure security during transmission. Several different types of client platforms can be linked together using cc:Mail and the cc:Mail Router to create a wide-area mail network.

Process methodology

cc:Mail is a client e-mail package that is designed to allow the interconnection of a number of different type of client platforms. Multiple networks can be linked together into a single mail system. Connectivity to other mail systems is provided by gateways to various mail standards such as SMTP and MHS. Gateways also provide connectivity to proprietary mail systems such as IBM's OfficeVision and MCI mail. The MHS and SMTP mail gateway also allow connectivity to a number of other mail systems.

Operating systems and hardware platforms

cc:Mail is available for DOS, Windows, OS/2, and Macintosh platforms. The cc:Mail Router provides gateways to SMTP, MHS, and IBM OV/VM PROFS mail systems.

Features

In addition to the functions described previously, cc:Mail offers the following features:

cc:Mail Mobile The cc:Mail Mobile allows PC's with modems dial-in access to the mail systems. Remote users such as sales representatives can use this feature to dial in periodically and retrieve and/or send mail messages.

cc:Mail Router The cc:Mail Router provides connectivity beyond a single network and can link multiple servers and LANs into a single wide-area mail network. Multiple LANs can be connected by network bridges or by modem. The router also provides connectivity to external mail systems as described earlier.

Emc2/TAO—Fischer International

Emc2/TAO is the e-mail portion of an integrated multiplatform workflow automation system. The product is available for a number mainframe, midrange, and PC LAN operating systems. In addition to basic mail functionality it supports electronic scheduling, electronic forms, and cross-platform directory services.[6] It serves as the basis for WorkFlow.2000, which is discussed later. Messages can be composed using a built-in text editor or another editor external to the mail system. Message recipients can be designated as To, Carbon Copy, and Blind Copy addressees. Users navigate through the mail application via a graphical user interface. Figure 6-8 shows the Emc2/TAO main menu.

Through the use of the button bar various functions can be selected. The major areas displayed include the Calendar, Inbasket, To Do list, and personal schedule. The Inbasket contains all messages received. New and unread messages are listed first in the Inbasket, other items are arranged by date. Items in the Inbasket can be read, filed, resent, printed, deleted, forwarded, or replied to.

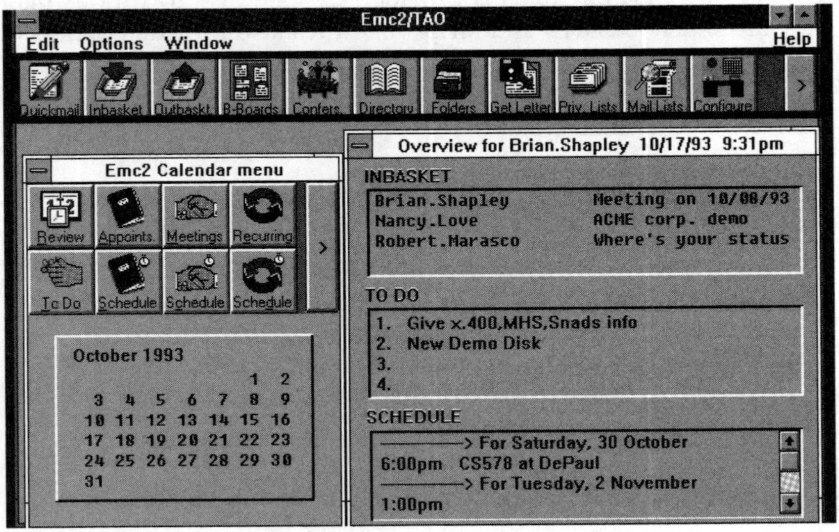

6-8 *The Emc2/TAO main menu.* Fischer International Systems Corporation

6 2/TAO Electronic Mail Communication Center (Naples, Florida: Fischer International Systems Corp.), 1993.

Figure 6-9 shows a user Inbasket. In this example, an attachment of bit-mapped graphics was included with the mail message. By selecting the attachment, the appropriate application is called to allow the graphics to be viewed. Once the message has been reviewed, it can be filed in a number of user defined file folders. File folders for Not Filed mail, Trash, and Letters Sent are automatically created.[7] The Trash folder retains messages for a preset time before permanently deleting them.

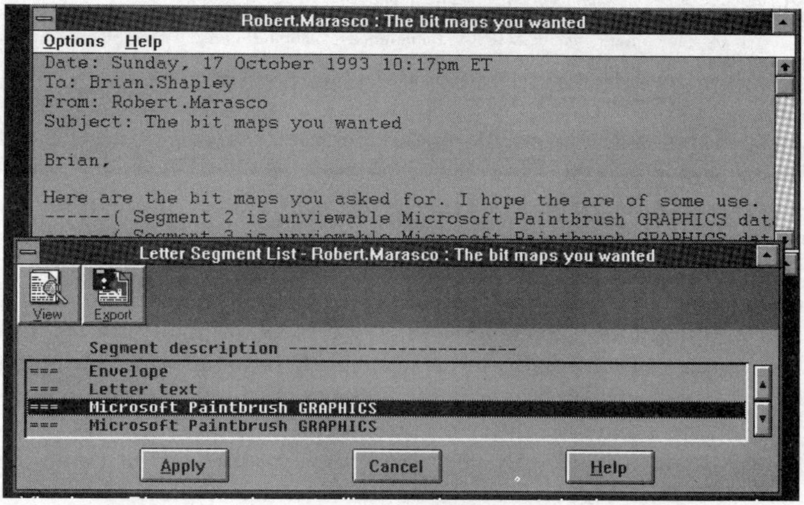

6-9 *Emc2/TAO's user in-basket.* Fischer International Systems Corporation

Messages can be created using the internal Quickmail editor that supports Windows cut and paste editing. It also supports spell checking, address look up, and attachment of other types of documents.[8] Addressees can be selected from a listing of all users on the connected platforms or from public or private mailing lists. Mail can be designated as "confidential" which limits automatic processing such as printing and forwarding. Figure 6-10 shows an example of a mail message created with the Quickmail editor. An out-basket is used to track messages sent and their status. Originators of mail can see if their message was received and acted upon by the recipient.

Another major component of Emc2/TAO is the scheduler. It supports individual and group scheduling, resource scheduling, appoint-

7 2/TAO Catalog of Features (Naples, Florida: Fischer International Systems Corp.), 1993, p. 16.

8 Ibid., p. 6

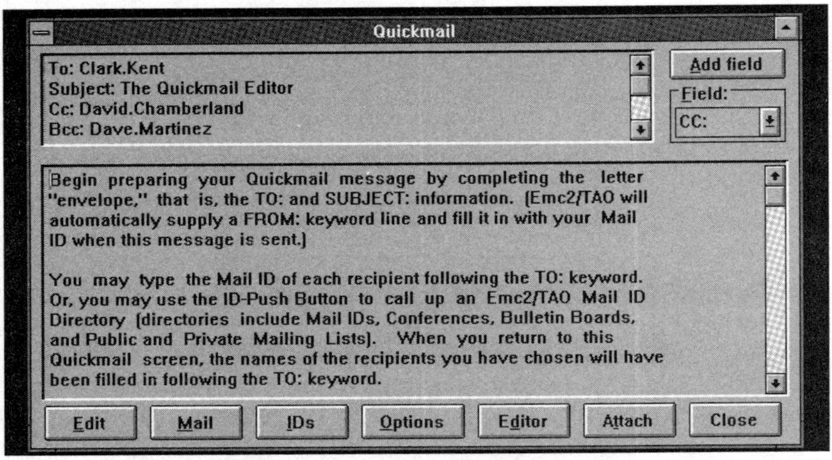

6-10 *An example of a mail message created with Emc2/TAO's Quickmail editor.* Fischer International Systems Corporation

ment and meeting coordination, and task management.[9] The calendar function utilizes the same messaging system as the mail product and offers the same cross-platform capabilities. Cross-platform scheduling with other systems such as PROFS, DISSOS, and OfficeVision is supported.[10] Users can selectively control access to their calendars by allowing others to view only certain periods of time or the complete details of events. Figure 6-11 shows the calendar display.

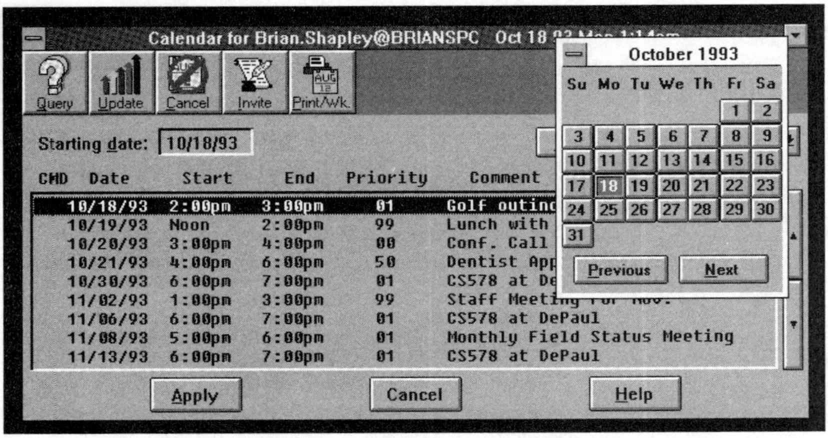

6-11 *Emc2/TAO's calendar display.* Fischer International Systems Corporation

9 Ibid., p. 19.

10 Ibid., p. 20.

A monthly calendar is displayed and the details of each days appointments are shown. Regularly occurring appointments can be automatically scheduled as recurring events based on a given schedule. Meetings with a group can be automatically scheduled and members notified via a message in their in-basket. The originator is notified of the attendees acceptance or rejection of the appointment and the schedules of all involved are updated.

Rather than automatically scheduling a meeting, the available times for all involved can be graphically displayed and an acceptable time selected. Figure 6-12 shows a display of availability for a group. Users can control automatic scheduling and if schedule conflicts are permitted. The availability of shared resources such as conference rooms, audiovisual equipment, and office equipment can be checked, as well as the availability of individuals for meetings.

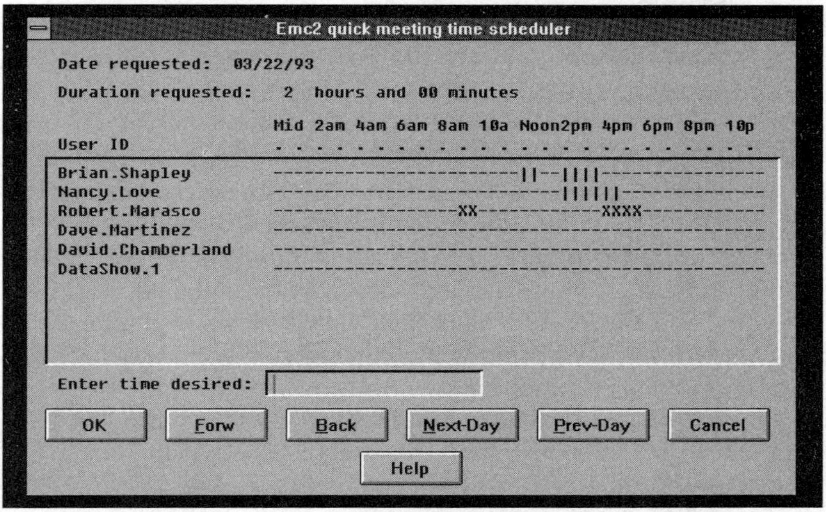

6-12 *Emc2/TAO's display of availability for a group.* Fischer International Systems Corporation

Process methodology

Emc2/TAO utilizes a single database architecture with communications links to various platforms and operating environments to maintain synchronization of mail directories for the entire organization.[11] The mail application on LANs or midrange platforms such as AS400s is linked via a distributed application to the central database. All users

11 2/TAO Comprehensive Architecture for Enterprise E-mail (Naples, Florida: Fischer International Systems Corp.), April 1994, p. 8.

share a common calendar, directory, and bulletin board, as well as gateways to external systems. In this type of configuration, all mail processing occurs on a centralized mail server.

Operating systems and hardware platforms

Emc2/TAO operates on the following server platforms and operating systems:[12]

- IBM AS400 OS/400
- IBM Mainframe MVS, VSE, VM
- PC/LAN OS/2

Supported client platforms include DOS, Windows, Macintosh, UNIX, and OS/2. The following network protocols and operating systems are supported:

- Banyan
- IBM LAN Manager
- NETBIOS
- Novell
- PATHWORKS
- TCP/IP

Features

In addition to the basic mail and scheduling functions described previously, Emc2/TAO offers the following features:

Emc2/TAO PC products A group of products are available to provide remote connectivity and download capabilities for DOS, Windows, and Macintosh mail clients. Windows-based graphical user interfaces for several types of mainframe terminal emulators are provided by various PC products.

WorkFlow.2020 and WorkFlow.2000 These two products offer electronic forms and electronic forms routing based on the Emc2/TAO mail system. WorkFlow.2000 is discussed in detail later.

Emc2/TAO paging gateway he paging gateway allows e-mail users to send messages and forward mail to mobile users via alphanumeric pagers, advisor message receivers, and pen-based computers.

MULTINET This product provides electronic data interchange (EDI) connectivity from other applications.

Microsoft Mail and Schedule+

Microsoft Mail is a LAN-based e-mail system with gateways to several external mail systems. Schedule+ is a LAN-based calendar and scheduling application. The mail product operates on Microsoft compatible

12 Ibid., p. 17.

and Novell networks. Support is provided for a number of client platforms. Mail and calendar functions are handled independently by the two applications. Within mail, messages are arranged in an in-box, an out-box, and various folders. Figure 6-13 shows the user in-box, out-box, and a list of private folders. Folders can be either private or shared among a group of mail users.

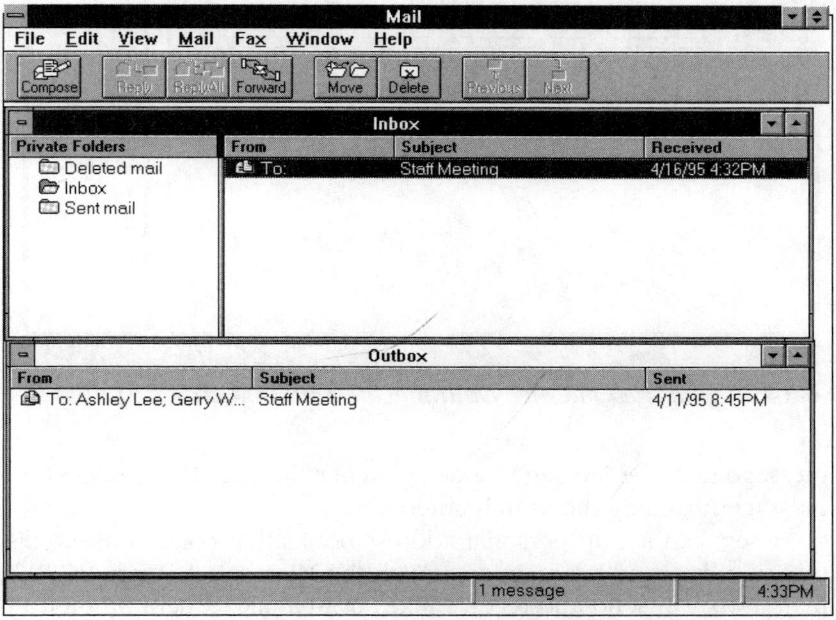

6-13 *Microsoft Mail's user in-box, out-box, and a list of private folders.*

By selecting the Compose icon, a blank message format is provided for the creation of a mail message. Addressees can be selected from a list of recipients contained in either private or shared address books. Documents can be attached to messages and message priorities set via the Options icon. The Check Names option verifies that the recipient names listed in the To: and CC: fields are valid mail addresses. Clicking on the send icon sends the mail message. A folder is provided for copies of outbound mail messages. Figure 6-14 shows a completed message waiting to be sent.

A series of icons allows incoming mail messages to be replied to, forwarded, moved to a folder, deleted, or paged through. Windows objects such as graphs or spreadsheets can be inserted into mail messages. A Message Finder is available to locate misplaced mail messages. By entering information such as sender, recipients, subject, or

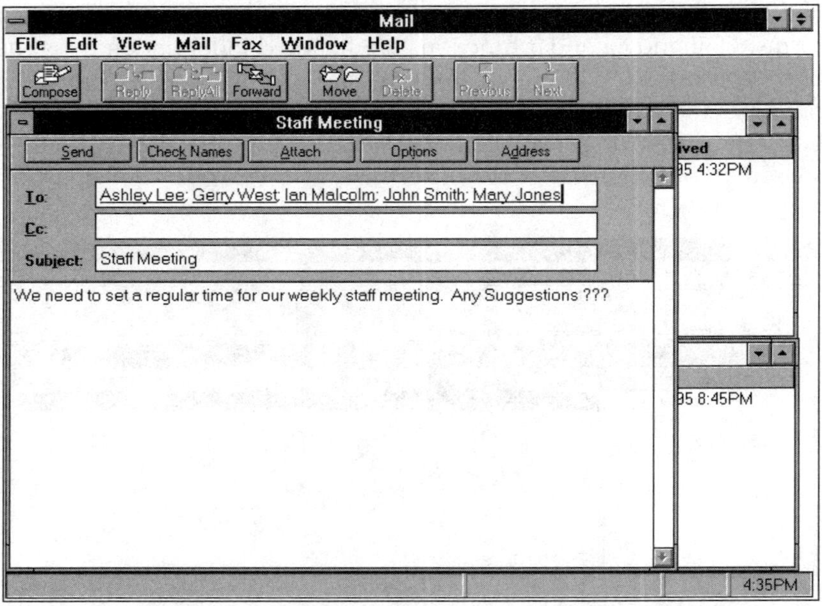

6-14 *A completed message waiting to be sent in Microsoft Mail.*

message text, the Message Finder searches the specified folders for a message matching the search criteria.

Users can set up personal address books that contain users, distribution lists, and fax recipients. With the Microsoft At Work PC FAX, mail users can send and receive faxes from a fax modem on their PC or shared on the network.[13] Figure 6-15 shows an entry in a personal address book for a fax recipient. When this entry is selected as the recipient of a message, the message is automatically formatted as a fax and routed to a modem for transmission.

Schedule+ provides individual calendar and group scheduling. It consists of an appointment book, task list, planner, and message windows. Each user maintains calendar files on their local computer and on the file server.[14] When connected to the file server after working off-line, the server and local calendar files are updated.

In addition to scheduling appointments, calendar users can be assigned tasks via Schedule+. Appointments and tasks can be estab-

13 User's Guide—Microsoft Workgroup Add-on for Windows (Redmond, Washington: Microsoft Corp.), 1993, p. 43.

14 Mike Magee, "Mail Models—Microsoft Corp.'s Microsoft Mail 3.0 Electronic Mail System and Microsoft Schedule+ 2.0 Add-on Desktop Accessory Utility," *PC User*, July 15, 1992, p. 39.

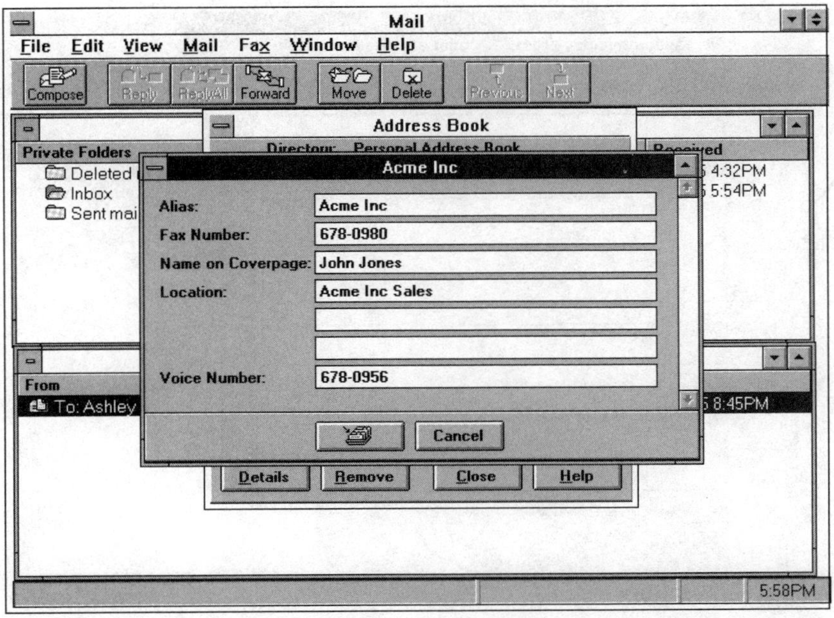

6-15 *Microsoft Mail's entry in a personal address book for a fax user.*

lished as either public or private, with the details of private events shown only to the originator. From a day planner type of interface, users can schedule daily appointments. A monthly calendar is used to select the month and day of an appointment. Figure 6-16 shows the appointments screen.

Appointments are established by selecting a month and day and then adding an appointment at the appropriate time. By selecting another user, their calendar can be viewed. Recurring appointments can be added to a user's calendar according to a preset schedule. Figure 6-17 shows an example for a recurring appointment setup. In this example, the appointment is scheduled for the first Wednesday of each month, starting on 4/25/95 with no ending date.

Group scheduling can be accomplished via an automatic scheduling feature that will attempt to locate a time that is open for all participants in the meeting. Users of both Schedule+ and Microsoft Mail are notified of appointments both in Schedule+ and via a mail message in the users in-box.

Process methodology

Microsoft Mail operates through the use of a workgroup "post office" created on a shared network drive and a client mail application that

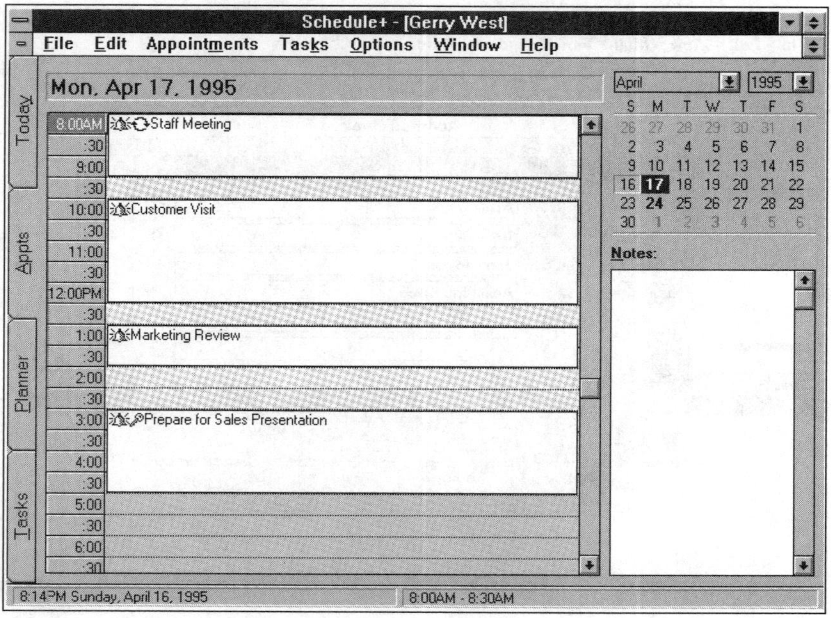

6-16 *The appointments screen in Microsoft Schedule+.*

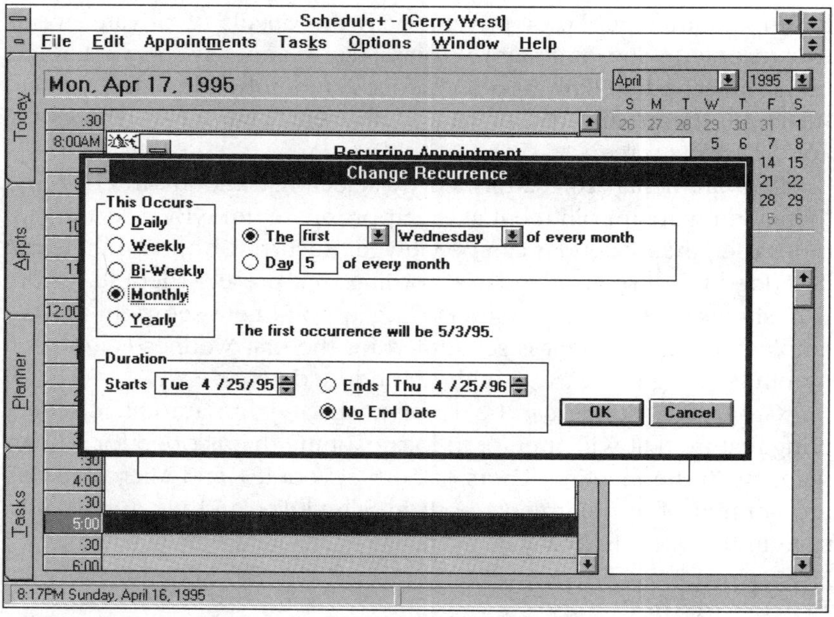

6-17 *An example for a recurring appointment setup in Microsoft Schedule+.*

runs on individual workstations. Additional software is used by the mail administrator to maintain the mail system. Each user must have an account established on the shared post office. When logging in to the mail application, users select the computer and shared directory that contains their post office. A local message file is stored on each user workstation and contains stored messages, message folders, and personal address books.

Schedule+ operates in a similar fashion, with a workstation application that creates local files that are updated when a connection is made to the shared mail server. Connections to external mail systems are handled through add-on gateway products for the base mail system.

Operating systems and hardware platforms

Microsoft Mail operates on the following client platforms:

- DOS
- Macintosh
- OS/2
- Windows

A number of PC network operating systems are supported including Microsoft WorkGroup for Windows, Novell, and AppleTalk.

Features

Microsoft Mail and Schedule+ offer the following additional features:

Microsoft Mail Remote Provides remote access via modem to the mail system. Messages can be created off-line and are then transferred when a connection to the mail system is established.

Microsoft Schedule+ for Macintosh This is the Macintosh version of the Schedule+ application. It operates on Macintosh clients and is designed to work with Microsoft Mail for Macintosh on AppleTalk networks.

Novell GroupWise—Novell, Inc.

Novell GroupWise is a LAN-based workgroup product that provides e-mail, calendar, group scheduling, and task management. It has a rule-based message management system that supports workflow routing. The client application runs on a number of platforms as does the GroupWise server application. Gateways are available to provide cross-platform messaging. GroupWise supports multiple message types and provides full message status tracking to include message delivery, opening, deletion, acceptance, rejection, and delegation.[15] The mail ap-

15 Technology Overview, GroupWise 4.1, p. 2.

plication can be accessed from within other applications such as WordPerfect. Each of the applications (mail, calendar, scheduling, and task management) are presented as individual icons in the GroupWise main menu. Figure 6-18 shows the GroupWise main menu.

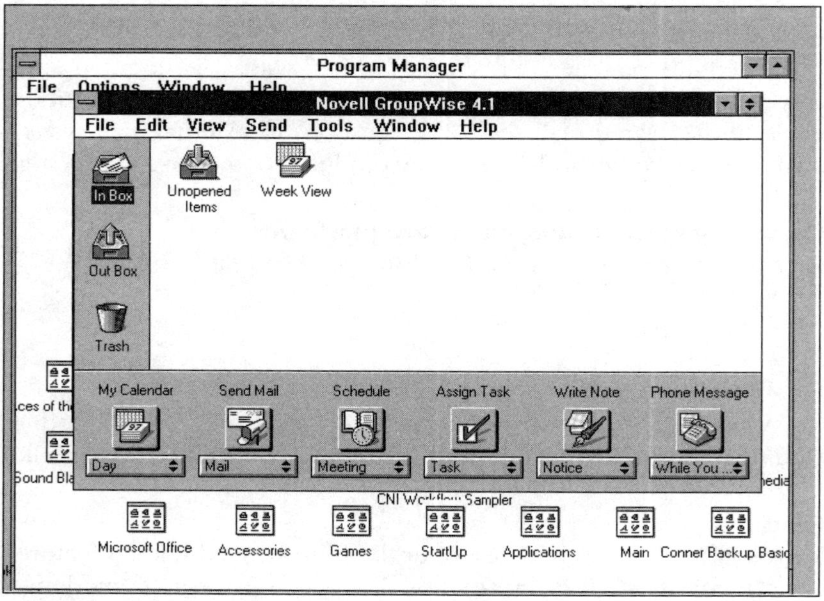

6-18 *The GroupWise main menu.*

From this view, the In Box shows mail messages that have not yet been opened as unopened letters. By selecting the In Box, a list of waiting items is displayed. An icon preceding each message indicates what type message it is—a mail message, a scheduling request, or a task assignment. Figure 6-19 shows an In Box with items waiting to be read. The Out Box shown below the In Box contains copies of mail that has been sent. The Out Box also is the means by which the status of outbound messages is tracked.

By selecting an item, it is displayed for action. By selecting various icons, items can be replied to, forwarded, or deleted. As the recipient takes action on a message, the status of the message is updated to provide the originator with the latest information on the message. By selecting the Info icon, status information on the message is displayed.

Each type of message has it own specific display format and associated action icons. Mail messages appear differently than schedule or task messages. Schedule and task messages provide the option to

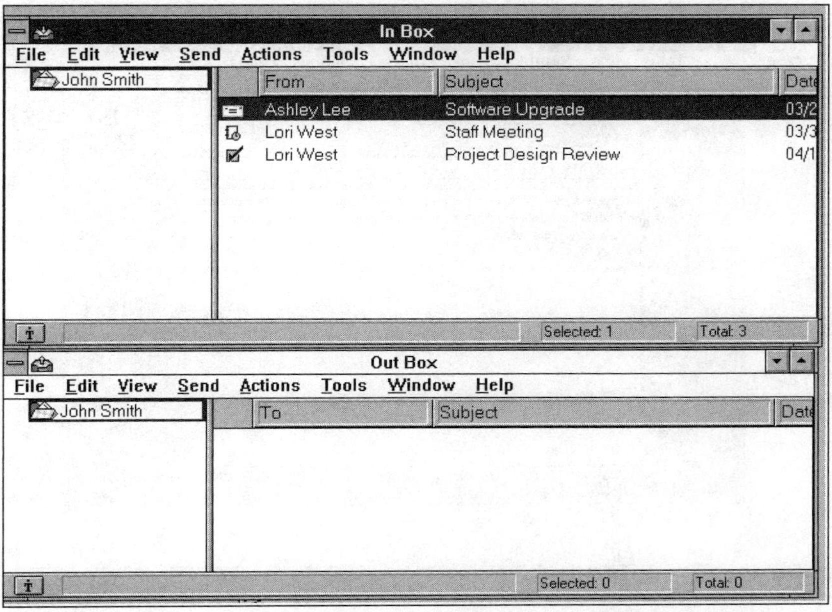

6-19 *An in-box with items waiting to be read in Novell's GroupWise.*

accept or decline messages. Figures 6-20, 6-21, and 6-22 show the various message formats. As with mail messages, appointments and tasks return status information to the originator when the recipient acts upon them. Acceptance of an appointment or task also updates the users calendar and task list.

In addition to the standard formats, customized formats for the various types of messages can be designed. The GroupWise View Design allows users to design customized message formats. These formats can become electronic forms that use the GroupWise messaging system. The basic objects of each type of message can be formatted as desired using a graphical design tool. Using object linking and embedding (OLE), other Windows objects can be imbedded in the customized message form. This allows the inclusion of word processing documents, spreadsheets, audio, or video in a message format. Figure 6-23 shows a simple example of a customized form for task notification.

In addition to creating customized message formats, rules can be defined for message handling. The rules can apply to a single type of message or to multiple message types. Rules can take such actions as filing, forwarding, or replying to messages. Specific conditions such as the message priority or originator can be used to determine when

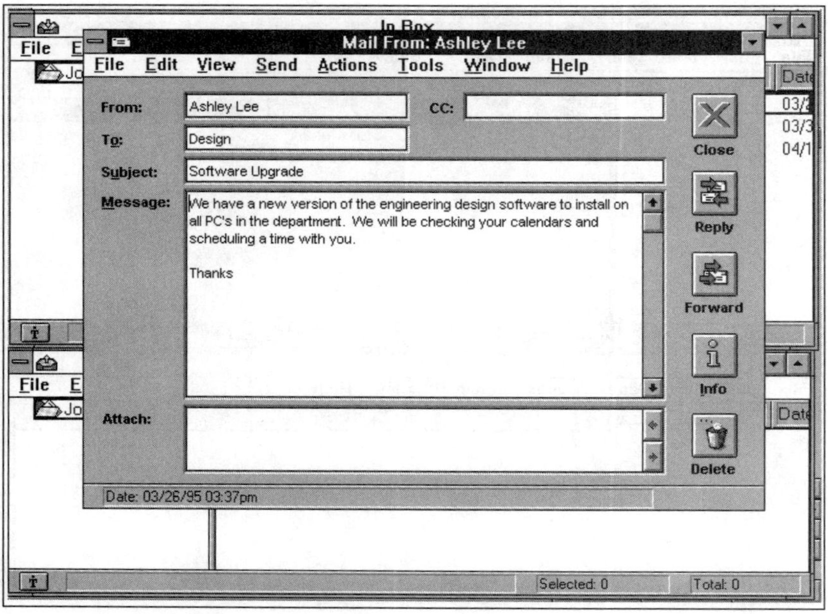

6-20 *Mail message format.*

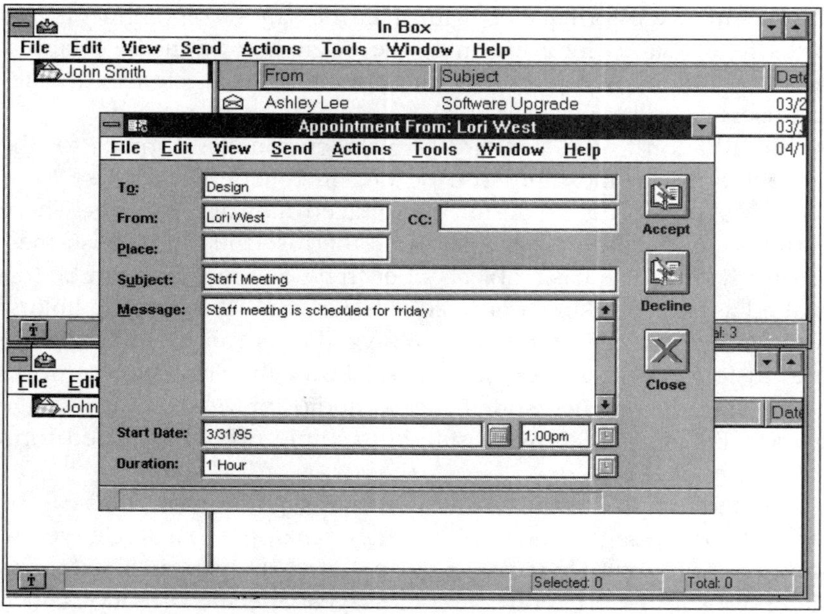

6-21 *Scheduler message format.*

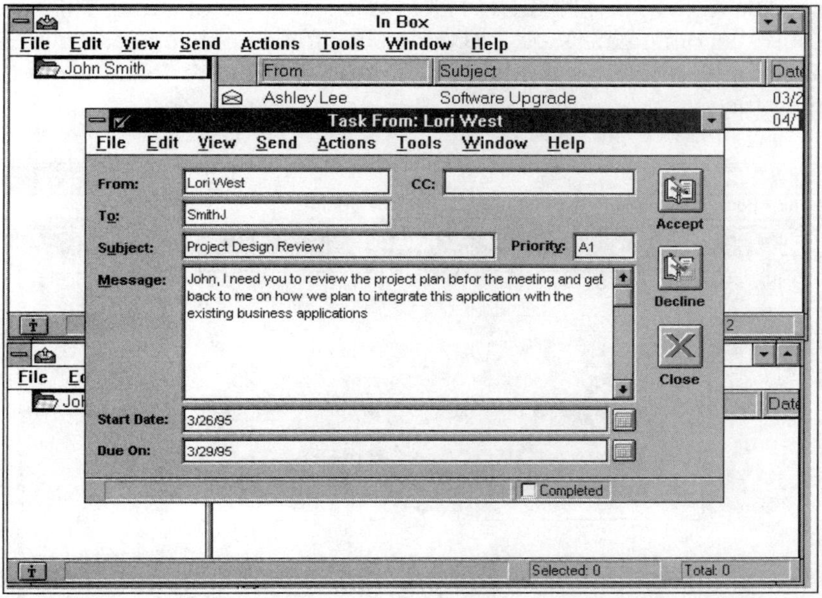

6-22 *Task message format.*

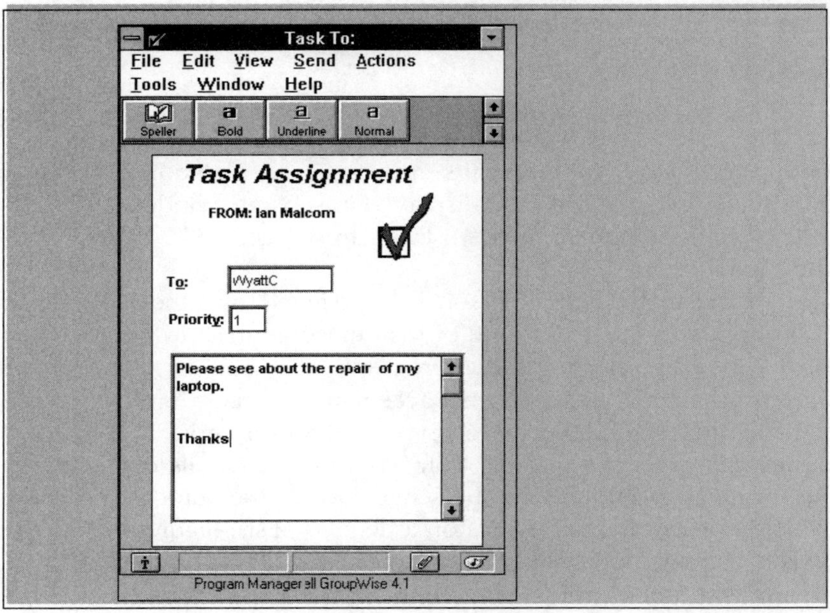

6-23 *A simple example of a customized form for task notification.*

specific rules apply. Figure 6-24 shows an example of a rule. This rule causes incoming messages to be filed in a folder and generates a message to the originator notifying him or her that the recipient is out of the office.

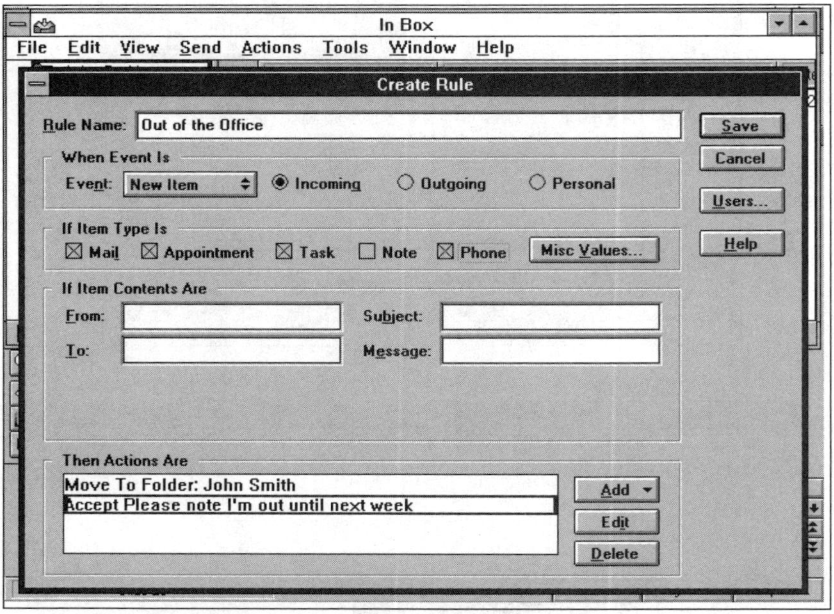

6-24 *An example of a rule in GroupWise.*

The calendar provides a day planner view of appointments, notes, and tasks. Appointments are shown on an hourly schedule. Notes and assigned tasks are displayed in separate windows. The details of an appointment, note, or task can be accessed by clicking on the desired item.

Tasks can be either personal or assigned by others. Assigned tasks appear as a special type of mail message that can be accepted or declined by selecting the appropriate icon. The originator of the task is notified of the recipients acceptance or rejection of the task. Personal notes and tasks are entered by the user and can be marked as private, preventing others from viewing the details of the event. Recurring appointments can be scheduled via the autodate function, which repeats calendar events on a defined basis. Figure 6-25 shows a daily calendar in GroupWise.

As with other group scheduling applications, GroupWise allows the schedules of others to be checked in order to find an available

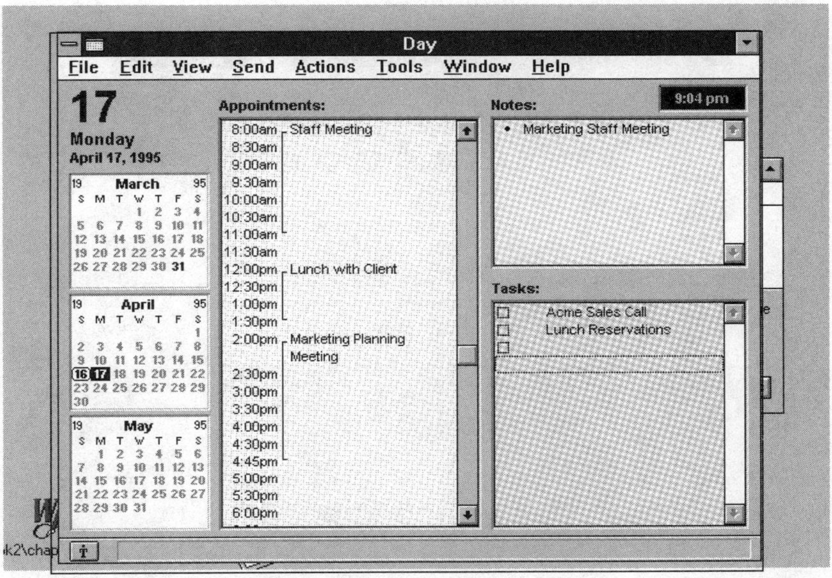

6-25 *A daily calendar in GroupWise.*

time for all members of a group to meet. By specifying an individual or a group of users, a meeting duration time, and a search date range, the busy function will search the appropriate calendars and present a graphical display of the activities of the selected group members for the specified time range. After selecting a meeting time, GroupWise notifies the group members via a scheduling message. As group members accept or decline the appointment the originator is notified and the appropriate calendars are updated. Figure 6-26 illustrates a busy search for an appointment.

Process methodology

GroupWise is a store and forward messaging system comprised of several components.[16] The Client component is the end user application that interfaces with the messaging system through either GroupWise applications or other mail-enabled applications. The Post Office is simply a directory structure on a network file server that provides a storage area for the messages of a group of users. The Message server is the transport agent that exchanges mail between post offices and mail gateways. Gateways provide connectivity between GroupWise and other messaging systems.

16 Technology Overview, GroupWise 4.1, p. 5.

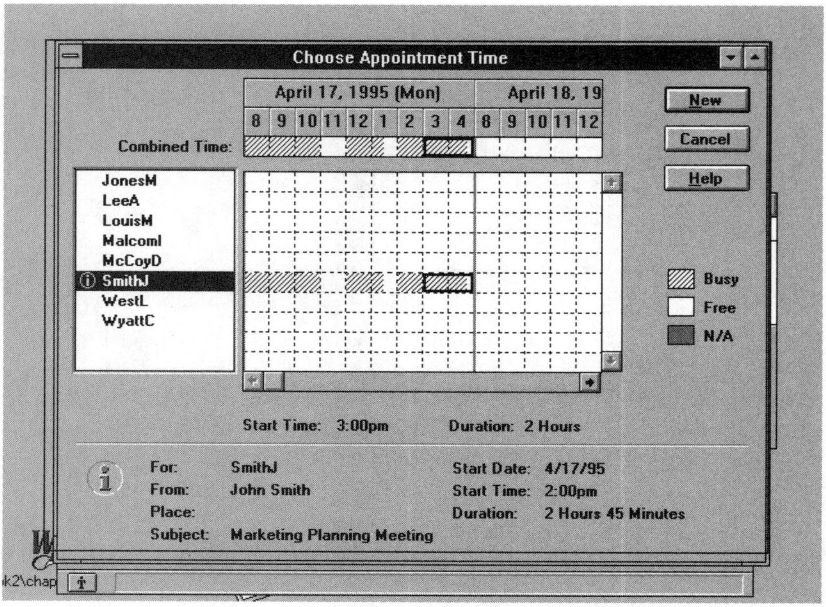

6-26 *A busy search for an appointment in GroupWise.*

The GroupWise messaging engine recognizes the various types of messages and applies messaging services such as rules folders and other functions to all messages it handles. This same type of handling applies to GroupWise gateways. This allows the translation of cross-platform messages into the appropriate message type for each type of system. For example, a meeting request originated in GroupWise and then passed to a proprietary e-mail and scheduling system, such as IBM's OfficeVision, is translated into the appropriate format for a meeting request in that system. The recipient sees the meeting request as they would normally see a meeting request on their system. This is in contrast to other types of gateways that simply translate all message types into a simple mail message format.

Operating systems and hardware platforms

GroupWise operates on the following client platforms:

- DOS
- Macintosh
- PowerMac
- UNIX
- Windows

Server platforms include NetWare NLM, OS/2, DOS, and UNIX. Each of the client and server applications are compatible.

Features

GroupWise offers the following features in addition to those listed earlier:

GroupWise gateways Gateways are available for the following:

- API gateway
- Asynchronous gateway
- cc:Mail gateway
- Fax/Print gateway
- Lotus Notes gateway
- Message Router gateway
- MHS gateway
- NetWare Global MHS gateway
- OfficeVision/VM/PROFS gateway
- Pager gateway
- SMTP gateway
- SNADS gateway
- Telephone Access server
- VMS Mail gateway
- X.25 gateway
- X.400 gateway

InForms InForms is the application development and forms design product of the Novell GroupWare division. This product is describe in more detail later.

SoftSolutions SoftSolutions is the document management product of the GroupWare suite of products. This product is described in more detail later.

Case study

Commercial real estate financing

A provider of commercial real estate financing was looking for a means to automate and better manage their lending process.[17] The traditional process was slow and consisted of the accumulation of documents into a file. The file was then passed from person to person in the loan process. It was often difficult to determine the status of a loan at a particular point in time. To obtain information on a loan in progress, the file had to be located and reviewed to determine the status of the application. At times documents were misplaced or missing. An effective way to manage and control loan applications was desired.

17 *OUTFRONT: Banking Solutions Using Enterprise Networks*, vol. I, no. 9 (Westboro, Massachusetts: Banyan Systems, Inc.), 1994.

A loan application processing system was developed that used BeyondMail and BeyondMail Rules. BeyondMail serves as the message transport system and BeyondMail Rules is used to automate the loan processing workflow. Member banks use a custom application that creates specialized forms that are routed through BeyondMail to a central processing facility. Remote locations are connected to the central processing facility via X.25, T1, or asynchronous connections.

The information contained in the electronic forms is added to a database and the forms are routed to the various steps in the loan process. At each step, the database is updated to reflect the status of the loan. In addition to updating the database, the system generates notifications of problems during processing. Additional documents such as spreadsheets and word processing documents can be attached to the loan application in lieu of a hard copy.

The end result of the system was a decrease in the amount of time required to process a loan application and more efficient management and control of the overall process. Managers have rapid access to loan application information, allowing them to adjust lending criteria to changes in the financial market. The routing and tracking features of the mail system minimize lost documents and provide greater accountability for application packages. The overall impact of the system was a shorter processing time and lower processing costs.

7

Electronic forms routing

The goal of many office automation projects has been to create the elusive "paperless" office. Often the result of such efforts has been just the opposite—automated systems have increased the amount of paper an organization must deal with. Electronic forms and electronic forms routing are one category of groupware that might actually succeed in the goal of reducing the amount of paper generated by computers and automated systems.

As was mentioned earlier, most electronic forms systems evolved from applications that electronically created paper forms. As network connectivity and e-mail became more common, the next logical step was to replace the printing of forms generated electronically with the routing of forms generated electronically.

In the previous chapter, many of the e-mail systems described include the capability to electronically route mail messages based on a defined set of rules. Electronic forms routing is essentially the same process with the exception that the message or electronic form has a format and data elements designed to support a specific business application.

For example, it is very easy to use a basic e-mail application as a customer order entry system. The person receiving the order simply completes an e-mail message and sends it to the shipping department. The problem now arises when the shipping department attempts to interpret the free-form text message received from the order taker. Has all the required information been included on the message? Has the order taker used the correct part numbers and customer shipping information? Do all order takers use the same format for messages? How can the status of the order be tracked?

It is easy to see that the information requirements are more complex than can be handled by simple e-mail. Electronic forms are generally used in situations that require the collection of information in a structured format. This is the same function that paper forms accomplish. Specific pieces of information are requested and captured by the form. Often the choices are limited to a range of acceptable responses. For example, yes, no, or a valid zip code or part number.

Once the information has been captured, it can be used to continue the processing workflow. This might take the form of passing the information to someone via e-mail or entering the data into a database for further electronic processing.

Electronic forms can also be used as a way to access information from automated sources. Once the information has been entered, a blank form can serve as the means to format an inquiry. Electronic forms often serve as the "front end" for database management systems. Access to databases from electronic forms is generally accomplished by either proprietary drivers or through Microsoft's Open Database Connectivity (ODBC).

Electronic form applications often consist of two components: the form design tool and the form filler. The form design tool is used to design and format the electronic form. These tools are generally independent of the form filler and routing software, in that they are used infrequently and only by a programmer or developer. Most design tools are Windows-based and graphical in nature.

Data fields can be defined and formatted as well as other objects such as boxes, lines, and menus. Many design tools allow the incorporation of mathematical functions and look-up tables in the form design. More advanced design tools provide for the inclusion of business rules and routing logic in the form design. The design tool can be a separate application or an add-on to an e-mail application.

The form filler is the application that allows the user to complete and route the electronic form. This may be a separate application or may be combined within an e-mail application. In the case of an e-mail system, a specialized mail message format is accessed and then routed as a mail message. Stand-alone form filler applications can be used to capture information that is then entered into a database and accessed by other users. Electronic forms-type applications can also be developed using Windows-based database tools such as Microsoft Access or Lotus Approach.

Electronic forms routing products

In this chapter we present several representative electronic forms routing products. This is not intended to be a complete review of all products nor a comparison of products. Specific products are used to illustrate the features of this category of groupware. A general description of the product is presented followed by a discussion of underlying process methodologies. Operating systems and hardware platforms supported are listed along with particular features of each product. Several of the products mentioned are companion products to specific e-mail packages and may not operate independent of the e-mail product. To get the most recent information on specific products, please contact the vendors.

BeyondMail Forms Designer—Banyan Systems Inc.

BeyondMail Forms Designer is the form design product for BeyondMail.[1] The design tool provides a graphical environment in which to build forms that can be used by the mail system. Data entered on forms can be entered into databases via the mail system database links.

The BeyondRules rule scripting language can be used with BeyondMail electronic forms. Processing rules can be based on the type of form or on data contained in the form.

Figure 7-1 shows an example of a BeyondMail form. In this example, a customer support form for computer support is completed

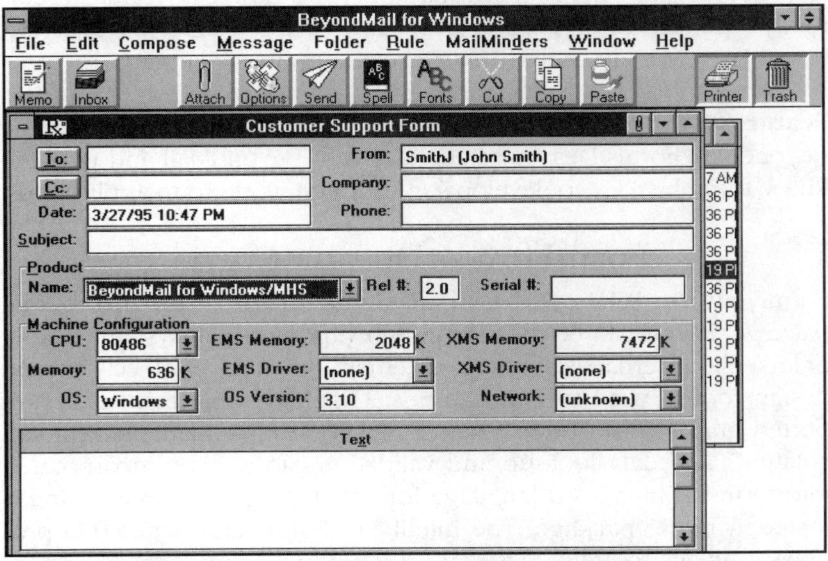

7-1 *An example of a BeyondMail form.*

1 BeyondMail Release 2.0, Product Overview (Westboro, Massachusetts: Banyan Systems, Inc.), 1994.

by the recipient of the support call. After entering some basic information about the configuration of the computer, the form is sent via the mail system to a customer support engineer. The form contains data fields with scroll boxes as well as free-form text fields.

Process methodology

Forms are developed using the BeyondMail Forms Designer and then used by BeyondMail. BeyondMail is a client e-mail package that is designed to interact with several different mail transport systems. Figure 6-6 shows the layered architecture of this product. The various user interfaces communicate with the mail interface and the rules interface. These two interfaces are built upon the forms layer, a rule engine, and a message transport access layer. The message transport access layer deals with the three mail transport systems. The GMHS and MHS transport systems are designed for Novell NetWare LANs. The MHS for non-NetWare LANs is designed for other LAN operating systems that conform to the MHS standard. The Banyan Intelligent Messaging for Vines transport system is also a supported transport system. This provides compatibility with existing BeyondMail 1.0 for Vines.

Operating systems and hardware platforms

BeyondMail Forms Designer runs under Windows. BeyondMail currently operates on DOS and Windows clients connected to a PC-based LAN. Macintosh and UNIX client support is planned.

Features

BeyondMail Forms Designer integrates with BeyondMail and BeyondRules. It can be used to develop sophisticated workgroup applications.

FormFlow—Delrina Corp.

FormFlow is a Windows-based electronic forms design and routing package. Forms can be routed through various e-mail systems, faxed, or linked to external database management systems.[2] An object-oriented design tool is used to create forms. Graphical objects such as imported graphics can be included in form designs. Mathematical calculations and data look-up and validation can also be incorporated into forms. A high-level language for developing rules and routing is included in the package. The Intelligent Forms Language (IFL) provides a means to create customized workflow solutions using FormFlow forms.

2 The Guide, Corporate Software, vol. 19 (Norwood, Massachusetts: Corporate Software, Inc.), 1994, p. 367.

Process methodology

Forms are developed using the FormFlow Designer and are then completed using FormFlow Filler. The completed forms are then routed via fax or passed to an e-mail system or a database. Access to databases is provided through ODBC drivers.

Operating systems and hardware platforms

FormFlow products run under Windows. E-mail support is provided for the following mail systems:

- cc:Mail
- Lotus Notes
- Microsoft Mail
- WordPerfect Office
- Other MHS-based e-mail systems

Access to the following databases is provided by ODBC drivers:

- Access
- Btrieve
- FoxPro
- Gupta
- Informix
- Ingress

Features

Sample form applications and form templates that can be customized for specific applications are included.

JetForm—JetForm Corp.

JetForm is a Windows-based electronic forms design and routing package. Forms can be printed, routed through various e-mail systems, or linked to external database management systems. Several products are available depending on the specific form-handling requirements. JetForm-Design is used to create forms for use with other JetForm products. The JetForm-Filler is used primarily to complete forms for printing as hard copy. JetForm-Server is a network-based product for managing forms in a multiuser networking environment.

The design tool provides a graphical environment in which to build forms. Data residing in an external database can be accessed for editing and validation of entered data. Calculated fields are supported through a number of mathematical functions. Windows objects can be included in forms through dynamic data exchange (DDE) and object linking and embedding (OLE). Forms can be designed with predefined routing lists. Security features include electronic signatures and form encryption. The case study at the end of the chapter illustrates the use of JetForm with an e-mail system.

Process methodology

Forms are developed using the JetForm-Designer and are completed using the appropriate JetForm-Filler application. The completed forms are then printed, routed via fax, or passed to an e-mail system or a database. Access to databases is provided through ODBC drivers. JetForm interfaces with e-mail systems through VIM or MAPI.

Operating systems and hardware platforms

JetForm applications run under Windows. E-mail support is provided for the following mail systems:

- cc:Mail
- Microsoft Mail
- VIM or MAPI

Access to over 20 databases is provided by ODBC drivers included with the product.

Features

Forms can be routed to a list of users with a return-to-sender option and a built-in audit trail. Electronic notes can be attached to the forms.

InForms—WordPerfect Corp.

InForms is a DOS- and Windows-based electronic forms design and routing package. Forms can be used to gather data to be routed through e-mail or entered into a database management system.[3] In addition to data entry, InForms can be used as a data access and data query tool. The InForms product consists of two major components: the InForms Designer and the InForms Filler. The Designer is used to develop forms for use by the Filler.

Forms can be linked to several different databases and present a combined view of fields in all connected databases. Calculations can be accomplished in forms to support processing of statistical or financial information. Graphical objects such as drop-down list boxes, check boxes, radio buttons, and spreadsheet-like tables can be included in forms. Viewers for word processing documents and graphics can be imbedded in forms allowing the viewing of such objects without including them in the actual form. Figure 7-2 shows an example of a form created with InForms.

3 Technology Overview, InForms Architecture (Provo, Utah: Novell, Inc.), September 2, 1994, p. 5.

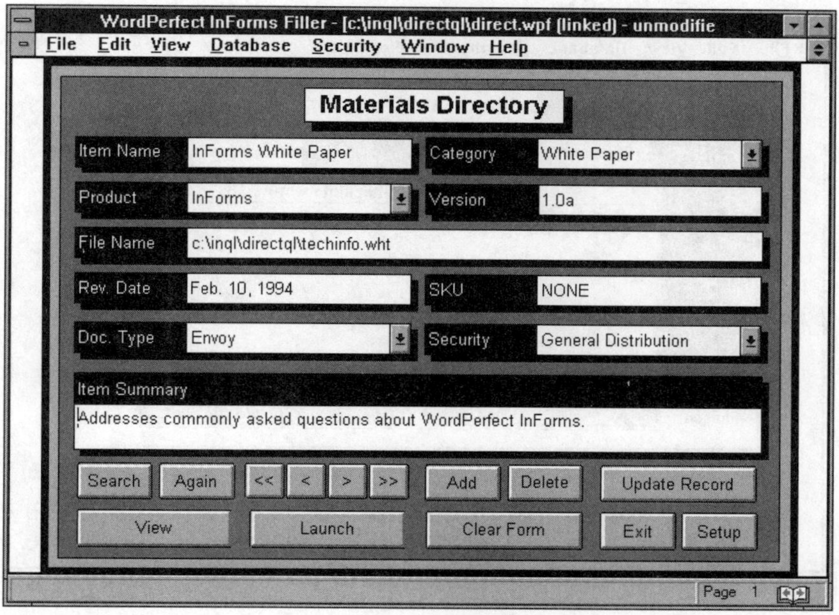

7-2 *An example of a form created with InForms.* WordPerfect Corporation

In this example, information can be entered into the database or the database can be queried for information. Data functions such as record paging, adding, deleting, and updating of records is controlled by a set of buttons. By selecting the appropriate button, the corresponding database action is accomplished. This form contains references to a word processing document that is accessible through the viewer. By selecting the View button the viewer displays the word processing document. Figure 7-3 shows the form with the viewer in use.

Business logic such as routing can be embedded in the form through the use of the Send Mail function. Based on data in a particular field or on specific actions taken, the form can be routed according to predefined distribution. For example, purchase requests can be routed for approval based on the total dollar amount of the request.

Data query is supported through the use of a graphical query screen. This screen provides complete query capabilities on any field on the form. By selecting the appropriate field and entering specific conditions, a query is built and executed. Figure 7-4 shows a query screen. In this example, a query was done on the field "Products" for the value "Informs." The report shown at the bottom of the screen lists the results of the query. Clicking on any row of the results screen displays a form view of the data.

7-3 *The form with the viewer in use.* WordPerfect Corporation

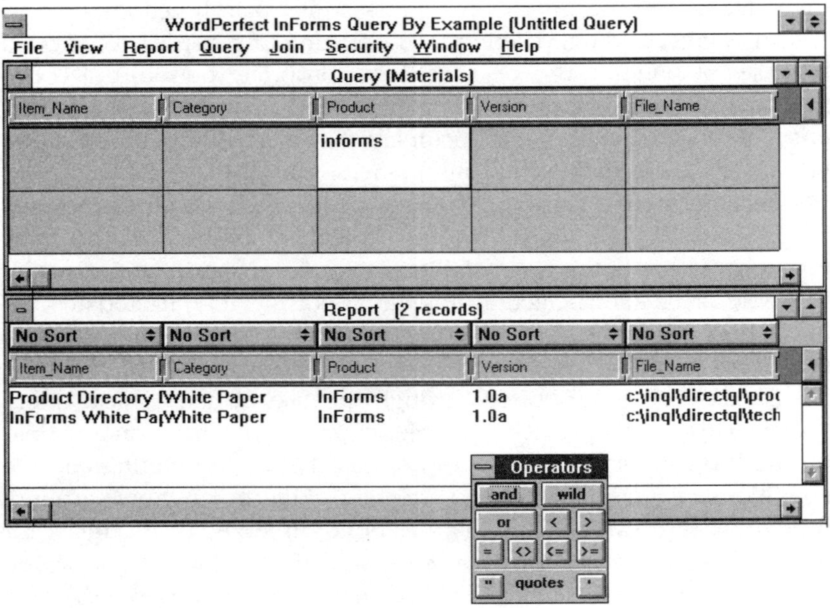

7-4 *A query screen in InForms.* WordPerfect Corporation

Forms can be mailed through a number of e-mail systems. From within the forms application the mail option can be selected. This calls the appropriate e-mail system and attaches the form with data to the mail message. Figure 7-5 shows a form that has been attached to a Novell GroupWise e-mail message. The form appears as an attached object at the bottom of the mail message.

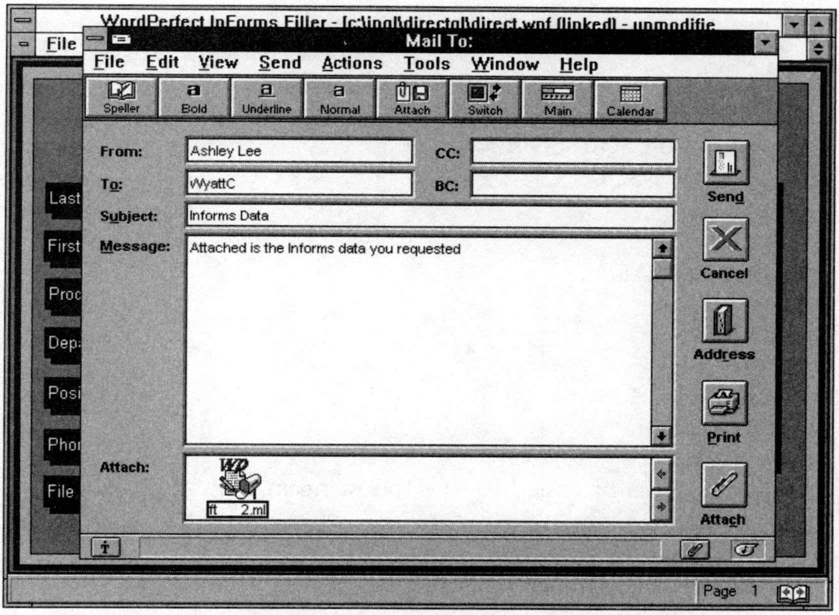

7-5 *A form attached to a Novell GroupWise e-mail message.* WordPerfect Corporation

Process methodology

The methodology under which InForms operates is based on the following design principles:

- Form independence from databases
- Form independence from end-user environments
- Easily used design tools

Database independence allows forms to access multiple databases transparent to the user and to present data from multiple databases as a single view in the form. Independence in end-user environments allows the forms to be ported to different end-user client platforms and still maintain the same look and feel. Easily used designs promote the development of customized workflow applications.

Operating systems and hardware platforms

The InForms Designer runs under Windows. The InForms Filler is available for DOS, Windows, and Macintosh. Database access is provided for the following:

- ASCII
- Btrieve
- Clipper
- DataPerfect
- dBase
- DB2
- FoxPro
- Informix
- Microsoft SQL server
- NetWare SQL
- ODBC
- Oracle
- OS/2 DBM
- Paradox
- SQLBase
- Sybase
- XDB

Lotus Notes

E-mail support is provided for the following mail systems:

- cc:Mail
- Microsoft Mail
- Novell GroupWise
- WordPerfect Office 3.1
- WordPerfect Office 4.0
- VIM or MAPI compliant e-mail

Features

One notable feature of InForms is its use of electronic signatures. Based on specific conditions, an electronic signature might be required on a form. Predefined approval groups can be used to determine who can sign a particular form. Specific fields on a form can be protected with the electronic signature. A tamper seal indicates if data on a signed form has been altered. In addition to electronic signatures, specific data on forms can be encrypted to further protect information.

Microsoft Electronic Forms Designer—Microsoft Corp.

Microsoft's Electronic Forms Designer is a Windows-based electronic forms design tool for Microsoft Mail. It provides a Visual Basic type of development environment for form design.[4] In addition to the graphical design of the forms, properties and custom behaviors can be attached to control buttons. Since the forms designer uses Visual Basic, the full procedure language capabilities of Visual Basic can be incorporated into the form design. Data from external sources can be accessed by ODBC. Windows objects can be included in forms through OLE. Forms can be designed with predefined addressing, sequential routing, and automatic notification.

Process methodology

Forms are developed using the Electronic Forms Designer and Visual Basic. They are then completed and mailed using Microsoft Mail or other MAPI-compliant mail systems.

Operating systems and hardware platforms

Microsoft Forms Designer runs under Windows and requires the professional edition of Visual Basic. E-mail support for completed forms is provided for Microsoft Mail and MAPI-complaint e-mail systems. Access to databases is provided by ODBC drivers.

Features

Forms can be composed off-line and then passed to Microsoft Mail through Microsoft Mail Remote. Sample forms and form templates are provided with the design product.

WorkFlow.2020—
Fischer International Systems Corp.

WorkFlow.2020 is an electronic forms design and routing application for Windows.[5] Forms are designed in an object-oriented "pick and click" environment. Objects are stored in libraries making them reusable in future applications. Figure 7-6 illustrates the design tool. In this example, a purchase order form application is being developed. A palette of graphical design tools is shown in the upper right corner of the screen. By selecting the appropriate design tools, text, graphics, and data fields can be added to the form.

The completed form can present a single view of data collected from multiple sources. Entered data can be validated prior to acceptance, and forms are automatically routed to the appropriate next step for processing or approval.

Secure electronic processing is provided by an electronic signature. Users sign a document by clicking on an icon and entering a

4 Microsoft Electronic Forms Designer Data Sheet (Redmond, Washington: Microsoft Corp.), 1995.

5 WorkFlow.2020 (Naples, Florida: Fischer International Systems Corp.), 1994.

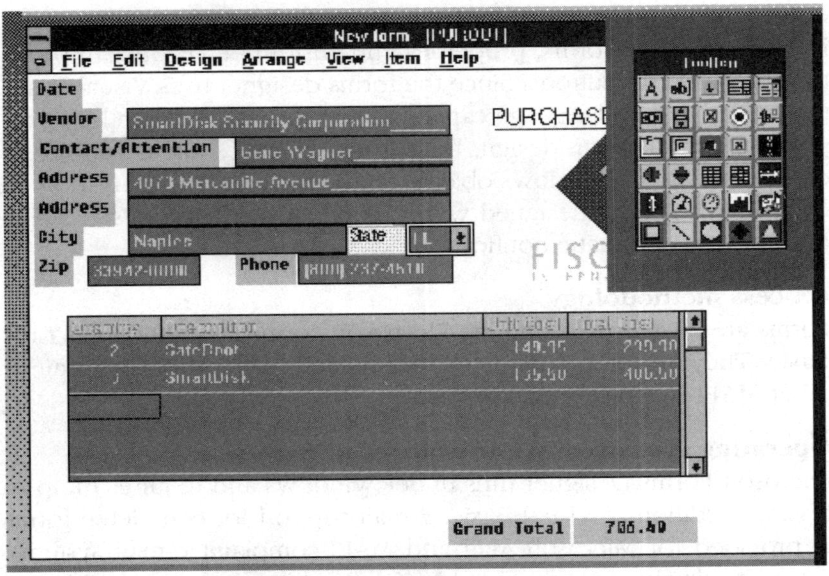

7-6 *The design tool in WorkFlow.2020.* Fischer International Systems Corporation

password. Restrictions and approval authorizations are checked prior to allowing an electronic signature to be placed on a document. For example, a users' authority to sign a purchase order and the amount they may sign for are verified before they are allowed to sign. More elaborate security such as token-based systems can be incorporated into the electronic signature.

Figure 7-7 shows a completed electronic purchasing form. The form will now be routed to the appropriate person for approval. WorkFlow.2020 can be integrated with EDI products allowing electronic forms to be sent via EDI to vendors, suppliers, and customers.

Process methodology

Forms can be processed either on a stand-alone PC or on networked PCs. WorkFlow.2020 supports DDE, DLL, and OLE. This provides integration with other Windows applications such as word processing, spreadsheets, and e-mail. It is written in the O'REXX standards-based, object-oriented language.

Operating systems and hardware platforms

WorkFlow.2020 runs under Windows on networked or stand-alone PCs. E-mail support for completed forms is provided for MHS-compliant mail systems. See Chapter 6 for information on the Emc2/TAO

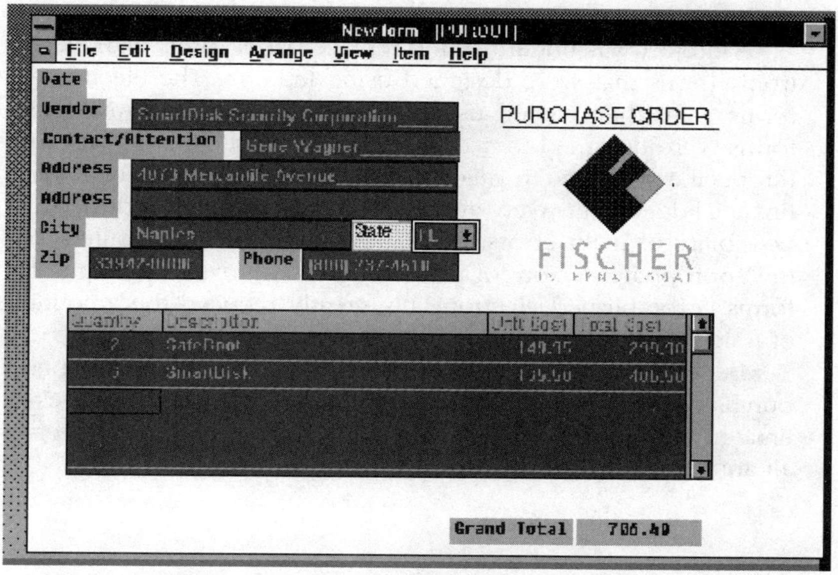

7-7 *A completed electronic purchasing form in WorkFlow.2020.* Fischer International Systems Corporation

e-mail system, also from Fischer International. Access to databases is provided by ODBC drivers.

Features

A toolbox of predesigned forms and object libraries is provided with the design tool. WorkFlow.2000 is another forms routing software that runs on mainframe, midrange, OS/2, DOS, and Macintosh platforms.

Case study

Government administration

The Ministry of Education and Training of Ontario, Canada, was seeking a way to reduce costs and enhance the workflow of administrative forms.[6] Paper forms were produced by an automated design tool, but paper, printing, and storage costs were a concern. The completion of paper forms, particularly those with calculations, were susceptible to error, adding time and cost to form processing. An automated solution that would eliminate paper forms and improve processing flow was sought.

6 Wendy Lavalle, "Electronic Forms a First for Ministry," *Computing Canada*, July 19, 1993, p. 29.

A project was undertaken to replace paper forms with electronic forms that were designed using JetForm. The electronic forms were then routed using Microsoft Mail on a LAN. The forms were designed to access data from existing databases to fill specific fields and to validate and edit entered data. Totals for financial documents were automatically calculated to reduce the possibility of math errors. Forms were automatically routed to the appropriate person for processing or approval. Redesign of forms accomplished electronically greatly reduced the amount of time required to introduce new forms.

Benefits were realized in terms of cost savings from paper purchasing, printing, and storing of hard copy forms. It was estimated that paper usage was reduced by 70 percent and overall annual costs were reduced by $50,000.

8

Image processing

As was stated earlier in the text, workgroup image processing evolved from early image storage systems. These systems were designed to eliminate the large volumes of paper forms and documents associated with business processes. Initially the goal was to create "electronic filing cabinets" to replace paper documents and their associated storage and handling costs. Most of these systems were simple filing and retrieval systems and did not incorporate electronic images into the business process. The imaging system existed at the end of a manual process that was still centered around paper documents. Hardware associated with image processing was relatively expensive and usually not widely used. While still providing major benefits, early image storage systems did little other than replace filing cabinets.

The major difference between image storage systems and image-based workflow systems is the addition of routing and business logic to an image. With these additional capabilities, the electronic image can become the focus of the business process rather than just a storage medium at the end of the process. This can, in many situations, lead to reengineering of the business process and not just automation of existing processes and flows. In some cases, image processing combined with reengineering efforts has resulted in savings of 30 to 60 percent over existing processes.[1] Many vendors of workflow products are incorporating imaging into existing products.

Images can be stored as several types of electronic media depending on the particular business need. Options include magnetic disk, write once read many (WORM) drives, and rewritable optical storage. As the volume of images stored increases, archiving often becomes a concern with image-based systems.

Several vendors of optical storage systems offer archival products that, after a predetermined period of time, move images to media that can be taken off-line and stored until needed. Under this type of stor-

1 "Supplies Reposition to go with the Flow," *Software Magazine*, February 1995, p. 69.

age architecture, images recently created are available for immediate recall, while older images are "spooled" to off-line storage. Images stored off-line are available but require an optical disk or other type of storage media to be recalled from the archive library and reloaded on the system.

In addition to specialized optical storage systems, many DBMSs support binary large objects (BLOBs). A BLOB is a type of field in a database that can be used to store images, graphics, and other types of binary data.[2] This allows images to be stored and retrieved as part of the database. Many commercial imaging systems are based on relational database management systems that support binary objects. Several notable database products include Informix, Ingress, and Sybase.

A concern in imaging is the indexing of images as they are entered into the system. Indexing is required to associate some key field or value with an image. For example, when imaging an accounts payable invoice, it might be indexed by invoice number, vendor number, or vendor name. This is the key by which the image is linked to a transaction in the business process. Depending on the application, one or more keys may be assigned to an image or a group of images that make up the image "folder" for a specific transaction.

The indexing of images can occur manually or may be automated as part of the imaging process. With manual indexing, an operator scans the document and then keys in an index value for the document—in the previous example, an invoice number. This is sometimes necessary because the source documents do not have a standard format from which index values can be easily located by means of optical character recognition.

Automated indexing involves the use of optical character recognition software to read data from the document image and then index the document. Generally this method is used in situations where the format of the source documents is fixed or when is it possible to determine the location of index data based on specific headings or titles. For example, an imaging system could look for the text string "Invoice Number:" and then use the value that follows to index the document. Several of the products listed later in this chapter use optical character recognition to automatically index documents during the scanning process.

Image processing products

In this chapter we present several representative image processing systems. Most systems consist of a combination of hardware and

2 Alex Berson, *Client/Server Architecture* (New York: McGraw-Hill, 1992), p. 310.

software. Some include workflow automation software as well as image processing software. This is not intended to be a complete review of all products nor a comparison of products. Specific products are used to illustrate the features of this category of groupware. A general description of the product is presented followed by a discussion of underlying process methodologies. Operating systems and hardware platforms supported are listed along with particular features of each product. To get the most recent information on specific products, please contact the vendors.

FileNet—FileNet Corp.

The FileNet product line consists of a number of imaging and workflow products for several operating systems and hardware platforms. Workflow automation is provided through the Visual WorkFlo suite of products. Visual WorkFlo consists of three components, Visual WorkFlo/Composer, Visual WorkFlo/Performer, and Visual WorkFlo/Conductor. The Visual WorkFlo/Composer is used to create WorkObjects that combine transaction data with instructions that define the work to be performed and provide status tracking information. Figure 8-1 illustrates an object definition in WorkFlo/Composer.

Defined objects can then be linked to graphically depict the entire workflow. Each graphical object represents a step in the overall

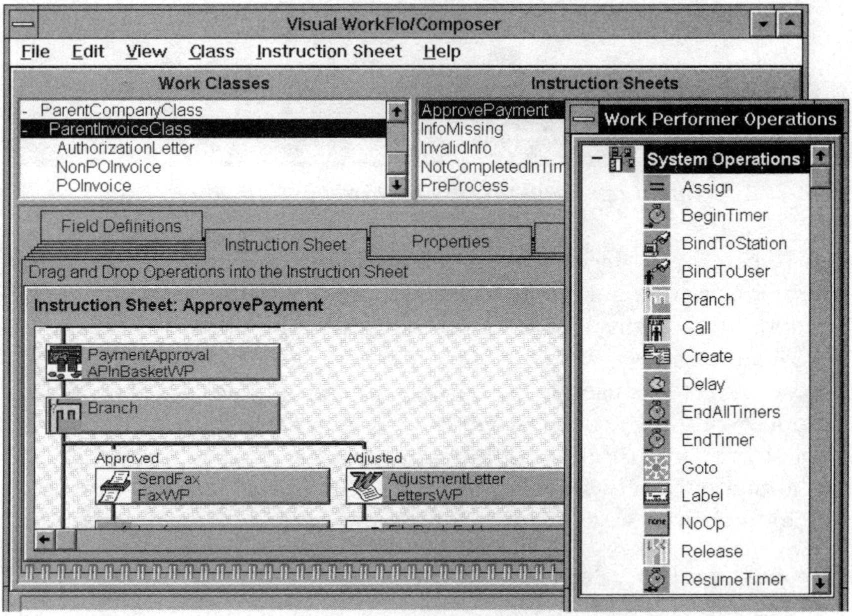

8-1 *An object definition in WorkFlo/Composer.* FileNet Corporation

process. Figure 8-2 shows a payment approval process in WorkFlo/Composer. In this example, the payment approval process involves branching based on approval or adjustment of a payment request. If the payment is approved, a mail message and then a fax are sent. If the payment request requires adjustment, a word processing application is called to generate a letter and then a document is placed in a folder. The Work Performer Operations window shows graphical objects such as branching, go to and waiting for events that can be used to represent specific operations when defining a workflow.

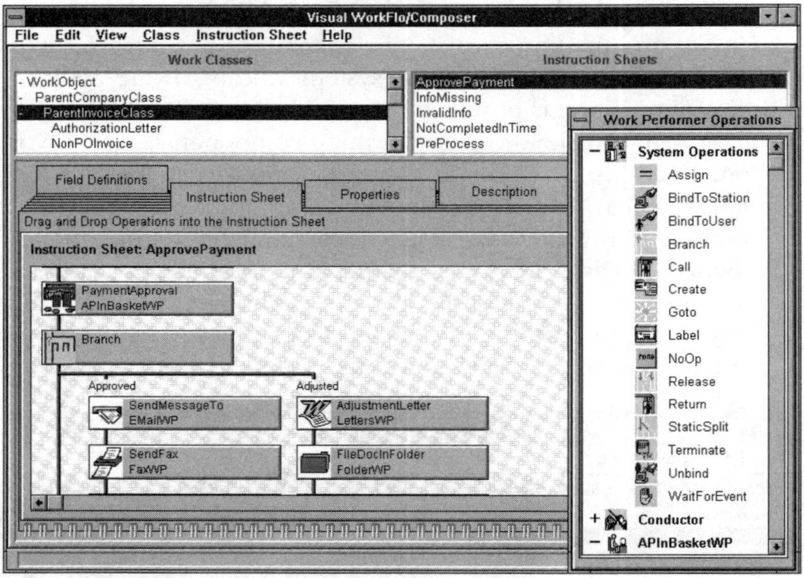

8-2 *A payment approval process in WorkFlo/Composer.* FileNet Corporation

Once WorkObjects have been defined, the Visual WorkFlo/Performer is used to link the objects with an information processing application. Applications can be developed with a number of development tools such as C++, Visual Basic, or other FileNet tools. Visual WorkFlo/Conductor is used to graphically administer, modify, analyze, and model workflow activity. A WorkFlo System Development Kit is available to create custom workflow applications for Windows and OS/2. In addition to software, FileNet offers a full line of hardware products including servers, scanners, printers, and optical storage systems.

Process methodology

In general, FileNet employs a client/server architecture for document imaging. Documents are imaged and then stored in the image management system (IMS). The IMS organizes, stores, and manages access to images, CAD drawings, data, text, photographs, and other multimedia data and acts as a server to client workstations. The workflow application runs as a client application on end-user workstations. Client applications are developed using an object-oriented graphical development tool.

Operating systems and hardware platforms

FileNet products run on the following host operating systems:

- AIX
- HP-UX
- MPE/iX
- Windows NT

The IMS software supports Token Ring, Ethernet, FDDI, TCP/IP, and Novell SPX/IPX networks and is fully integrated with Oracle and Sybase database management systems. Workflow and document imaging software is supported on the following client platforms:

- AIX-6000
- HP-UX
- Macintosh
- OS/2
- SunOS
- Windows

Features

In addition to the products described earlier, the FileNet product line offers the following:

WorkFlo/ICR WorkFlo/ICR is an optical character recognition subsystem that automates data entry and document indexing by extracting data from designated input fields on a scanned image. Machine-printed as well as hand-printed text, checkboxes, and other data on scanned images can be read and used to index documents.

COLD software Computer output to laser disk (COLD) software is used to archive and access computer-generated output. This replaces hard copy reports, microfilm, and microfiche. Computer-generated output files are processed by the COLD software and are then accessed using FileNet imaging applications.

WorkFlo/Payables WorkFlo/Payables is a complete image-enabled accounts payable application. It runs as a client/server application using the FileNet document imaging and WorkFlo software.

AutoForm System Development Kit The AutoForm System Development Kit is a forms toolbox for the design of electronic forms to be used in conjunction with WorkFlo and document imaging applications. A graphical design environment is used to develop forms for Windows and OS/2 Presentation Manager.

KeyFile—KeyFile Corp.

KeyFile is a Windows-based document imaging and workflow product. It can process both images and electronic documents. The JobMaker workflow tool provides a form-based interface for creating job steps in a workflow. A Windows graphical interface is used for access to scanned images and electronic documents. Images can be received from several types of scanners, and DOS-compatible files from word processing applications, spreadsheets, CAD, and other PC applications can serve as the source of electronic documents. Third-party OCR products can be used to process scanned documents.

Workflow tracking and monitoring is provided for each job step and task recipient. DDE access to KeyFile functions is available from DDE-compliant application development tools such as Visual Basic, PowerBuilder, and ObjectVision. OLE links to KeyFile documents can be inserted into OLE-compliant applications such as Lotus Notes, Microsoft Access, cc:Mail, and Microsoft Mail. A development kit provides application programming interfaces (APIs) for application development in the C programming language.

Process methodology

KeyFile provides an open architecture by supporting Windows DDE, OLE, and KeyFile Open Access Layer (KOALA). Support for third-party scanning and optical storage hardware is provided, making the imaging application hardware independent. Links to an MHS communications server and e-mail systems provide a way to develop customized, integrated applications.

Operating systems and hardware platforms

KeyFile requires a Windows workstation with a VGA display. The document server requires a Windows- or OS/2-capable PC with VGA display and sufficient disk storage for the application. Optical storage is optional. The following networks are supported:

- Banyan Vines
- DEC Pathworks
- LAN server
- Microsoft LAN Manager
- Novell NetWare
- Windows for Workgroups

Features

The KeyFile product includes workgroup mail and network fax. These products support shared and private address books and distribution lists.

ViewStar—ViewStar Corp.

ViewStar is a Windows-based document and workflow product. Workflow automation is provided through the Process Architect product. Process Architect is a graphical business process modeler and application development tool. Workflow processes are visually depicted as connected workflow tasks. A simulation feature allows processes to be modeled to predict throughput and predict potential bottlenecks. A set of predefined functions such as folder matching, review routing, and decision branching can be graphically associated with a task.

Once a process has been mapped using the Process Architect, the Application Designer can be used to develop the user application. The Application Designer is used to build display windows, menus, action bars, and buttons. Objects created during the design process can be utilized in future applications.

To add further business logic to an application, scripts can be incorporated into an application from a 4GL scripting language. A library of example scripts—the Process Script Assistants—can be used for customization of an application. These scripts are based on existing business objects and the Process Script macro language. Utilizing this library of existing code can reduce application development time.

Image-enabled applications can be linked to existing applications through the Business Process Automation server. The Business Process Automation server provides a link to existing database management systems through SQL. Several interface modules are available to link image applications with legacy systems and various types of hardware devices such as printers, scanners, and fax servers.

Process methodology

ViewStar utilizes a client/server architecture for its document imaging application. Documents are imaged and then stored on a host image server. The Repository Manager software provides scalability in document storage through library partitioning.[3] This allows document libraries to be spread across multiple servers. The client application

3 ViewStar, The Product for Business Process Automation (Alameda, California: ViewStar Corp.), 1994, p. 4.

resides on networked Windows workstations. Workflow analysis and application design are accomplished using object-oriented tools. Support of Windows DDE and OLE provide integration with other Windows-based applications. The use of standard SQL allows the use of a number of relational database management systems as data sources.

Operating systems and hardware platforms

ViewStar runs on PC LAN and UNIX servers and supports the following database management systems:

- DB2
- Gupta SQLBase
- Microsoft SQL server for Windows NT
- Sybase SQL server for NetWare
- Sybase SQL server for UNIX

ViewStar software supports Token Ring, Ethernet, FDDI, TCP/IP, and Novell SPX/IPX networks and is fully integrated with Oracle and Sybase database management systems. Workflow and document imaging software is supported on the following client platforms:

- AIX-6000
- HP-UX
- Macintosh
- OS/2
- SunOS
- Windows

Interfaces to legacy systems on IBM mainframe and midrange AS400 systems are provided through 3270 and 5250 gateways. Integration with Lotus Notes is available through a Notes Integration Toolkit.

Features

In addition to the products described earlier, ViewStar offers the following:

OCR/ICR OCR/ICR is optical character recognition software that can be used for forms processing of machine-printed or hand-printed text and checkbox form entries. Contextual rules based on expected data in specific fields are used to increase data accuracy.

Process Replicator Process Replicator allows workflow processes designed in Process Architect to be exported from one system to another. This provides a way to develop workflow applications on a test system and then transfer them to a production environment on another system.

System administration tools Various tools are available to aid in system administration and maintenance. These include debugging utilities, on-line help, and on-line documentation.

Case study

Insurance processing

Connecticut Mutual Life Insurance is one of the top 30 U.S. life insurers with over 1.2 million policyholders.[4] Like most of the insurance industry, Connecticut Mutual's operations were primarily paper driven. Employees in several functions were overwhelmed by paper documents, and procedural inefficiencies caused delays and redundant processing. A number of unconnected information systems in different departments complicated information exchange. Upper management realized that operations were labor-intensive and inefficient and that the organization could not meet its service and financial objectives.

A reengineering effort that included the introduction of document imaging and WorkFlo software from FileNet was undertaken to streamline operations. At the core of the effort was the "command center" integrated workstation. From a command center workstation, users have access to all needed information including images, data, voice, and video. By establishing a common interface and access method, redundant systems were eliminated and common functions such as document scanning and indexing were provided through a single set of utilities. Overall access to information at all levels within the organization was improved.

Benefits were realized in a number of areas. Customer response time for beneficiary change was reduced from days to seconds and the number of human interventions was reduced from 22 to 2. Operating productivity for all areas of the company increased by 35 percent or more. Dependence on hard copy documents was greatly reduced, while access to information was increased. The initial investment in one division was paid back within 18 months of introducing the image-enabled workflow application. Based on the successes in the initial implementation, additional imaging applications were planned to take advantage of the existing investment in imaging technology.

4 Connecticut Mutual Insures Success with Imaging and WorkFlow Software (Costa Mesa, California: FileNet Corp.), 1993.

9

Document management

The term "document" tends to bring to mind images of hard copy textual material generated by some type of word processing software. But in terms of workflow and workgroup computing, document management confers an entirely different meaning.

Word processors do indeed generate documents, but a document in today's business context may be much more complicated than just a single textual file. In some businesses, the document has become the primary product. The "document" has become a complicated product that is developed in a collaborative environment and involves a great deal of work to complete. It is the complex nature of the document and the management of the collaborative work process that has given rise to document management software. Let us take a brief look at the concept of a business document before looking at representative document management products.

A document may be comprised of a number of different types of materials. Generally documents are thought of as being only text, but in reality they may contain graphics, audio, video, and other types of electronic information, as well as text. Consider an architectural document for the design of a building. The document may contain textual material that describes the project, along with graphics and computer-aided design drawings. Spreadsheets could be included that contain lists of materials and cost estimates. Full motion video showing the building from different elevations and simulating traffic flow could be combined as well.

Taking this example even one step further, a virtual reality simulation of the building could be included to allow prospective occupants of the building to take a tour of the building before it is built. While this might seem a bit extreme, it illustrates the point that a document can be a complex entity comprised of a number of different elements.

Given that a document can be extremely complex, it can also become a collaborative effort for a workgroup. In the architectural example, there might be designers, engineers, architects, and graphic artists all working on the project simultaneously. This is somewhat different than other workflow products previously mentioned, in that work might be occurring simultaneously rather than serially.

Often workflow infers a sequential process, in that one step is completed before the next processing step is started. With a group document workflow, there may be many concurrent processes all interrelated. This gives rise to the need for shared information and centralized version control and change control.

The specifications for various parts of the overall project might change and that information must be updated and communicated to all involved. An audit trail of changes and modifications is necessary particularly in regulatory or contractual situations. Different options may be designed for presentation to a client, and each of those options needs to be tracked throughout the project. As each element of the overall document is being worked on, it must be accounted for, and any changes and the originator of those changes tracked. This is commonly referred to as *check in/check out* and is used to control who has a particular element of the document. As changes or revisions to elements of the document are made, they are recorded. This is referred to as *version control.*

In many situations, elements of one document might also be elements of other documents. Given the previous example, engineering drawings in the client presentation document might also be part of a building permit document, or a purchase request document. Designs for a single building in one document might be part of a larger document for the design of an entire complex. The elements of one document might have many complex relationships with other documents. This makes the management and control of individual elements even more important.

A relational database serves as a good analogy of a document management system. Each element of the document is similar to a record or table entry in the database. Each document is similar to a particular view of the database in which data from several tables is linked together and presented as a single view of the data. The same data might be presented in several different views of the database.

Document management systems often utilize relational databases. Document management products in general deal with some or all of the concerns listed. Less complex products primarily deal with check in/check out and version control, while more advanced products deal with the management and interrelationships of document elements as well.

Document management products

In this chapter we present several representative document management systems. Most systems are primarily software-based and are designed to run on a number of platforms. Some include workflow automation software as well as document management software. This is not intended to be a complete review of all products nor a comparison of products. Specific products are used to illustrate the features of this category of groupware. A general description of the product is presented followed by a discussion of underlying process methodologies. Operating systems and hardware platforms supported are listed along with particular features of each product. To get the most recent information on specific products, please contact the vendors.

Documentum—Documentum Inc.

Documentum is an enterprise document management system that is based on a client/server architecture. It is comprised of three major components: the Documentum Workspace, the Documentum server, and the Documentum Toolkit.[1]

The Documentum Workspace is a graphical user environment for managing and processing documents. A number of graphical client platforms are supported. The Documentum server is an object-oriented application that runs on a UNIX server. The server manages document storage, library services, workflow management, and application development. The Documentum Toolkit is a set of high-level application programming interfaces that support programming languages and application development tools. Figure 9-1 illustrates the components of the Documentum system.

The Documentum server services both Workspace and custom clients. On the server, documents are stored in an object-oriented repository called DocBase. Objects in DocBase can be stored in several different ways, including relational databases, network file systems, and optical storage systems.

Workspace client applications can be integrated with other client applications. Custom applications that access the Documentum server can be developed using the Toolkit APIs.

1 Documentum Announces Enterprise Document Management System (Pleasaton, California: Documentum, Inc.), 1994, p. 2.

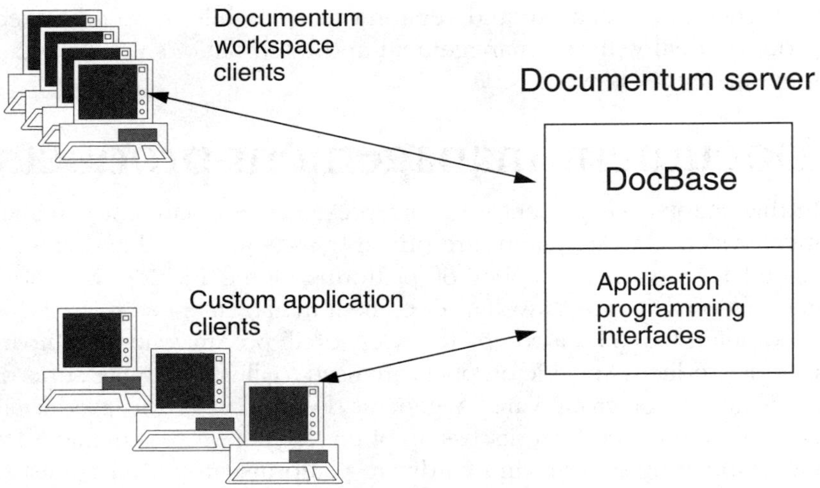

9-1 *Documentum document management.*

The Library Services feature of the Documentum server automates the storage and management of documents. It maintains version control and cataloging, and organizes documents based on user-specified naming conventions. Included in Library Services is a document query language (DQL) that provides an SQL-type query language to access documents. Queries can be based on business content, document attributes, or text.

The Documentum Workflow Management application is another component that runs on the server. Workflow Management automates the processing and production of documents across workgroups. Business rules and routing can be incorporated into workflow management, and both serial and parallel routing logic can be incorporated into workflows.

Process methodology

The Documentum system is based on an object-oriented client/server architecture. The client/server architecture was described in detail in the preceding section. Of particular interest is the object-oriented methodology used for documents. The basis of this object-oriented approach is the DocObject, which is an object-oriented representation of reusable document components. These objects support the creation of virtual documents, which are unique combinations of objects from any information source that can be assembled on demand.

DocObjects include not only information, but also incorporate business rules into the object. Each DocObject contains four parts: the actual document, and its attributes, operations, and relationships. Attributes include such items as name, title, and author. The creation of virtual documents is handled by the Dynamic Document Assembly (DDA) application. This application automates the assembly of DocObjects based on business rules stored on the Documentum server. Figure 9-2 shows the relationship between DocObjects, DDA, and a virtual document.

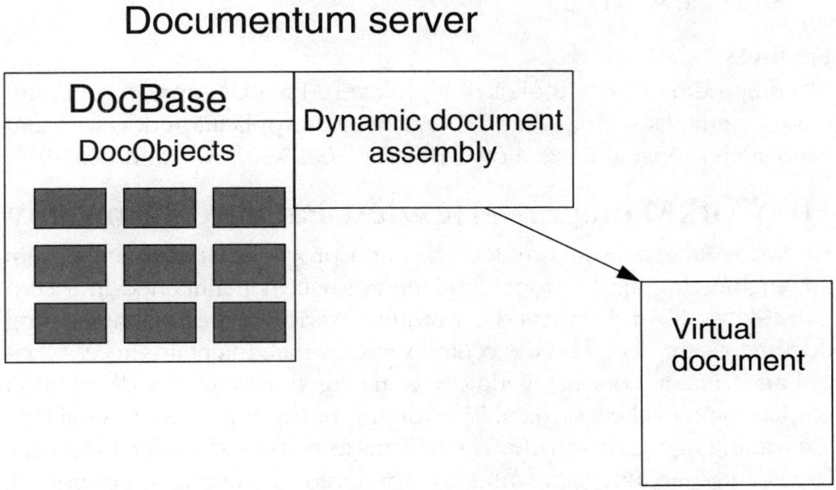

9-2 *The relationship between DocObjects, dynamic document assembly, and a virtual document in Documentum.*

In this example, DocObjects stored in the DocBase are accessed by the Dynamic Document Assembler, based on predefined business rules, to produce a virtual document. For example, architectural design DocObjects that have been finalized could be combined to produce a virtual specification document for customer review and approval. Integration is provided with word processing applications such as FrameMaker, Interleaf, Microsoft Word, and WordPerfect.

Operating systems and hardware platforms

The Documentum server application runs under the following operating systems:

- AIX
- HP-UX
- Sun Solaris
- Windows NT

The client document management application is supported on the following platforms:

- AIX
- HP-UX
- Macintosh
- Motif
- Sun OS
- Windows
- Windows NT

Features

Documentum offers a toolkit of high-level APIs that support programming languages such as C and C++ as well as application development tools such as Visual Basic, PowerBuilder, SQL Windows, and OMNIS 7.

HP WorkManager—Hewlett Packard Company

HP WorkManager is a complete data and process management system for engineering applications. Engineering data is maintained in a centralized "vault" and retrieved on request. Various types of engineering documents are stored on the central server, which maintains access control and version control. Workflow is managed through the distribution of electronic packets of data. The routing of these packets is similar to the routing of e-mail and electronic forms as discussed earlier. Electronic forms and electronic signatures for approved documents is supported. Integration with other engineering and manufacturing applications is supported. The WorkManager product consists of the server application, the client applications, and application integration products. Figure 9-3 shows the various components of HP WorkManager.

The server application includes data vault and process management capabilities. The Engineering Client is designed for engineers and project managers and has complete application functionality. The Design Client contains a subset of the functions contained in the Engineering Client. The Basic Client is designed for clerical and management users and has view-only capabilities.

Process methodology

HP WorkManager relies on a centralized database to maintain control of engineering data. A hierarchical security system is used to provide various levels of access to users or groups of users. The basic method of distributing data is through electronic "packets." Packets are similar to file folders in that they contain all required data such as design drawings, electronic forms, notes, and other documentation relating to a specific task or project. The packet itself does not actually contain the data but has a reference to the appropriate documents in the

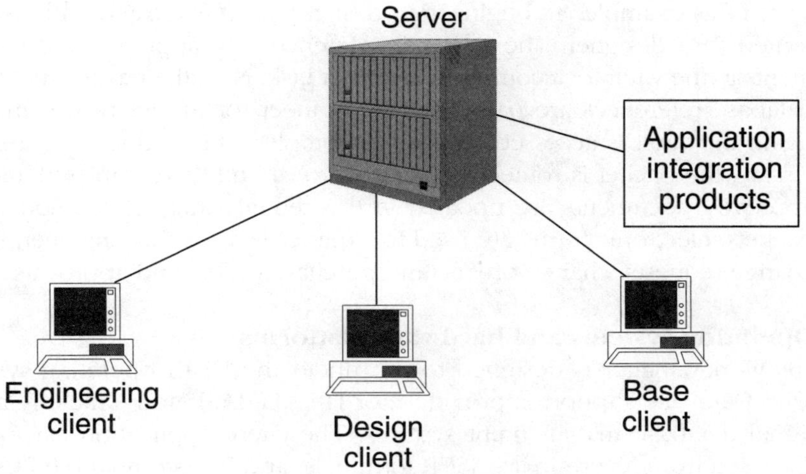

9-3 *Various components of the HP WorkManager.*

central data vault. Recipients of the packet can then access desired information from the vault. Routing lists can be used to send packets from one group member to the next. As tasks are completed and approved, the latest information is posted back to the central vault. Figure 9-4 illustrates the packet concept in relation to the electronic vault.

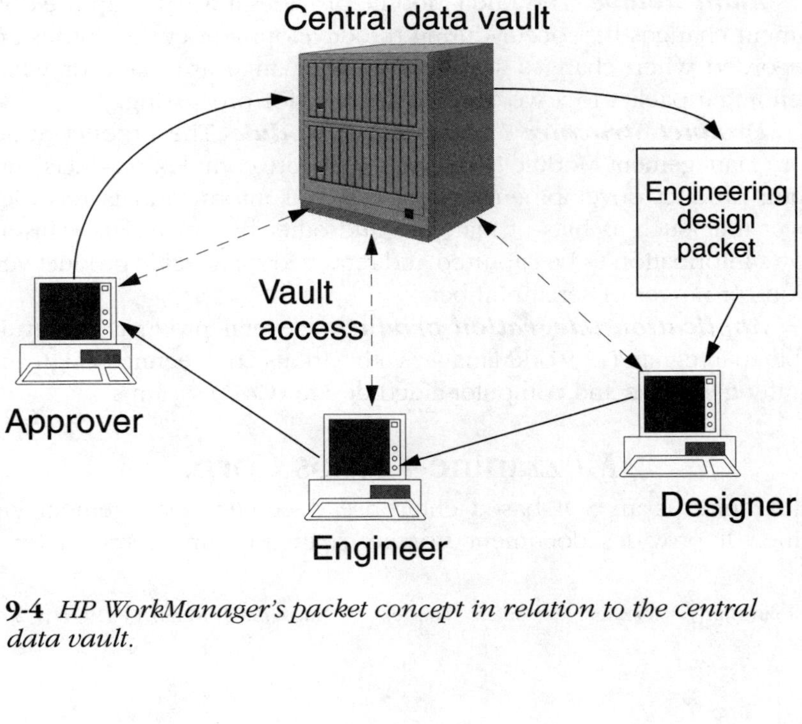

9-4 *HP WorkManager's packet concept in relation to the central data vault.*

In this example, an engineering design packet is created and then routed to a designer. The designer references the appropriate documents in the vault to accomplish his or her task. Next the packet and its database references are passed to an engineer for further processing. Again the vault is accessed for data to complete the engineering task. Finally, the packet is routed for final approval and the completed and approved documents are updated in the central vault. In addition to packets, electronic forms are used to capture data such as engineering change requests, change orders, and purchase orders and approvals.

Operating systems and hardware platforms

HP WorkManager is designed to run under the UNIX operating system. Database support is provided for HP ALLBASE and Oracle relational database management systems. The client application can be accessed from X-terminals, ASCII terminals, and IBM-compatible PCs.

Features

In addition to the products described earlier, the following additional modules are available for HP WorkManager:

Classification Module The Classification Module provides the capability to define a comprehensive classification scheme for data contained in the vault. It allows a logical grouping of parts or assemblies and the creation of customized classification hierarchies.

Audit Module The Audit Module provides a way to capture document changes that occur during the development cycle. Entries are recorded when changes such as a state change are made or when sending a packet to a workgroup member for processing.

Product Structure Management Module The Product Structure Management Module is designed for more complex products with long product development cycles. Detailed information is recorded over time such as bills of materials and other historical data. This allows information to be captured and retrieved for specific product versions or ranges of serial numbers.

Application integration products Several products are available to integrate HP WorkManager with various engineering design and drafting systems and computer-aided design (CAD) systems.

Mezzanine—Saros Corp.

Mezzanine is an SQL-based enterprise document management engine.[2] It provides document storage, searching, and retrieval for a

2 John Garris, "Mezzanine/Document Manager," *PC Magazine*, November 8, 1994, p. 2.

number of client applications. It features a scalable architecture in that multiple servers can be utilized for a single document library. As the size of the document library increases, additional servers can be added as needed. Version control facilities track documents as they are "checked out" and prevent simultaneous alterations. As documents are returned, they are stored as new versions. Document Manager is the graphical client application that provides access to stored documents. Other client applications and add-on products for Windows applications can be used to access documents stored under Mezzanine. A software development kit is available to create customized applications with Mezzanine document access.

Process methodology

Mezzanine utilizes a client/server architecture in that the document management system operates on one or more servers and supports requests from LAN-based client applications. It utilizes Microsoft's SQL server as a database. Documents are organized into libraries and libraries are structured into shelves that contain documents. This is analogous to the storage of hard copy documents in a manual filing system. A user-definable tree-like structure can be used to create a document structure that mirrors the logical structure of documents in actual practice.

Operating systems and hardware platforms

The Mezzanine document server can be loaded on OS/2 or UNIX platforms. Packaged Windows-based client applications are available or custom applications can be created for Macintosh, OS/2, UNIX, and Windows clients.

Features

Saros offers a Software Development Kit (SDK) in addition to the products listed earlier. The SDK provides a way to develop customized applications for several client operating systems.

Revise—FileNet Corp.

In addition to the document imaging products described in the previous chapter, the FileNet product line includes several technical document management tools. These tools include Revise-Review for Windows, Revise-Review/Sun, Revise-Markup, and Revise-Edit. They are primarily used to review, mark up, and edit technical documents. Revise-Review for PC and Sun workstations provides a way to view scanned images and mark up layers of engineering drawings and other large format documents. Panning, scrolling, rotating, and zoom capabilities are included. Revise-Markup contains all the viewing features of Revise-Review as well as tools to mark up existing images by drawing vector layers on top of scanned images. Revise-Edit merges markup layers with underlying raster images to create new documents and drawing revisions.

Process methodology

In general, FileNet employs a client/server architecture for document imaging. Documents are imaged and then stored in the image management system (IMS). The IMS organizes, stores, and manages access to images, CAD drawings, data, text, photographs, and other multimedia data, and acts as a server to client workstations. The Revise products work in conjunction with other FileNet products and view or modify existing images or create new images to be managed by the FileNet system. See the preceding chapter for more information on the FileNet image management system.

Operating systems and hardware platforms

FileNet products run on the following operating systems:

- AIX
- HP-UX
- MPE/iX
- Windows NT

The Revise product line is supported on Windows and Sun workstations.

Features

In addition to the products described earlier, the FileNet product line offers the following:

Image eXchange Facility/Sun and CALS eXchange/Sun These two products support the transfer of document images and other files between CAD or raster workstations and the FileNet document imaging system. Image eXchange Facility/Sun allows drafting workstations to access documents stored in FileNet IMS. The CALS eXchange software provides a common exchange format for importing files from CAD or other third-party applications that use the CALS standard.

WorkFlo/Scan Image Import This software allows document image files created by non-FileNet scanners to be imported to the FileNet system. Once imported, the images are available for full processing.

SoftSolutions—Novell Inc.

SoftSolutions is the document management component of the Novell GroupWare product line.[3] It manages storage, searching, and retrieval of a number of different types of documents including word processing documents, spreadsheets, image files, and e-mail. SoftSolutions provides document storage, tracking, retrieval, and security. Multiple versions of a document can be stored and tracked. Up to 999 versions of a document can be maintained with 99 active versions.

Full text search is provided for stored documents. An add-on module provides an intelligent searching capability with concept, numeric, approximation, phase, proximity, and root word search types. Integration is provided with popular word processing, spreadsheet, imaging and workflow products.

The SoftSolution Document Desktop provides a customizable graphical user interface for the document management system. Various icons can be used to represent documents, folders, searches, document management functions, and other Windows applications. An object viewer provides the capability to display a number of different types of documents including text, drawings, bit maps, and spreadsheets.

Process methodology

The SoftSolution product is based on an open architecture that supports multiple operating systems, platforms, and desktop applications. The Universal Filing System manages documents stored across multiple platforms. Each document includes a profile that contains such information as title, author, document type, security, and creation date. This profile is used for storing and retrieving the document. A client/server architecture is utilized by the Server Enhancement Module which allows access to document data from client applications. This module runs as a NetWare loadable module or as a process on UNIX platforms.

Operating systems and hardware platforms

SoftSolutions runs under the following operating systems:

- AIX
- DG/UX
- HP-UX
- NCR Unix

3 Technology Overview, SoftSolutions Document Management Architecture (Provo, Utah: Novell, Inc.), September 9, 1994.

- NetWare
- SCO Unix
- Sun Solaris
- VMS
- Ultrix

Features

In addition to the products described earlier, SoftSolutions offers the following:

Multiple language versions SoftSolutions is available in English, French, Japanese, Spanish, Danish, Hungarian, and German language versions.

SoftSolutions Intelligent Search The Intelligent Search Module provides advanced searching capabilities based on meanings, concepts, or ideas contained in the document.

Case study

Telecommunications manufacturing

A manufacturer of telecommunications equipment was looking for a way to manage the large volumes of documentation associated with the manufacture and support of its products. Many of its products are custom designed and require complex technical documents that are produced through the collaborative efforts of engineers, designers, technicians, writers, and editors. Creating and maintaining this documentation was becoming a major challenge. Existing information systems were fragmented and not totally automated. Some documents were available only in hard copy. Document searches at times required that several different databases be accessed. Information retrieval was difficult and time-consuming. Updates to documentation were equally as difficult, with changes often being made to hard copy documents. Management was interested in automating document management to reduce costs, improve their competitive position, and improve their level of customer service. Additional requirements included an open architecture and object-oriented technology.

A document management system from Documentum was implemented on UNIX servers with PC and Macintosh clients. This system provided an architecture for the creation, sharing, reuse, and management of documents throughout the entire organization. The new system has eliminated redundancy in the documentation process and allows more rapid production cycles. The company has been able to respond more quickly to customer inquiries and overall productivity has improved. The documentation application is being expanded throughout the organization and it is planned that it will be provided to select customers.

10

Business process automation

This category of groupware is somewhat different from the categories previously discussed in that the emphasis is on the business process rather than on the underlying data. While a few of the products profiled in the previous chapters contained workflow design and analysis tools, most dealt primarily with the management of data in one form or another. If we look back at the categories covered to this point, we see that each dealt with a different type of data, from e-mail to electronic forms to electronic images and finally to electronic documents.

The emphasis in business process automation is on automating the business process regardless of the underlying data. For example, the process might be accounts payable processing, and the data might come in the form of scanned images, electronic forms, and e-mail. The business process automation application, while relying on various data sources, focuses on the management of the process. The application is built to support a specific business process, hopefully one that has been well engineered.

This is important because the automation of a poor process might provide some benefit, but the real benefit comes from an approach that combines automation with process reengineering. Reengineering is a popular term, but many organizations have found that there has been very little engineering of processes to begin with. Often existing business processes simply evolved from existing manual methods. Attempts at automating these types of legacy processes have simply automated much of the redundant and inefficient processing required in manual systems. For example, many organizations use multipart forms in business processes. What is the reason for multipart forms?

In most manual systems, the multipart form served as a way to provide each step in the process with a copy of the transaction. Each individual step in the process kept a copy of the form for their own record keeping. Given a four-part form, that suggests that four separate filing systems, all containing the same data, existed in the organization. That also equates to four times the cost for document storage and management. Add to that the cost of redundant automated systems in each processing step and the true cost of the business process becomes more evident. Automation of this same process might simply replace the four-part form with an electronic form that is routed to each processing step in the existing manual system. Each processing step would then print a hard copy of the form or use the electronic form as input to their automated system.

Automation of the process that involves reengineering results in a different solution. For example, the number of steps might be reduced based on a set of business rules such as the dollar amount of the transaction. A single copy of the transaction is centrally stored rather than storing multiple copies either on hard copy or electronically. Redundant applications and databases can be eliminated or consolidated. The overall impact of this process automation would be far greater than with simple automation.

While this all sounds very attractive, there are several practical concerns regarding business process reengineering. Probably the most obvious question is how do you reengineer a business process? This is in many respects a management question rather than an automation problem. The focus of total quality management (TQM) is often on process reengineering, and several methods such as process action teams and quality circles are used to evaluate and reengineer processes. Many management consulting firms specialize in business process reengineering (BPR). While this might be a management issue, there is a fast growing market for BPR design and analysis tools. Chapter 11 deals with this category of software in detail.

Once the process reengineering is accomplished, how is the new process to be implemented? That is the focus of the products covered in this chapter. These products are designed to implement an automated business process independent of underlying data sources. A process focus infers that there is a structured process flow to enforce and that there is some process management provided. Management includes where a particular transaction is in the process, and perhaps some means of gathering and analyzing statistical information on the efficiency of the overall process.

Other concerns of process automation software include process methodologies and data integration. Process methodologies stem from the design and analysis tool or methods used to construct the process.

These process methodologies use some type of model to describe various interactions during the business process. These methodologies can carry through to the design of the actual application. For example, if the process methodology is based on a model that requires feedback from the customer to determine if the process is completed successfully, that might require that the application have some type of feedback mechanism to determine if and when the process is completed.

Data integration is a concern since these products primarily deal with process. Data is still a very necessary part of the process. The concern is, does a particular process automation software support the various types of data required? Most process automation software is fairly generic and, either directly or through third-party add-on products, deals with specialized data such as relational databases, electronic forms, images, voice, or video.

Business process automation products

In this chapter we present several representative business process automation products. Some include workflow automation software as a part of the process automation design tools, while others offer standalone companion products for process design and reengineering. (See Chapter 11 for more detailed information on process design tools.) This is not intended to be a complete review of all products nor a comparison of products. Specific products are used to illustrate the features of this category of groupware.

A general description of the product is presented followed by a discussion of the underlying process methodologies that may apply. Operating systems and hardware platforms supported are listed along with particular features of each product. Significant third-party products are mentioned for some products. To get the most recent information on specific products, please contact the vendors.

Action Workflow System—Action Technologies

Product description

The Action Workflow System is comprised of several components that provide workflow computing solutions based on an open, object-oriented, client/server architecture.[1] The complete system in-

1 Corporate Backgrounder (Alameda, California: Action Technologies), 1995, p. 7.

cludes Action Workflow Analyst, Action Workflow Builder, and Action Workflow Manager.

The Action Workflow Analyst is used to model, analyze, and reengineer business processes. Detailed information on existing processes, such as costs in terms of time and money, can be incorporated into the model. Through a graphical interface, the process model can be changed and the results on the overall process studied. Variations in the existing process can be modeled and analyzed to determine if they will provide the desired result. Detailed information on the Action Workflow Analyst is provided in chapter 11.

The Workflow Builder is used to design and develop workflow applications based on graphically generated business process maps.[2] These maps can be generated within Workflow Builder or from the Action Workflow Analyst. These maps depict the workflow within a business process and define several parameters key to the business process. Maps are independent of the environment in which the application will be implemented.

Design can be performed in either of the two supported environments—SQL server or Lotus Notes. The choice of environment is often driven by the type of application. Lotus Notes is preferable in applications that are somewhat free-form and require frequent accessing and updating of forms. The Lotus Notes version of Workflow Builder automatically generates Notes Forms and Views. Existing Notes functionality such as security and directory services can be utilized in Workflow Builder applications.

High-volume, transaction-based applications that are integrated with other business applications are suited to an SQL environment. The SQL server version writes workflow definitions and application data to SQL databases. Developers can specify application data and database form names. Front-end applications can be developed using C, C++, Visual Basic, and other Windows-based design tools that can call Windows dynamic linked libraries (DLLs).

Business process goals and objectives can be embedded within the application. This provides tracking of actual performance against objectives. This can be accomplished by specifying cycle times for individual workflows and the entire process. Automatic actions such as escalation and notification can be triggered when expected cycle times are exceeded. To provide workflow functions that cannot be easily expressed in a graphical form, a scripting language is used. A script assistant facility is provided to simplify the development of scripts.

2 Action Workflow Builder—A Design and Development Tool for Workflow Networks (Alameda, California: Action Technologies), 1994.

Action Workflow Manager is the administrative component of the Action Workflow System.[3] It provides a way to monitor, administer, and control workflow functions for either SQL server or Lotus Notes environments. The Manager provides a way to start and stop server processes, set authorization levels, schedule processes, and delete, suspend, or cancel ongoing processes. New applications can be managed by the Workflow Manager and moved into production to run concurrently with existing applications. Performance can be monitored by a follow-up and reminder function as well as by statistical reports on process performance.

Process methodology

The Action Workflow System is based on a workflow methodology that defines business processes. This methodology utilizes a "loop" metaphor to describe how work is performed in a business process and to define parameters such as the work to be done, the participants, and the requirements for successful completion.[4] The participants in a workflow consist of a performer, who does the work, and a customer, for whom the work is being completed. Each loop divides work into four phases—preparation, negotiation, performance, and acceptance. These phases define the specifics of the workflow. The final phase—acceptance—is used to determine if the work was successfully completed. Figure 10-1 shows the graphical depiction of an Action Workflow.

In this example, a customer-compliant system is modeled. The units of work are represented as interconnected loops. In each loop the various participants and the associated costs for each workflow are identified.

Operating systems and hardware platforms

The Action Workflow Builder is designer to run on a Windows-based PC. The Action Workflow Manager runs under OS/2 or Windows NT and requires either SQL server or the server edition of Lotus Notes.

Features

In addition to the products listed earlier, Action offers the following:

Action Workflow DocRoute DocRoute workflow enables document management applications. It integrates with Saros Document

3 Action Workflow Manager—A Management and Administrative Tool for Workflow Networks (Alameda, California: Action Technologies), 1994.

4 Action Workflow Analyst—A Modeling and Analysis Tool for Business Processes (Alameda, California: Action Technologies), 1994.

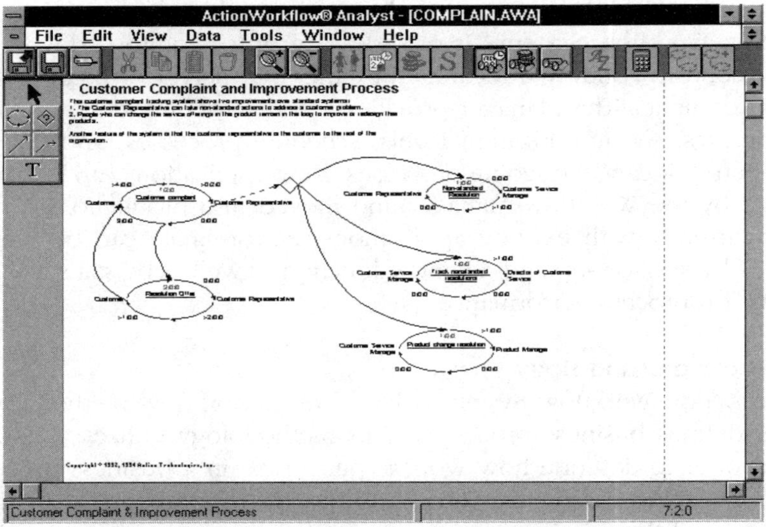

10-1 *The graphical depiction of an Action Workflow.* Action Technologies

Manager, PC Docs OPEN, and Novell SoftSolutions.[5] This product allows Workflow Builder applications to access documents from other document management systems.

KI Shell—UES, Inc.

Product description

KI Shell is an object-oriented, database-enabled work management system. It is used to create a basic activity network model and then to define workflow processes. KI Shell workflows are database-enabled as opposed to mail-enabled. This allows KI Shell to utilize different database management systems in a client/server architecture. The focus of the workflow design process is to identify the roles, decision support for each role, activities, rules, and information objects associated with a workflow. In a graphical environment, workflow objects are created and linkages between them established. Figure 10-2 shows an example of a workflow designed in KI Shell.

This graphical representation is used to define the activities and interactions that occur in the business process. Rules are incorporated into the model through the RuleWriter which uses the C programming language. Using reusable System Integration Library functions, process data can be examined and specific actions initiated. These functions

5 Corporate Backgrounder, p. 9.

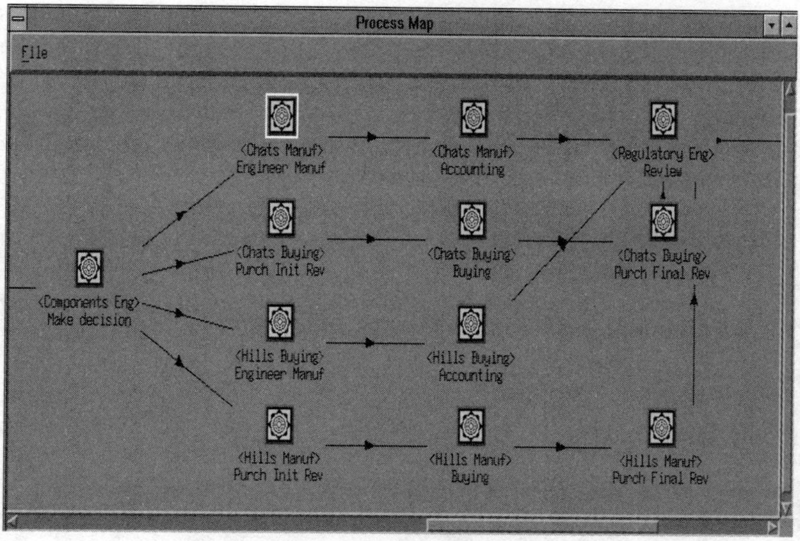

10-2 *An example of a workflow designed in KI Shell.* UES, Inc.

are also used to prepare data, launch applications, and interact with users. Figure 10-3 shows a set of rules developed in RuleWriter.

After a workflow has been designed and rules programmed, the application is implemented and managed by the Runtime system. The

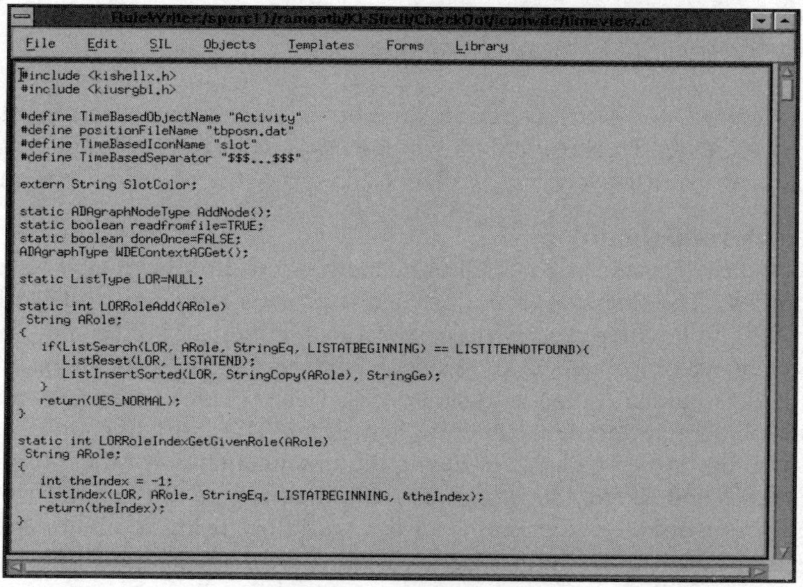


```
#include <kishellx.h>
#include <kiusrgbl.h>

#define TimeBasedObjectName "Activity"
#define positionFileName "tbposn.dat"
#define TimeBasedIconName "slot"
#define TimeBasedSeparator "$$$...$$$"

extern String SlotColor;

static ADAgraphNodeType AddNode();
static boolean readfromfile=TRUE;
static boolean doneOnce=FALSE;
ADAgraphType WDEContextAGGet();

static ListType LOR=NULL;

static int LORRoleAdd(ARole)
 String ARole;
{
   if(ListSearch(LOR, ARole, StringEq, LISTATBEGINNING) == LISTITEMNOTFOUND){
      ListReset(LOR, LISTATEND);
      ListInsertSorted(LOR, StringCopy(ARole), StringGe);
   }
   return(UES_NORMAL);
}

static int LORRoleIndexGetGivenRole(ARole)
 String ARole;
{
   int theIndex = -1;
   ListIndex(LOR, ARole, StringEq, LISTATBEGINNING, &theIndex);
   return(theIndex);
}
```

10-3 *A set of rules developed in RuleWriter.* UES, Inc.

Runtime system interprets the workflow model to control work queues, invoke applications, collect process data, and provide decision support. Figure 10-4 shows a sample KI Shell application. In this example, the various users of the system interact with the workflow system via a graphical interface. As decisions are made, rules are interpreted and appropriate actions taken.

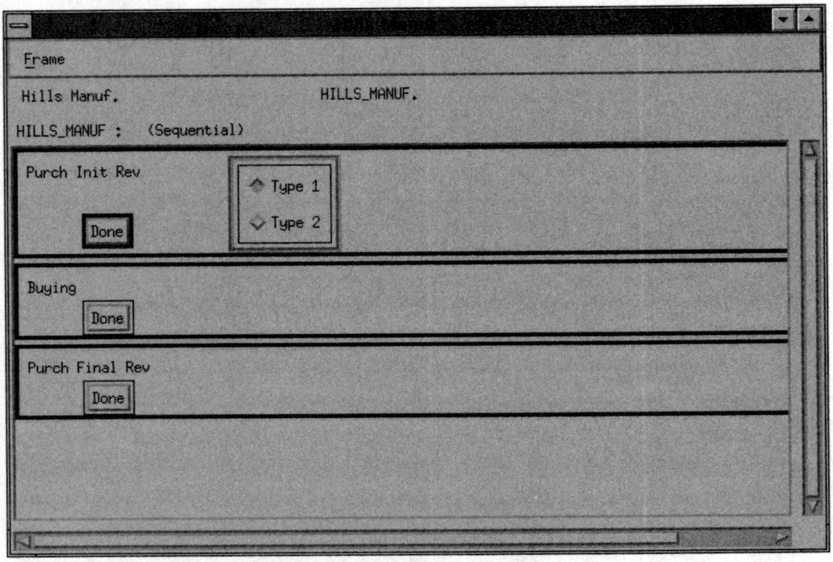

10-4 *A sample KI Shell application.* UES, Inc.

Metrics on workflow performance are automatically collected and a history of decisions made during a process is maintained. This information can be displayed graphically for analysis of the workflow system.

Process methodology

Workflow design in KI Shell is accomplished through a seven-step process. The first step in the process is process modeling and clarification. In this step, legacy processes are identified and reviewed. This step is accomplished in conjunction with the second step, which is the documentation of the as-is process. This provides a baseline from which design and reengineering can occur. The third step—process simplification—involves reviewing the documentation of the existing process and looking for areas in which the process can be improved. Step four involves the design of the workflow using the automated design tools. In the fifth step—workflow implementation—rules are programmed into the workflow design, again using the automated tools. The sixth step is the actual production deployment of the application. The seventh step—process extension/improvement—provides feedback on the performance of workflow applications and involves changes if necessary.

Operating systems and hardware platforms

KI Shell runs under the following operating systems:

- AIX
- HP-UX
- OS/2
- Sun OS
- Windows

Since KI Shell is a database-enabled workflow system it requires an SQL database to operate with. KI Shell utilizes the following databases:

- DB/2 for OS/2
- ORACLE
- Sybase

Features

KI Shell offers the following additional products:

Track-It Track-It is a ready-to-use workflow product that manages tasks for a collaborative workgroup environment. Tasks and documents can be created, assigned, distributed, and tracked. Applications include marketing, product development, and consulting.

Connect-It Connect-It provides integration with IBM mainframe and midrange applications. Data can be captured from host applications or be sent back to the host application via a high-level language applications programming interface (HLLAPI) to 3270 and 5250 terminal sessions. A development environment that includes screen mapping facilities and a Runtime system are available.

Lotus Notes—Lotus Development Corp.

Product description

Lotus Notes is a client/server application for developing workgroup computing solutions. It differs from traditional operational data systems and personal productivity applications in its approach to data and the interactions of workgroup members.[6] Operational data systems are generally transaction-oriented and personal productivity applications deal with the accomplishment of a single task.

Notes has been characterized as a "Strategic System" because of its extended workgroup support, its communications model, and

6 Lotus Notes: An Overview, A Lotus Development Corporation White Paper (Cambridge, Massachusetts: Lotus Development Corp.), 1995, p. 2.

its unique information model. Extended workgroups are supported through enterprise-wide application connectivity and support for remote users. The Notes communication model is based on users sending messages and sharing information from a commonly accessible source. The information model differs from traditional data systems in that it accommodates semistructured information in the form of documents, reports, faxes, letters, and scanned images, as well as video and sound.

The Notes application requires a server application and a client application. Both applications are available for a number of operating systems. Clients on one operating system can access data on the servers of other operating systems. A key feature of Notes is its ability to replicate data across an enterprise on multiple servers. This eliminates the need to access individual servers to obtain information.

Replication is bidirectional, in that changes made to a document at any location cause the updated document to be replicated on all servers that access the document. When databases are replicated, only those documents that have changed are replicated. This reduces the telecommunications resources required to link the distributed servers. In addition to servers, remotely connected client applications can be the recipient of database replications as well. Client workstations can specify conditions for the documents they wish to have replicated on their client workstation. The replication process for remote clients can occur as a background process.

Security is provided through authentication, access control, encryption, and digital signatures. Authentication confirms the identity of users accessing the Notes server. Access control specifies the users and type of access they have to resources, databases, documents, and data fields. Field- and document-level encryption is provided. Digital signatures are used to verify the originator of documents and to detect altered documents.

Notes contains its own e-mail system and it can integrate with other e-mail systems. A single directory is used to manage user's names and system addresses. Due to the replication feature, a single integrated directory is maintained.

An object-oriented graphical design environment is used to design Notes applications. A number of integration tools and third-party application integration products are available. Appendix B contains a listing of Notes applications, add-on products, and design tools.

Process methodology

Notes is a database that stores information in semistructured documents. These documents can contain a variety of different data types including text documents, reports, faxes, letters, and scanned images, as well as video and sound. Documents are defined by forms which specify the data fields contained on the document. Figure 10-5 shows an example of a Notes form.

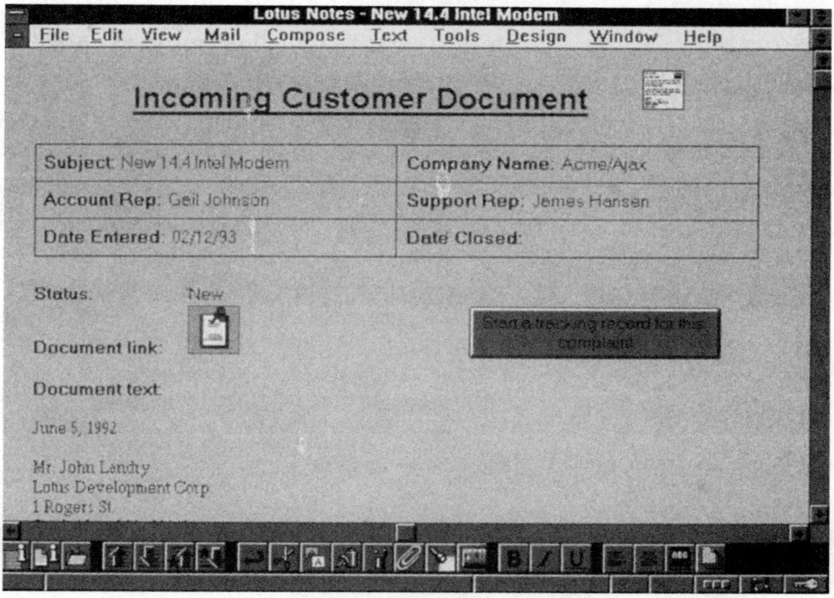

10-5 *An example of a Notes form.* Lotus Development Corporation

In addition to the types of data mentioned, forms can contain linked or embedded objects. Documents are browsed in views that present data in a columnar form. Figure 10-6 shows an example of a Notes view.

In this example, documents are listed in a columnar spreadsheet form. A hierarchical structure is used for multiple generations of documents or for documents with parent/child relationships. A Windows File Manager-type collapsible view is used for multiple levels of documents. The document is the lowest level of data management within Notes and it is essentially a "container" for data. By selecting a document, the form view is shown. Full text searching and version control are provided for documents.

The application development environment provides basic facilities, advanced programming facilities and extensions for database integration, desktop application integration, and application programming interfaces. Basic development facilities allow for the creation of forms, fields, and views in an object-oriented, graphical

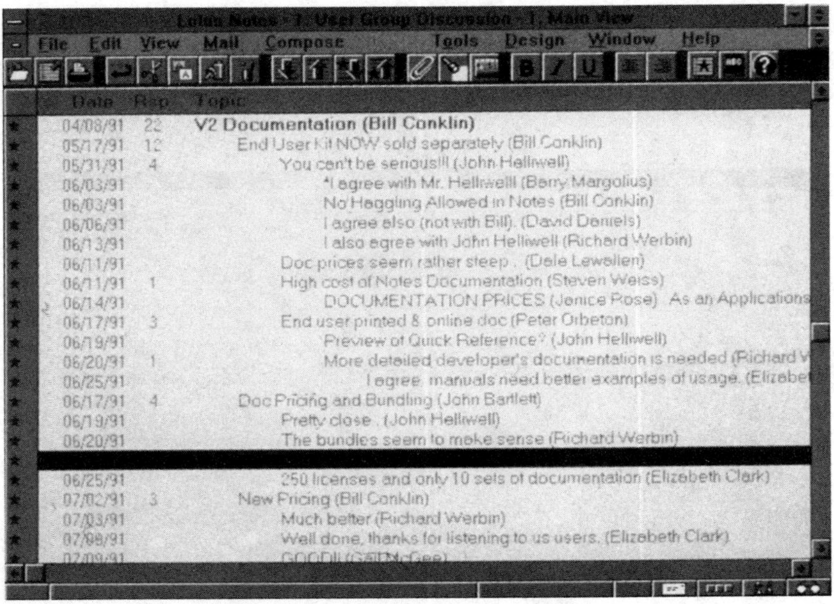

10-6 *An example of a Notes view.* Lotus Development Corporation

environment. Advanced functions allow the use of formulas, Lotus @ functions, macros, and design templates. Database integration is provided by a number of products including Open Data Base Connectivity drivers for Notes. A number of development tools and add-on products are available for Notes.

Operating systems and hardware platforms

Lotus Notes server runs on the following operating systems:

- AIX
- HP-UX
- Novell
- OS/2
- SCO Unix
- Sun Solaris
- UNIX
- Windows
- Windows NT Advanced server

The client application operates on

- AIX
- HP-UX
- Macintosh

- OS/2
- SCO Unix
- Sun Solaris
- Windows

Features

The following products are available for Lotus Notes:

Lotus Notes Vip Vip—the Visual Programmer—is a visual programming environment for Notes developers. It contains a complete set of tools including a debugger, a script editor, and a development object toolbox.

Lotus Notes HiTest Tools for Visual Basic These tools provide access to core Notes services through Visual Basic.

Phone Notes This is a development environment that provides access to Notes through touch-tone telephone systems. This tool can be used to develop applications that gather data, including voice data, for entry into a Notes database. Several sample applications are included in the development kit.

Lotus Forms Lotus Forms is a development tool for creating electronic forms. Data can be placed in Notes or other ODBC-compliant databases. In addition to the Designer, a Forms Filler application provides users with a sophisticated editor, a highlighter pen tool, and a pop-up note editor.

Notes Express Express is a subset of the full Notes client application. New applications cannot be developed with Express; however, several application templates are provided.

Case study

Transportation

A major rail carrier was looking for an executive information system to replace costly fixed format mainframe reports. Hard copy reports from a mainframe-based information system provided statistical data on the previous day's business. This information was used by senior management to make business decisions. The hard copy reports were in fixed formats and provided one "view" of the data. Depending on their particular area of interest, various managers wanted to view the data in different ways. The cost of the mainframe reporting system was causing concern as well. Increased demand for processing time would require the purchase of additional mainframe computer capacity. Management was looking for a flexible, cost-effective executive information system to replace the existing mainframe reports.

An executive information system based on Lotus Notes was implemented to replace the mainframe reporting system. Managers now have instant access to data each morning. Reports can be viewed by a variety of parameters as desired by each manager. Mainframe usage and cost have been reduced. Total cost savings were estimated to be in excess of $70,000 each year. New reports can now be quickly and easily added to the system. Data is provided more quickly and managers are able to respond to changes in the business environment more rapidly.

11

Business process analysis

This category of groupware covers the tools used to analyze and reengineer business processes. Some of the products listed in other groupware categories include graphical design tools, but few include business process analysis tools. The products covered in this chapter are primarily stand-alone applications that can be used to reengineer processes independent of business process automation software. In some situations, reengineering has occurred using these products and the reengineered processes have been implemented without the use of process automation software. These tools are concerned primarily with process analysis and not necessarily with application design and building. Some products, however, do integrate with application development software and can deliver a complete workflow application based on the design from the process analysis tool. What exactly is process analysis? Let us briefly define what comprises a business process analysis tool.

Business process analysis tools are used to define, analyze, and reengineer business processes. These tools are for the most part for management analysts and industrial engineers. These are not primarily tools for applications developers, although there may be some interaction between the analysis tool and applications design tools.

As a starting point, most tools provide a way to graphically depict the existing business processes. This is necessary to form a baseline from which reengineering efforts can begin. This baseline is important for documenting how the existing process works and to provide baseline metrics from which to measure the effectiveness of the new process. Often business processes evolved out of necessity and little design or engineering occurred. Documenting the existing process helps to formalize what really happens in a process and identify opportunities for reengineering.

Often the question is asked, "Why are we doing it this way?" All too often the answer is, "Because we have always done it this way." Tradition seldom adapts to changes in the business environment and past inefficiencies seldom change with technology without a concerted examination of processes and procedures. Baseline metrics are necessary for determining the impact of reengineered processes.

These metrics can be in many forms. Dollar cost and cycle time are popular metrics. Often the lowest cost and shortest cycle time are desirable outcomes. Other metrics that are often considered are quality and customer satisfaction. At times these are difficult factors to quantify. Quality can be measured in terms of defect rates or returns. Customer satisfaction is somewhat more difficult to measure and often cannot be captured as part of the business process. It can be measured in terms of survey results, repeat requests, or complaints.

When determining metrics to measure, the metrics should be related to the overall goals of the business organization. If costs and productivity are key measures, then the process model should capture these metrics and the process optimized for results in these areas. If customer satisfaction is a key organizational goal, then metrics for response time and customer satisfaction should be captured and the process engineered to provide acceptable results in these areas. Often metrics in several areas are used to determine the relative trade-offs involved in changes to the business process. For example, in an order processing application, the process could be maximized to reduce costs, but order processing time could be increased, resulting in lower customer satisfaction and potentially lost business. On the other hand, a process that handles orders very quickly may prove to be too costly to support. Often processes are interrelated and the results of reengineering a single process must be taken in the context of its impact on the entire organization.

After the process has been defined, analysis can begin. This can be accomplished by either manual or automated means. Some products look at the various steps in a business process and their interrelations and suggest ways to reengineer that process. Other products provide a mechanism for the user to alter the process model and then review the results of the change. Depending on the complexity of the process model, changes may be intuitive or may require further study and analysis. "What if?"-type simulations can be useful in studying the results of proposed changes. Various factors, such as inputs and process flow, can be changed and the resulting impact on key metrics analyzed.

Based on the analysis of the process model, reengineering of the business process can occur. Here the various steps of the new process are defined and the process flow formalized. During analysis, the behavior of the process model is studied. In the reengineering phase, the new process is constructed. The result of the reengineering may be new procedure documents or process maps, or even specifications for new workflow applications.

After the reengineered process is implemented, process analysis tools can be used to study the new process and determine if it is actually producing the desired results. Metrics should be designed into the new process to provide a measure of its performance against the baseline process. The process can then be refined if necessary to produce the desired results.

Business process analysis products

In this chapter we present several representative business process analysis products. Some are part of workflow automation software products described earlier in the text, but they also operate as standalone products. Products that are integrated as part of an application design tool are not included in this section, but are covered in their respective groupware category. This is not intended to be a complete review of all products nor a comparison of products. Specific products are used to illustrate the features of this category of groupware. A general description of the product is presented followed by a discussion of underlying process analysis methodologies that may apply. Operating systems and hardware platforms supported are listed along with particular features of each product. To get the most recent information on specific products, please contact the vendors.

Action Workflow Analyst—Action Technologies

Product description

The Action Workflow System is comprised of several components that provide workflow computing solutions based on an open, object-oriented, client/server architecture.[1] The complete system includes Action WorkFlow Analyst, Action Workflow Builder, and Action Workflow Manager. Action Workflow Analyst is used to model, analyze, and optimize business processes. Analyst is used to create graphical maps that model business processes. In the maps, metrics on the

1 Action Workflow Analyst—A Modeling and Analysis Tool for Business Processes (Alameda, California: Action Technologies), 1994.

process, as well as who work performers are, what their role is, and how they interact with others in the process, are defined. Through a graphical interface, the process model can be changed and the results on the overall process studied. Variations to the existing process can be modeled and analyzed to determine if they will provide the desired result. Time and value data can be exported from the process model to word processing applications. Workflow maps generated by Analyst can be imported into the Action Workflow Builder to create workflow applications.

Process methodology

The Action Workflow System is based on a workflow methodology that defines business processes. This methodology utilizes a "loop" metaphor to describe how work is performed in a business process and defines parameters such as the work to be done, the participants, and the requirements for successful completion. The participants in a workflow consist of a performer, who does the work, and a customer, for whom the work is being completed. Each loop divides work into four phases—preparation, negotiation, performance, and acceptance. Figure 11-1 illustrates an Action Workflow loop.

Each phase defines the specifics of the work to be performed in that phase. In the preparation phase, the customer requests that work be accomplished or the performer offers to do work for the customer. In the second phase—negotiation—the customer and the performer agree on the work to be done and specifications of the terms of satisfaction. This is similar to the process of entering into a contract. Each party specifies what is to be accomplished and what the requirements are for the contract to be considered complete. The third phase—performance—is where the work is actually accomplished

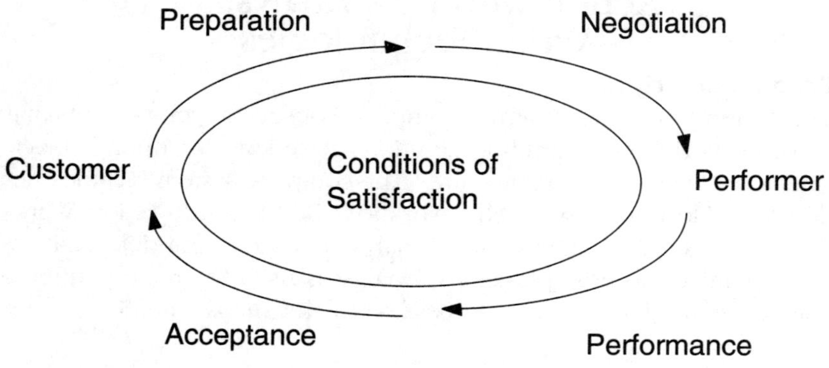

11-1 *An Action Workflow loop.*

and delivered to the customer. The final phase—acceptance—is used to determine if the work was successfully completed. Within Analyst, workflows are associated with each phase. Figure 11-2 shows the graphical depiction of an Action workflow.

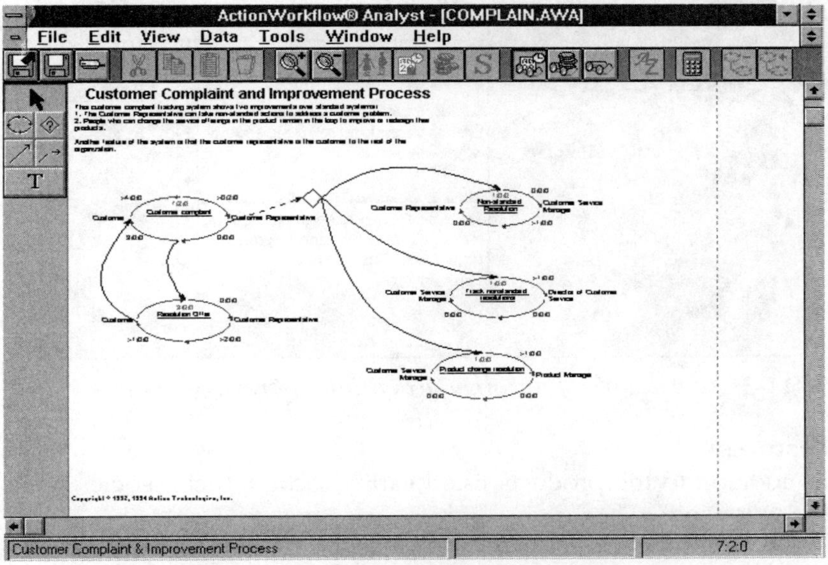

11-2 *The graphical depiction of an Action Workflow.* Action Technologies

In this example, a customer-compliant system is modeled. The units of work are represented as interconnected loops. In each loop the various participants and the associated costs for each workflow are identified. Costs, in terms of time and dollars, are entered for each phase in the process for the entire workflow. The entire workflow is defined through a graphical user interface. Figure 11-3 shows an example of a workflow definition screen. Here the workflow is identified along with the workflow type, the customer, the performer, and the conditions of satisfaction.

Built-in consistency checking reviews workflow maps and identifies errors such as erroneous links, inconsistent time allocations, or missing participants. The visual workflow map can then be reviewed for reengineering opportunities. These might include duplicate workflows and sequential workflows that are performed in parallel.

Operating systems and hardware platforms

The Action Workflow System is designed to run on a Windows-based PC.

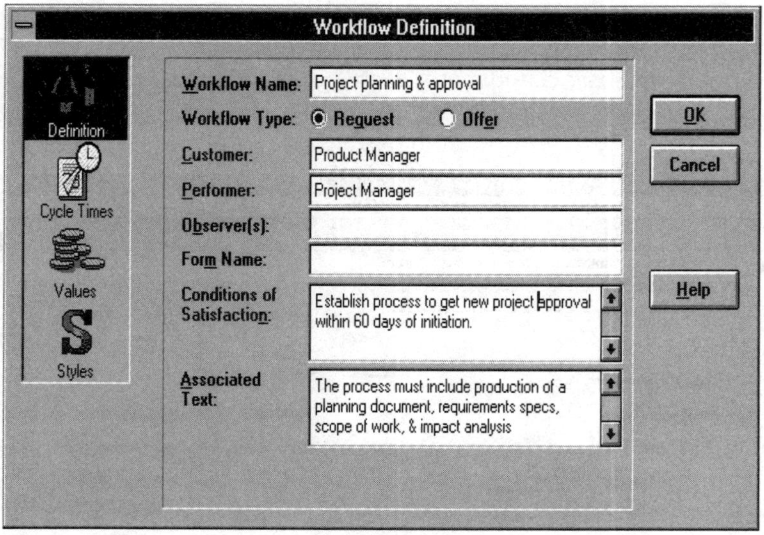

11-3 *An example of a workflow definition screen.* Action Technologies

Features

In addition to the products listed earlier, Action Technologies offers the following:

Action Workflow Builder The Action Workflow Builder is used to design and develop workflow applications based on graphically generated business process maps. These maps can be generated within Workflow Builder or from the Action Workflow Analyst. See the preceding chapter for more information on Workflow Builder.

Action Workflow Manager Action Workflow Manager is the administrative component of the Action Workflow System. It provides a means to monitor, administer, and control workflow functions for either SQL server or Lotus Notes environments. See the preceding chapter for more information on Action Workflow Manager.

Action Workflow DocRoute DocRoute workflow enables document management applications. It integrates with Saros Document Manager, PC Docs OPEN, and Novell SoftSolutions.[2] This product allows Workflow Builder applications to access documents from other document management systems.

BPwin—Logic Works

Product description

BPwin is a Windows-based business process design and analysis tool. It provides a graphical environment in which to design and model

2 Corporate Backgrounder (Alameda, California: Action Technologies), 1995, p. 9.

business processes. Various metrics and process costs can be designed into the business model. The process model can be viewed from a number of perspectives depending on the needs of the participants in the design process—a tree view might be desirable for mangers, while a process-oriented view might be used by designers and analysts. Figure 11-4 shows an example of a node tree view of a process. The node tree shows the functional hierarchy of the process.

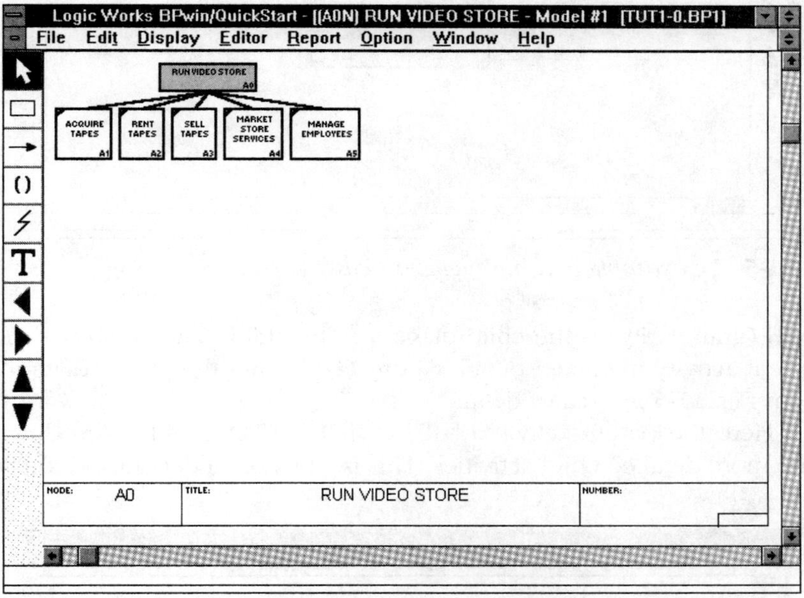

11-4 *An example of a node tree view of a process.* Logic Works, Inc.

BPwin interfaces with other database design tools to help ensure quality and consistency in the data model. It supports activity-based costing and "what if?"-type modeling.

Process methodology

BPwin models activities and their relationships. Activities are actions or series of actions that have a purpose and create some type of output. The models created in BPwin capture activities, their definitions, and how they relate to other activities. Activities are hierarchical and are broken down or decomposed into finer and finer detail to clearly explain what happens in the process. Figure 11-5 shows an example of a high-level process.

The arrows flowing into and out of the activity represent the inputs and outputs of the activity. From the parent diagram, the next

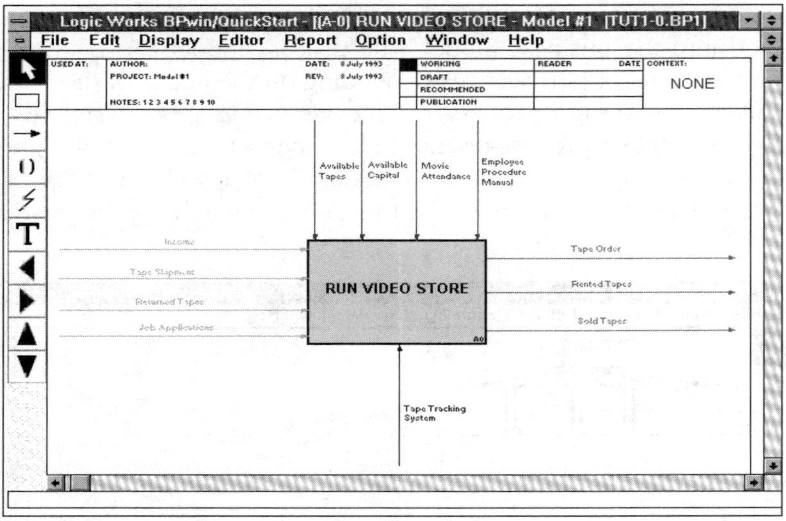

11-5 *An example of a high-level process.* Logic Works, Inc.

level (granularity) is the child diagram. The child diagram shows the parent activity in greater detail. Figure 11-6 shows the parent diagram from Fig. 11-5 in greater detail.

Here the parent activity of RUN VIDEO STORE is broken down into more detailed child activities. This is a first-level decomposition of

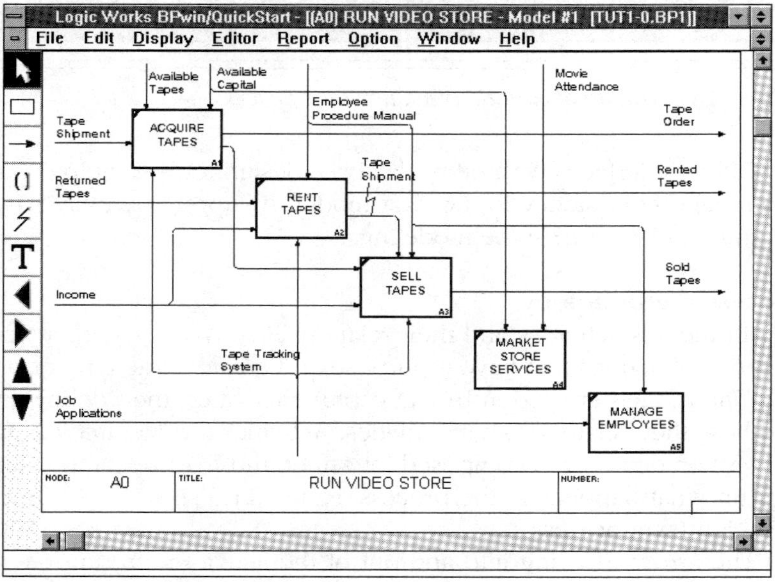

11-6 *The parent diagram from Fig. 11-5 in greater detail.* Logic Works, Inc.

the parent activity. Individual activities are defined by the Activity Definition Editor. The Editor is accessed by pointing at the desired activity and clicking on it. Figure 11-7 shows the Activity Definition Editor entry for the activity MANAGE EMPLOYEES from the earlier decomposition diagram.

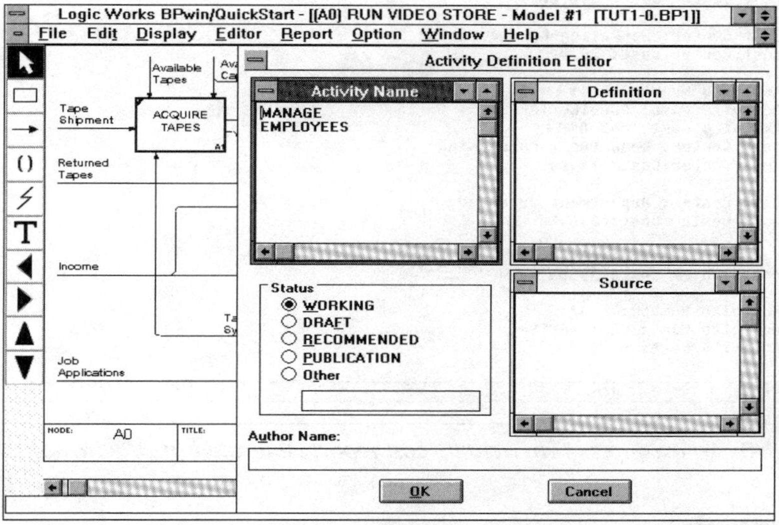

11-7 *The Activity Definition Editor entry for the activity MANAGE EMPLOYEES.* Logic Works, Inc.

Using this method, all activities for a process can be defined. The complete process design is accomplished in a graphical environment. Designs can be completed by a single person or by a workgroup and consolidated into a single larger view of the complete process. Process definitions can be annotated with multimedia data such as data entry screen captures, sound, video, or graphics.

Activity-based costing can be used to determine costs for activities. The costs at each subordinate level can be rolled up to higher levels. These costs can be used as metrics to determine a cost baseline for the current system or to estimate the costs associated with a proposed system.

Reports can be generated from BPwin or data can be exported to external word processing and spreadsheet programs. More advanced report generation is available through integration with the RPTwin reporting tool. Figure 11-8 shows an example of an activity cost report generated in BPwin.

Operating systems and hardware platforms

BPwin runs on Windows-based PCs.

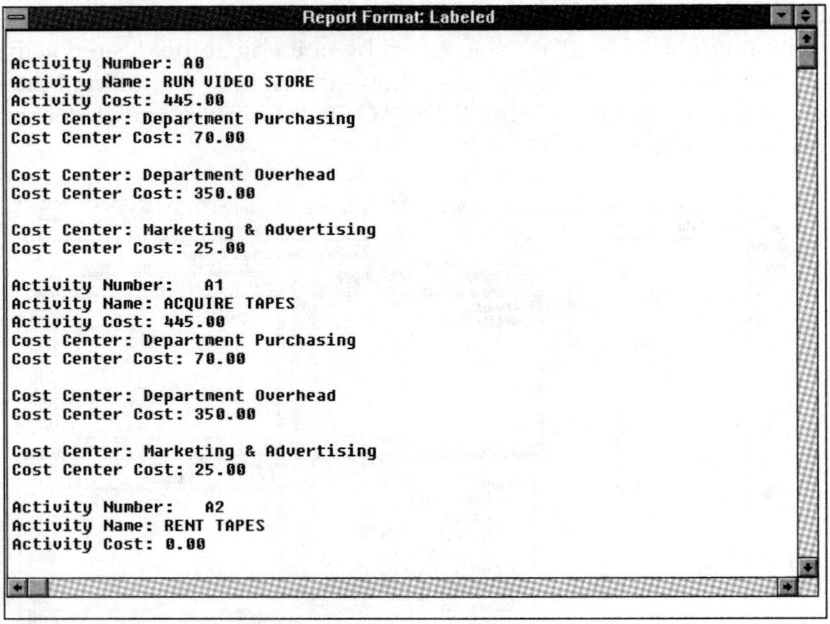

11-8 *An example of an activity cost report generated in BPwin.* Logic Works, Inc.

Features

In addition to BPwin, Logic Works offers the following products:

ERwin ERwin is a graphical application modeling tool for developing client/server database applications. Various products are available for several popular database management systems. It interfaces with BPwin.

RPTwin RPTwin is a report design tool that can produce sophisticated reports. Windows fonts are supported and a built-in drawing tool is provided to customize report layouts. RPTwin interfaces with BPwin.

Extend+BPR—Imagine That, Inc.

Product description

Extend+BPR is a graphical business process design and analysis tool.[3] Using icons, the steps of a business process can be defined and linked. Specialized simulation and modeling techniques can be included in the model of the business process. Once the model is complete, it can be run in an animated simulation mode so that the behavior

3 Extend+BPR, Business Process Reengineering, Product Information (San Jose, California: Imagine That, Inc.), 1995.

of the model can be observed and analyzed. Results of key metrics can be displayed as numeric values or graphically during the simulation. Complete process models can be created graphically without programming. Figure 11-9 shows an example of a process model created in Extend+BPR.

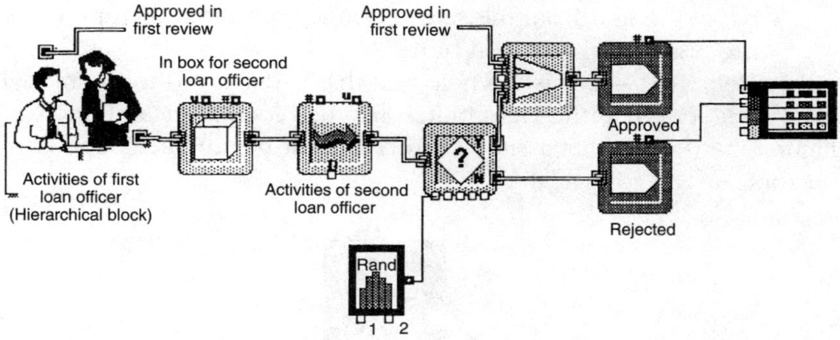

11-9 *An example of an activity cost report generated in BPwin.* Imagine That, Inc., portions copyright 1987–1995 Imagine That, Inc., San Jose, CA

In this example, a credit application approval process is modeled. Applications approved by the first loan officer move to an approved basket. Those that require further review move on to a second loan officer. There is a delay for processing time for each application before they are finally approved or rejected. This entire process model was created using graphical process blocks.

Process methodology

Extend+BPR is based on an iconic process model that uses a series of "blocks" and "connectors" to represent a business process. A number of standard blocks along with libraries of special-purpose blocks are available for model building. Blocks contain the following components:[4]

- Dialog—This is the dialog presented to the model builder and specifies the buttons, text, and entry boxes associated with the block.
- Script—This is the program logic for the block. The program reads information from the input connectors attached to the block, processes it according to the script, and then produces output for other blocks. Scripts are written in a C-like language called ModL.

4 Application Development Strategies, vol. VII, no. 1, Business Process Reengineering: Tools and Techniques (Alameda, California: Cutter Information Corp.), 1995.

- Icon—This is the visual icon that is shown in the model. It can be designed using Extend's drawing tools or other Windows or Macintosh drawing programs.
- Connectors—These are the input and output connectors attached to the block. A single block may have multiple inputs and outputs. This is the means by which information is passed to and from the script. Connectors are shown in the process model between blocks.
- Help Text—This is the help text that is displayed to the model builder when the Help button for the block is clicked on.

Figure 11-10 illustrates a simple process built using blocks and connectors.

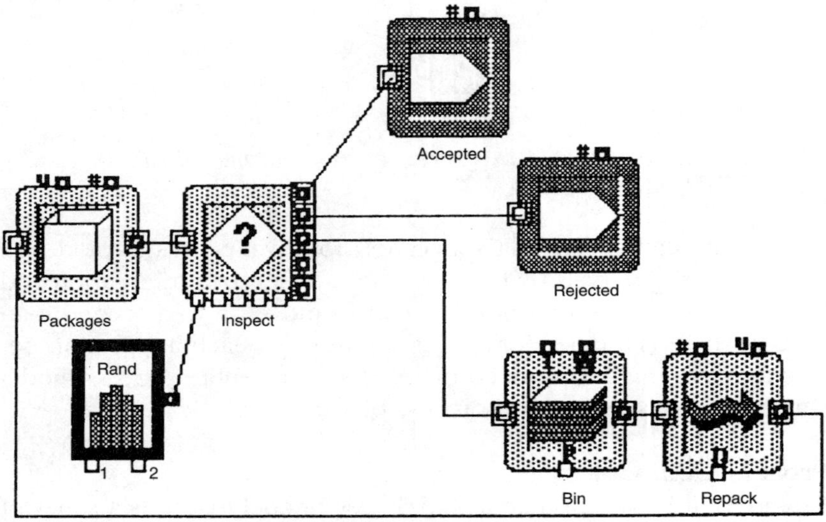

11-10 *A simple process built using blocks and connectors.* Imagine That, Inc., portions copyright 1987–1995 Imagine That, Inc., San Jose, CA

In this example, packages are inspected according to a set of criteria and then accepted or rejected. Each step in the process is represented by a block and the connectors between blocks represent the passage of information between blocks as well as the linkages between steps in the process. The Inspect block is represented by an icon with a question mark. This denotes that a decision must be made and that the result will be to accept or reject a package. The script of the Inspect icon contains the logic that specifies the criteria for the accept/reject decision. The connectors component of the Inspect block show that the block is connected to other blocks such as Packages, Accept, Reject, Bin, or Rand. Once the process model is completed, a simulation of the process can be run and the results viewed graphically. Figure 11-11 shows a completed model with the results of a simulation.

The process model shown in the background is for an invoice approval process. The smaller window in the foreground displays the results of the simulation both graphically and numerically. Various factors in the model can now be altered and the simulation run again and studied to determine if the changes produced the desired results.

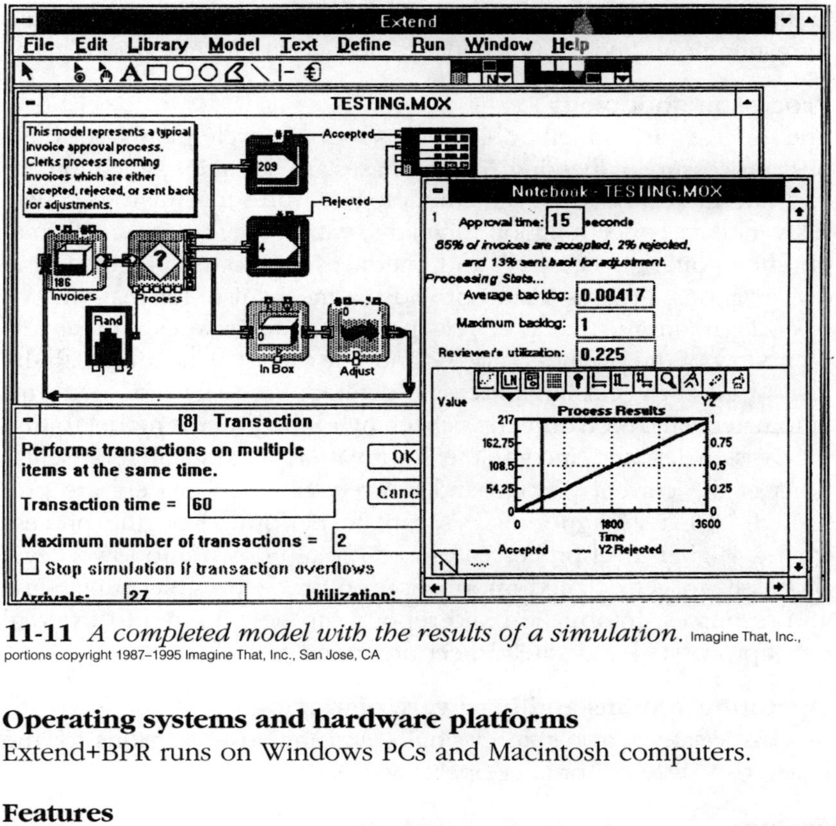

11-11 *A completed model with the results of a simulation.* Imagine That, Inc., portions copyright 1987–1995 Imagine That, Inc., San Jose, CA

Operating systems and hardware platforms

Extend+BPR runs on Windows PCs and Macintosh computers.

Features

In addition to Extend+BPR, Imagine That, Inc., offers several other simulation and modeling products.

Extend Extend is a graphical simulation and modeling tool. It can be used to conduct "what if?"-type analyses of engineering, scientific, and business applications.

Extend+Manufacturing Extend+Manufacturing is an operations research, industrial engineering, and manufacturing modeling application. It contains a library of specialized blocks for modeling manufacturing environments.

Process Vision—Antares Alliance Group

Product description

Process Vision is a graphical business process reengineering tool.[5] It captures and validates the various factors of business activities including the "who," "what," "where," "when," and "how" of processes. Competitive factors such as underutilized capacity, overburdened resources, and unclear accountability can be identified during analysis and graphically depicted. Detailed analysis of workflow, cycle times, data flow, and policies are supported. Applications can be developed from the information flows and data dictionaries defined in Process Vision.

Process methodology

The Process Vision methodology uses four life cycle phases for business process reengineering. These phases are definition, initiation, interview, and analysis.[6] This methodology ensures that analysts collect relevant data concerning job functions, workflows, policies, information flow, internal structure, and interfaces with other processes and organizations. Process Vision provides a mechanism for real-time visualization during the interview process. Interviewees can review their view of the business process and fine tune it as needed with the analyst. After the existing process is defined, Process Vision performs automated validation and error checking of the process model to find inconsistencies and incomplete information. Graphical representations of the current process and the reengineered process are presented. "What if?"-type analysis can be performed on the process model. Higher level processes can be broken down into lower level processes to get detailed information on procedures, accountability, and resources. Information and reports can be exported to external word processing and spreadsheet programs.

Operating systems and hardware platforms

Process Vision is available in single- and multiuser versions for the Macintosh System 7 or later operating system.

Features

In addition to the Process Vision product, the Antares Alliance Group offer the following:

RAPID RE Rapid RE is a high-level, management-oriented business process reengineering application. It is a Windows-based tool that incorporates the widely accepted Rapid RE methodology.

5 Process Vision, the difference between reaching your destination and reaching for it (Dallas, Texas: Antares Alliance Group), 1994.

6 Application Development Strategies, vol. VII, no. 1.

Case study

Education

Babson College, a private business college, was looking for a means to analyze and reengineer the way it provided services to students.[7] This included such services as academic planning, registration, financial services, degree audits, grading systems, and student profile information. It was the desire of the college administration to reduce the amount of time and effort required by students to complete administrative activities. There was great deal of paperwork and long processing delays were experienced with the existing system. The costs of administrative functions were becoming a concern as well for the independent institution. A business process reengineering task force was created to improve the administrative processes serving the students. Specific goals were set to increase customer satisfaction and to reduce the costs of administrative services.

After reviewing available workflow products, the Action Workflow System from Action Technologies was selected. Using the Action Workflow Analyst, current administrative processes were graphically modeled. These models were analyzed for inefficiencies in the current paper-based system. New processes were designed that eliminated redundancies and reduced process times. The costs associated with processes were identified. The redesigned processes were used to build custom workflow applications with the Action Workflow Builder.

The results of the implementing the reengineered processes have been improved administrative services to students and lower administrative costs. When fully implemented, it is estimated that the new workflow system will save approximately $2 million a year in administrative costs. Additional reengineering efforts are planned for other nonacademic administrative processes.

7 Babson College Selects Action Technologies for Workflow Solution (Alameda, California: Action Technologies), Press Release ATI-11, October 17, 1994.

12

Groupware trends

As with all areas of high technology it is difficult to keep pace with new developments and products. This is especially true with workflow and workgroup computing. Compared to other types of products, workflow is relatively new and the market is extremely fluid. Aside from Lotus Notes, there are no clear market leaders, and new products are being introduced at a rapid rate. Competing products and different approaches to workgroup computing are even now threatening the dominance of Notes. Given that this text is but a snapshot in time, it is still important to look at the current market and its potential direction. In this chapter we look at what may be in store for the workflow/groupware market in general, and then examine some specific developments in the industry that may influence the future direction of workflow and workgroup computing.

Future outlook

Groupware is a relatively new phenomena in the computing industry, and it is a rapidly growing market. Estimates are that by 1996 the market will expand to $5.5 billion annually.[1] This rapid growth is fueled by promises of more efficient, less costly, and higher quality business operations. As with client/server computing, as the demand for products increases, more and more vendors will provide a variety of products to meet the demand. Workgroup Computing is no exception. The rapid growth in third-party products for Lotus Notes is an excellent example of this.

Many vendors are seeking to workflow enable their products. This is done by either integrating their products with other workflow

1 David Coleman, Groupware: Past, Present and Future. Paper presented at GroupWare '94.

applications, such as Action Workflow Manager or Lotus Notes, or by integrating workflow features into their products. This is apparent in several of the image processing and document management products discussed in the text. Most are including graphical process modeling tools which then feed application development tools. This move to workgroup integration can be expected to continue with most networked applications.

Any application that requires collaborative work by multiple group members will need to include some type of workgroup management functions to remain competitive. Tools for rapid application development are a necessity for successful products. Long development times are no longer acceptable in today's fast-paced competitive business environment.

In addition to workgroup features, it seems likely that workgroup products will in the future incorporate business process reengineering tools. As discussed earlier in the text, these tools provide a way to model, analyze, and reengineer business processes. While many groupware products offer graphical workflow design tools, not all include modeling and analysis capabilities. These features are important in that they provide not only modeling but a methodology to quantify various costs and products of a business process. The ability to change various parameters of the process and run simulation models greatly enhances reengineering efforts and promotes analysis of methods and processes. As the groupware market matures, more modeling and analysis tools can be expected to be integrated with workflow software.

Interoperability in an enterprise environment can be expected to be a major feature companies look for in groupware solutions. Most organizations have a number of different and usually incompatible computer systems. Groupware will need to deal with multiple server operating systems, client operating systems, and user interfaces. The future of groupware may well be to serve a middleware in organizations.

Enterprise computing has been discussed for some time, but groupware may provide the impetus for organizations to look at establishing an enterprise-wide connectivity. By its very nature, groupware depends on wide dispersal in an organization. The growth of local area networks and data communications can only help to spread groupware. Groupware may also evolve into a common user interface for access to corporate data. Many organizations have multiple disparate computing systems, several of which a single user might need to access. This creates a platform-centered computing environment in which the user must conform to each computing system they access. Figure 12-1 shows a platform-centered environment.

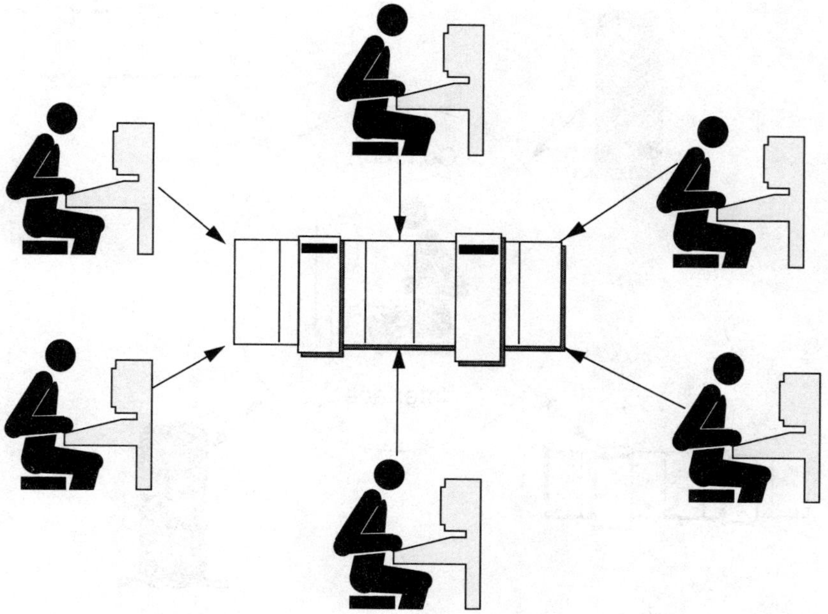

12-1 *The platform-centered environment.*

This is in contrast to the user-centered computing environment prompted by groupware. In a user-centered environment, the user is at the center of the computing universe and all corporate data is available to them through one standardized interface, which may well be their groupware application. Figure 12-2 shows a user-centered computing environment. Here the user is insulated from the intricacies of each data source they access. A single graphical interface replaces multiple terminals or terminal emulations.

Given the ability to access all individuals in an organization, the way work is structured can be expected to change as well. Physical and organizational boundaries to workflows would be eliminated. Every member of an organization would become a potential member of a workflow team. New types of workflows across the organization can be expected to evolve. Access to data will be enhanced, providing new opportunities. The possibilities are endless.

So given this optimistic outlook for groupware, what concerns need to be considered? Probably the most important concern is choosing a groupware product that is appropriate for your organization. Often groupware is as much about management and organizational philosophy as it is about technology. This is particularly true of products that utilize design tools based on a certain workflow methodology,

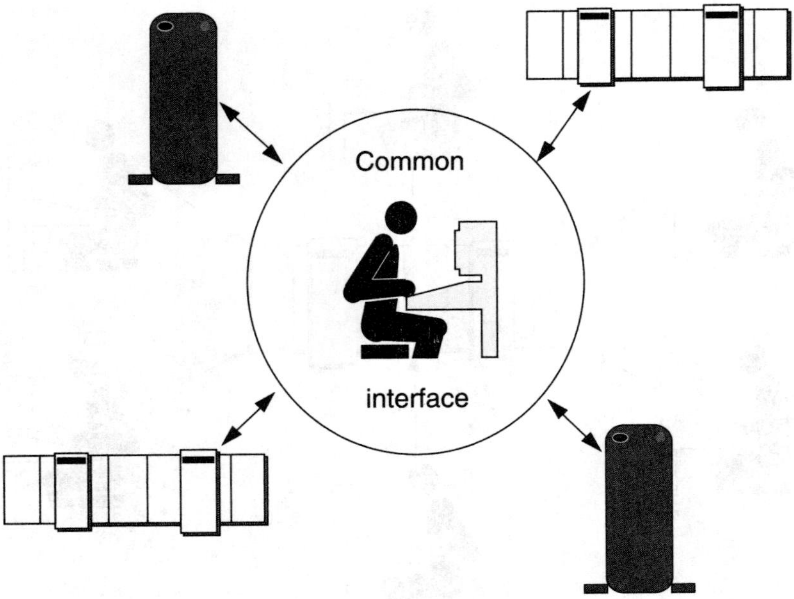

12-2 *The user-centered environment.*

such as Action Workflow Analyst or KI Shell. Each has its own way of approaching the way work is organized.

Consider if the methodology behind the product you select will work in your organization. As well as the methodology, there are the usual technical questions in terms of hardware, software, and database compatibility. Support for various types of data is also a consideration. While you might not be dealing with imaging or voice today, it may be wise to consider a product that can handle these type of data in the future. Flexibility and the availability of third-party products may be a consideration as well.

Given that a careful selection is made and all requirements are met, ensure that your workgroup computing solution is implemented as a group effort. This may require some organizational change, particularly in highly centralized organizations. Again groupware causes people to look differently at how work is done and gives them the opportunity to change the way things are done, hopefully for the better. Remember, in groupware the emphasis is on "group."

Market forces

The workflow/workgroup computing market is in its infancy. There are several major players and aside from Lotus Notes, no clear market leaders. Even Notes is seeing competition from other products. Technological developments and recent changes in the market may impact Notes current market lead and the future direction of workflow and workgroup computing in general. Four major developments that are sure to impact the market are the purchase of Lotus by IBM, the introduction of Notes networks, the Growth of the Internet, and the introduction of new groupware products. Let us look at each on these developments in more detail.

Lotus and IBM

The purchase of Lotus Development Corp. by IBM was one of the biggest stories in the computing industry in recent years. While mergers and the purchase of software companies by larger firms is not uncommon, the IBM/Lotus purchase signaled a major change in strategy for IBM, an industry leader. With this purchase, IBM acknowledged that its own line of groupware and workflow products were not a success in the market and further acknowledged Notes as the market leader.

IBM has begun replacing its line of workflow and workgroup products with Notes and other associated Lotus products. Current IBM workgroup products such as Ultimail and Time and Place will be dropped in lieu of updated Lotus products.[2] The Lotus product line will incorporate some of the functionality of the IBM products and will be expanded to include OS/2 versions of products such as Approach, the Lotus database offering.

To further the integration between IBM and Lotus products, DB2 access is being added to Lotus products. A major advantage to a suite of IBM/Lotus products is that it provides a multiplatform, enterprise-wide workgroup computing solution. Previously, Notes was targeted primarily at LAN users and multiplatform support was minimal. With the combination of Notes and IBM DB2 servers, Notes users can access data on a variety of platforms throughout an enterprise. This leverages IBM's multiplatform connectivity products. Notes has become the center of IBM's client/server strategy and will serve as the primary desktop user interface.[3] Other Notes technologies and companion products such as Notes Document and Imaging software will become the IBM imaging client in its imaging product line.

New versions of Notes are planned to provide greater scalability, centralized administration, and better network utilization.[4] These features are being incorporated to provide better management in large,

2 IBM lays plans for Notes-centric world, *Infoworld*, July 24, 1995, p. 1.

3 Ibid.

4 Notes 4 to improve scalability, management, *Infoworld*, October 2, 1995, p. 8.

distributed network environments. Database server capacity will be increased, along with the number of users allowed per server. Server replication performance will be improved in conjunction with changes in messaging to reduce network utilization. New administration tools will ease administrative tasks and allow for decentralized administration of geographically dispersed servers. Again these features are designed to move Notes from a simple LAN-based product into a full-featured groupware product designed for large-scale distributed environments.

A major question to be answered is the impact of the IBM merger on Notes and its future direction. By purchasing an existing product line and integrating it with their vast product line, IBM may have positioned itself well in the groupware market. In addition to providing software, IBM with its consulting, support, and integration services will be in a position to provide a full-service solution for corporations looking for groupware expertise. Given IBM's current share in the mainframe and midrange market, they may seem the logical provider of groupware products and services for organizations looking to move from or enhance legacy systems environments.

While these may be positive points to the merger of the two companies, there is some concern that Notes will become too closely tied to IBM legacy environments and might not move quickly enough to keep up with the changing marketplace. Given IBM's recent problems, some are hesitant to become dependent on proprietary or seemingly proprietary solutions. The large third-party market of Notes products tends to support the conclusion that Notes is a widely supported de facto standard as opposed to being a proprietary solution. The continued growth in Notes base and add-on products will determine if Notes maintains its status as a market leader and de facto standard.

Notes Networks

As the current revolution in data communications continues and organizations become linked by wide-area and even global networks, the need to provide integrated groupware solutions grows. Notes, through its data replication technology, fits well into a distributed environment such as exists in an organization linked by a wide-area network (WAN). The issue for most firms is the cost of building and supporting WANs, particularly if the sole use is for an application such as Notes. When the inclusion of remote sites, customers, and suppliers is considered, the problem becomes more complex and more expensive to solve.

The solution would seem to be something akin to using the public telephone system to provide connectivity between the various users in a distributed groupware environment. Not surprisingly, AT&T

in conjunction with Lotus Development is offering AT&T Network Notes. This is a service that allows companies to use Notes groupware over their global network.[5] Distributed Notes applications can be implemented without the expansion of corporate networks. Access for users such as customers and suppliers can be added with relative ease.

The agreement between AT&T and Lotus was completed prior to IBM's acquisition of Notes. AT&T is offering Network Notes as a subscription service over its public network at a modest monthly cost.[6] This provides groupware connectivity with the convenience of telephone service and eliminates the high capital investment of installing a WAN. Greater flexibility is provided in that as the locations of various groups within an organization changes, their connectivity can follow them.

In addition to AT&T, IBM has also announced that it will provide Notes connectivity over its own global network starting in 1996.[7] IBM has maintained a global network for quite some time and has provided connectivity for its own internal use and for its customers. The IBM network differs from the AT&T network in that it is a private network as opposed to AT&T's public network. IBM plans to offer Notes on its Global Network as part of a systems integration plan in which IBM can provide a complete Notes solution.

Another indication of the potential growth of Notes is an agreement with 11 international telecommunications carriers to provide Notes services on their public data networks.[8] This move will provide wide-ranging access for firms wishing to connect distributed business units, customers, and suppliers. When combined with the IBM and AT&T networks, this consortium handles 80 percent of the world's data communications traffic.[9] Additional agreements between carriers on billing, security, and support standards will further establish the global Notes network as a corporate groupware tool that may become as commonplace and convenient as telephone service.

While IBM's acquisition of Lotus might seem to complicate the initial Lotus/AT&T Notes Network agreement, the end result may still be a positive one for IBM. While they may have competition as a provider of Notes connectivity, IBM will still benefit from the sale of Notes software. As deregulation has increased the number of long-distance carriers in the telecommunications industry, the same may hold true for the "Notes connectivity" market.

5 AT&T, IBM to Offer Notes, Public and Private, *Information Week*, August 21, 1995, p. 16.

6 Ibid.

7 Ibid.

8 Lotus Notes Ascends World Stage, *Information Week*, October 16, 1995, p. 5.

9 Ibid.

IBM may have some advantages in that it can offer a complete solution including software, consulting, connectivity, and support. On the other hand, some firms may tend to shy away from a private network and instead look for solutions that will provide more open connectivity for themselves and potential external users. Given the agreements of major global telecommunications carriers to support Notes networks, the groundwork is in place for Notes to become the de facto standard interface for network and groupware computing.

The Internet

One of the most phenomenal events in the computing industry in the past few years has been the growth of the Internet. From its tiny beginnings, the Internet has grown to over 30 million users.[10] Designed originally as a means to link research facilities and educational institutions, the Internet has become the "Information Superhighway" of the 1990s.

Just a few years ago the Internet and World Wide Web were mostly a curiosity, and few saw any real commercial potential for the Internet. This has changed dramatically as more and more firms do business on the Web. *Information Week* magazine reports that in the first seven months of 1995 over $25 million in revenues were generated by 11 companies doing business over the Web.[11] Those figures can be expected to multiply many times over as Web technology continues to mature. The major business areas on the Internet include direct marketing of goods and services, advertising, information (data access), and Internet access.

The market for Internet products and services continues to grow. All of the big-name providers of communications services are vying for the Internet market. AT&T is planning to offer Internet access along with other services to its existing base of customers.[12] Other Internet-related services planned include providing information and entertainment services and providing assistance to businesses wishing to promote and market products over the Internet.

As the communications industry becomes more deregulated, industries outside the traditional telecommunications providers are attempting to enter the Internet market. In many locations, cable television firms are attempting to provide Internet and voice services to their cable customers. From a technical perspective cable operators are in a

10 AT&T Hits the Net, *Information Week*, August 28, 1995, p. 114.

11 Making Money on the Web, *Information Week*, September 4, 1995, p. 31.

12 AT&T Hits the Net

good position to provide high-bandwidth communications to a large population. In many areas, cable operators have installed fiber-optic cabling in hopes of providing a high-speed, multiuse connection to consumers. This type of installed infrastructure is better suited to providing Internet connectivity than voice-grade phone lines and modems, the access method currently utilized by most Internet users.

In addition to providing Internet access and access-related services, telecommunications providers are forming alliances with companies to provide entertainment, e-mail, and other on-line services. Clearly the telecommunications industry is preparing for a rapid expansion of Internet connectivity and services.

The major concern with conducting business over the Internet is security. While at this time security is still the primary impediment to widespread commerce over the Internet, this issue can be expected to be resolved in the near future. Several encryption technologies are in the development stage, and as proven products and standards emerge, business on the Internet can be expected to grow dramatically.

The most likely growth areas will be in the electronic purchasing of goods and services, much like today's 800 number service. The Internet offers firms the opportunity to put catalogs and product information on-line and make it available to millions of potential customers. In addition to goods, services will likely become a commodity purchased via the Internet. These services could range from access to databases to professional services such as accounting and consulting. Currently firms such as newspapers and on-line information services are operating on the Internet. These services provide information on a subscription basis to their users.

While this view of the future on the Internet and its impact on electronic commerce may have been entertaining, you might question the relationship between the Internet and the subject matter of this text. In reality, the two are very much related. The Internet is in essence one of the first groupware products. Initially designed as a mechanism for research and educational institutions to share and exchange information on government-funded research projects, it attempts to solve the problems associated with collaborative work on a large project by a number of individuals. Since its inception, the Internet has grown, but the basic purpose remains the same—to share and exchange information among a large group of people.

Many of the capabilities of workgroup computing products described earlier in this text are accomplished by Internet products. For example, e-mail and document distribution and management are all groupware functions that are possible on the Internet. According to the *GroupWare Report* (available on the Internet) from the University of Georgia, Groupware applications on the Internet generally fall into the following categories:[13]

Communications

The major communications applications on the Internet are e-mail, bulletin boards, audio conferencing, and video conferencing. E-mail is discussed in great detail in earlier chapters, and suffice it to say that it provides a basic communications medium for a group of people.

The generic mail format used by the Internet provides an open mail messaging environment in which any user can communicate with any other user on the Internet. The cost and complexity of setting up a private e-mail system are removed. Many commercial firms are turning to the Internet rather than setting up in-house e-mail systems. AT&T is using the Internet for e-mail for over 2500 of its employees.[14]

In addition to mail, there are other e-mail-type products that permit the simultaneous two-way exchange of information. These Chat-type programs allow two or more users to enter into a real-time dialog over the Internet. Many of the on-line services, such as America Online, Prodigy, and CompuServe, offer these types of programs. Bulletin boards provide a means to "post" information for a large group to access.

Relatively new to the Internet are audio and video teleconferencing. These applications are still in the early development stages and widespread use may be several years away.

Information sharing

The largest usage of the Internet to date has been to search for information. "Surfing the Net" has become a colloquialism for searching Web servers for information of interest to a user. While most searches might be for entertainment or curiosity, the potential for research and business-related information sharing is enormous.

There are several applications available on the Internet that search servers on the Net and compile an index of keywords, subjects, and titles on information contained on that server. By accessing one of these search engines, users can obtain a complete listing of servers, documents, and applications that meet their search criteria. This is similar to a card catalog or telephone directory for the Internet. Given the large number of servers on the Internet, finding information would be difficult if not impossible without some type of search facility.

13 Rick Watson, *Groupware Report*, University of Georgia, July 1994.

14 AT&T Hits the Net

Transferring information

In addition to accessing information, the Internet provides a way to transfer files. This allows users to access servers and download documents, data, and programs to their local workstations. Many software vendors are using the Internet as a way to distribute software patches and fixes. Some vendors are even using the Internet to distribute software. Graphical user interfaces for the Internet simplify the process of transferring data in what had been a somewhat user-unfriendly UNIX environment.

Software distribution

As was mentioned earlier, files can be easily transferred over the Internet. While the examples listed earlier dealt primarily with commercial applications, the Internet is being widely used to distribute shareware or free software. Many of the applications developed by universities and other public institutions are available on the Internet at no cost. While this might not appeal to commercial software developers, it allows the distribution of software that may actually enhance and increase usage of the Internet, and may ultimately benefit the commercial software industry.

A fundamental advantage to the Internet is its widespread use. Few private networks can come close to the number of users on the Internet. This removes the connectivity problem that is inherent with private networks. Access to the Internet can be provided in a number of ways, generally more easily and at a lower cost than installing a LAN and attaching it to a corporate WAN. The possibility of "virtual workgroups" emerges as well, since groups of people can be assembled to work on a project regardless of where they physically reside. Groups of engineers, researchers, designers, and writers from several different organizations could collaborate on a project. The virtual workgroup could then be disbanded and reassembled as needed for other projects.

The concept of the work environment would change as well, since now the need for collocated physical space would no longer exist. The virtual workgroup could consist of people working in offices, at home, on the road, or in any location where they could connect to the "Net." As has happened with the telecommuting concept, the traditional concept of work changes as well. Work by members of a virtual workgroup could occur at any time and any place. The eight to five workday in the office would no longer be the model for workers in the information age.

One need only look at what is currently available in terms of applications on the Internet to see that workgroup computing is possible today. E-mail is common on the Internet. Most of the existing groupware products have been developed by universities and research institutions, but the commercial market is rapidly developing products for the Internet. Some currently available groupware products for the Internet include[15]

ShowMe Whiteboard This is part of the Sun ShowMe suite of software and includes a shared "whiteboard" or electronic chalkboard. Users of the system can place drawings, equations, or other items of discussion on the whiteboard. Members of the electronic workgroup comment or draw on the whiteboard and all members of the group see the updated whiteboard image. In addition to the whiteboard, an application window can be used to execute an application, the results of which are available to all members of the group.

NCSA Collage Collage provides a shared whiteboard and shared text editing. Users can share a whiteboard image and collaboratively edit documents. An interactive chat feature allows text communications between group participants.

XTV XTV provides a shared application environment in which one user controls an application that all participants can view. A user can request and be given control of the application. Users are granted control of the application in the order that their request is received.

ShowMe SharedApp ShowMe SharedApp is part of the Sun suite of ShowMe software. It provides a means for a number of group participants to view and share control on an application.

These are examples of the some of the software currently used on the Internet. The purpose of these applications is to allow groups of users to participate in discussions and conferences via an electronic conference room. These tools provide a means for all to view text, documents, and diagrams via the Internet. The shared applications facilities allow an application such as a computer model to be shared among a group simultaneously. These tools evolved from the initial purpose of the Internet, to share information between research institutions. While there has been some commercial development of Internet groupware, most applications have been developed by universities and other educational institutions.

While the commercial market for Internet groupware has been somewhat limited, there are indications that vendors are preparing for an increased demand for these products. Recent announcements by Netscape Communications and Lotus show that they are preparing to provide Internet groupware products in the near future.

Netscape has emerged as a leader in the fast-growing Internet software market. Their products include Web browsers and Web

15 From Introduction to GroupWare, DT-5: Enabling Technologies (Blacksburg, Virginia: Virginia Tech), April 11, 1995.

server software for a number of platforms. In existence for only a few years, Netscape has become synonymous with the Internet. Their recent announcement of the acquisition of Collabra Software signifies a strategy that integrates Internet access with groupware.[16]

The Collabra Share software (described earlier in the text) was one of the first commercial groupware products. This product provides electronic discussion forums where users can distribute and discuss information. Designed to be independent of messaging infrastructure, Collabra Share functions with major e-mail systems such as Microsoft Exchange, Microsoft Mail, Novell Groupwise, Banyan BeyondMail, and Lotus cc:Mail.

According to Netscape, they plan to incorporate the collaboration and messaging capabilities of Collabra Share into future versions of Netscape products.[17] This is significant in that groupware functionality will be included in both client and server products. Given the open architecture of the Internet, this may mean that workgroup computing environments can be easily established among users on the Internet. This would definitely impact vendors of more proprietary groupware products such as Lotus and Microsoft.

Support for open mail protocols such as SMTP, IMAP, POP, and MAPI will allow the exchange of messages between a number of messaging systems and Netscape. The Netscape server software may evolve into an Internet mail and messaging gateway for other proprietary mail systems. Clearly this announcement will have major consequences on groupware and workgroup computing in the coming years. Many industry analysts feel that the acquisition of Collabra will put Netscape in direct competition with Notes for the title of de facto groupware standard.[18]

Realizing the need for more advanced applications on the Web, Netscape is expanding its product line to include sophisticated application development tools.[19] These tools provide a way to develop applications that access most major SQL databases. Applications will be portable to a number of platforms and operating systems. This provides a pseudo-open environment in that Netscape and the Internet provide the "middleware" to connect disparate platforms and operating systems. Companies could develop Internet applications that utilize existing hardware and databases. Database access is a major prerequisite for building highly functional business applications. This

16 Netscape to Acquire Collabra Software (Mountain View, California: Netscape Communications), Netscape Press Release, September 21, 1995.

17 Ibid.

18 Netscape to Buy Collabra, *Information Week*, October 9, 1995, p. 86.

19 Netscape Offers Application Development, *Information Week*, October 2, 1995, p. 98.

will be a very attractive product for firms wishing to do business on the Internet and may be a major competitor to the dominance of Notes as an application development environment and database front end.

Given the rapid growth of the Internet, vendors of proprietary groupware products must include it in their overall strategy. Lotus Notes is no exception, and in spite of their efforts to develop separate Notes networks with IBM and AT&T, Lotus is planning to incorporate World Wide Web access for Notes.[20] This integration will provide integration between Notes and Web clients, provide a means to exchange data between Notes and Web servers, and allow the use of the Internet for data replication. Notes users will be able to access the Internet through an internal Web browser without leaving Notes.

Besides the client software, Lotus plans to develop a Notes Web server that will provide basic Web server functionality but will offer additional capabilities for Notes clients who access the server. The server Web pages will act as a front end for the collection of data to be entered into Notes databases. Simplified administration tools will facilitate the replication of data among Notes servers over the Internet.

Lotus is pursuing a number of avenues for Notes and it can be expected that Internet integration is going to be of great interest to a number of Notes clients. While the IBM and AT&T network Notes offerings can provide access, the Internet may be the communications medium of choice. An appealing feature of the Internet is its widespread access. A Notes client may be able to provide information and services to a number of customers via the Internet without special connectivity. The Internet comes with the added attraction of millions of potential new customers that might not exist in the proprietary IBM or AT&T networks. Companies can develop internal Notes applications for sales and marketing and then link those applications to the Internet via a Notes Web server. Clearly this will have a great deal of appeal to current and potential Notes customers.

While the Internet may offer some new opportunities for Notes, it may also offer some challenges. As was previously discussed, the inclusion of groupware features in Web browser and server software may offer some competition to Lotus in the future, but today some firms are using Web servers and browsers rather than Notes.[21] This is a relatively new strategy and has only recently become a viable option to Notes as Web software has become more functional.

In most situations, these types of applications are being used internally and not over the Internet. Over 70 percent of the sales of

20 Lotus Will Leverage Notes With Web Links, *Infoworld*, September 18, 1995, p. 1.

21 Internet Looms Over Global Notes Efforts, *Infoworld*, August 14, 1995, p. 1.

Netscape Web server and Web browser software has been to support internal networks.[22] The use of internal networks addresses the security concerns that many have today, and given a corporate WAN that covers the members of a workgroup, access to the Internet or another proprietary network is not required.

Many of the features available only in Notes or other groupware products are now found in Web server software. Web server software that provides news groups, interactive discussions, and e-mail are often used in place of other groupware software. A primary consideration in choosing an internal Web server over Notes is cost. The estimated cost of installing Notes is approximately $200 per user, as compared with around $30 per user for Web software.[23] While perhaps not providing as complete a groupware product, an internal Web server may serve the needs of many organizations.

In addition to Netscape, there are a number of other providers of Web server and browser software. Many terminal emulation products and graphical operating systems such as OS/2 and Windows 95 either have or plan to incorporate a Web browsing application. The proliferation of client software will make the internal Web server an even more cost-effective alternative to proprietary groupware products.

Even with the previously cited adoption of Notes by major telecommunications carriers, the Internet may provide increasing competition to Notes networks. Announcements of secure Internet access by carriers such as AT&T and MCI provide an alternative to Network Notes.[24] These services are designed to provide the same level of security and reliability as Network Notes. Security concerns have been addressed using specialized hardware and software.

Internet usage may provide more access to customers than Notes Networks and may be less costly to implement and support. On the other hand, Notes Networks provide more a more full-featured application development environment and there are numerous third-party Notes products. The choice between Notes Networks and the Internet will most likely be based on a number of factors not just communications costs. Underlying business needs may prove to be the primary factor, with communications costs being a secondary consideration.

Use of the Internet as a means to enable workgroup computing potentially has many benefits. As was discussed earlier, the Internet is widely accessible, provides access to a wealth of information, and currently has groupware tools in use with new products expected in

22 Netscape to Buy Collabra

23 Internet Looms Over Global Notes Efforts, p. 20.

24 Carriers to Compete with Network Notes, *Infoworld*, October 2, 1995, p. 8.

the near future. In addition, the Internet has the advantage of being an "open" environment. This may prove to be the compelling reason for firms to opt for Internet-based groupware solutions.

A major problem in most large organizations is the integration of many disparate computing platforms, operating systems, and electronic messaging systems. Using the Internet alleviates the need to integrate internally and may provide a solution for internal as well as external workgroup computing environments. Often, projects are not solely internal, and outside consultants, subcontractors, and even customers may need to be involved in a particular project.

By using the Internet, the problems associated with creating the "virtual workgroup" described previously are minimized. The particular computing systems of each of the parties involved need only connect to and operate with the Internet. Special network connections are not required nor is proprietary client software. The virtual workgroup can be configured as needed, exist for the duration of the project, and then be disbanded until needed again. The cost of collaborative computing is reduced and becomes something akin to using the telephone for business.

Many promising new groupware applications such as video teleconferencing are on the horizon for the Internet. If these and other conceptual products prove to be practical, the future of workgroup computing many well be tied to the Internet.

New groupware products

As the interest in groupware continues to grow, the market for groupware products will continue to expand. Currently Lotus Notes is the clear leader in the groupware market. The e-mail and scheduling market has a number of major players such as cc:Mail, Microsoft Mail, Novell Groupwise, and Beyond Mail. Specialized products such as document imaging and document management products will most likely continue to provide their own integrated workflow applications.

Vendors of other types of software are looking to integrate workgroup computing into their traditional products. For example, the Oracle Workgroup/2000 product offers a client/server workgroup application development environment. Several other vendors are offering similar products or development toolkits that provide a way to integrate applications with messaging and e-mail systems.

In terms of the groupware market, there are some potential contenders for Lotus Notes. Microsoft Exchange may be one of the prime contenders for Notes. Originally planned to be incorporated into the much awaited release of Microsoft's Windows 95, the initial release of Exchange has been delayed.

Exchange is intended to provide a "Note"-type, folder-based desktop environment. The folder concept used by Notes and Exchange organizes information into folders of related data. For example, a folder can contain all documents relating to a particular project. These documents can be of several different types, such as word processing documents, spreadsheets, e-mail messages, or other types of electronic information. While similar in functionality to Notes, Exchange may have an advantage in the sheer number of Microsoft Windows users. This would be particularly true if Exchange is bundled as part of a future Windows release.

A relatively new product in the U.S. market is the TeamWARE suite of groupware products from ICL. Originally developed in Europe, TeamWARE consists of a complete line of e-mail, scheduling, and workflow tools designed to run on a number of platforms. The TeamWARE concept is based on an underlying message transport system that is utilized by a number of different products. Figure 12-3 illustrates the basic architecture of the TeamWARE product suite.

In this illustration the Messaging Server provides a means to connect the Office Groupware product with the TeamWARE Workflow system. To provide an enterprise-wide groupware solution, the Mes-

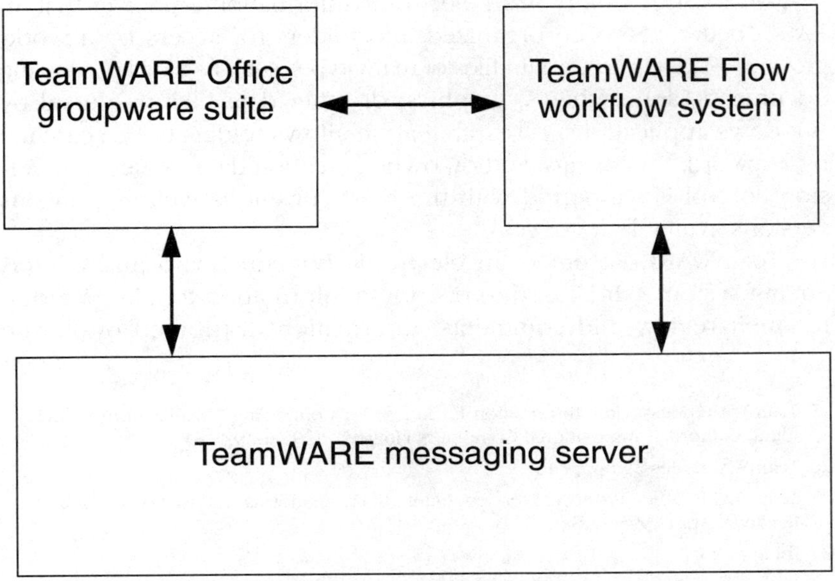

12-3 *The basic architecture of the TeamWARE product suite.*

saging Server is available with a number of TeamWARE Connectors that provide connectivity to other messaging systems such as[25]

- Bidirectional FAX
- Lotus Notes
- Microsoft Mail
- MIME (SMTP)
- Verimation Memo
- X.400
- X.500

Connections to other messaging systems such as cc:Mail, IBM SNA, and DEC VAX systems are planned.[26]

The TeamWARE Office offerings include e-mail, calendaring, a library function, and an electronic forum product. These applications are multiplatform and are supported on OS/2, Windows NT, Novell NetWare, and SVR4 UNIX servers.[27] Client applications are available for Windows, Macintosh, OS/2, and MS-DOS.

The mail product is organized as an in-box, an out-box, and a series of folders for organizing sent and received mail. TeamWARE Calendar is an electronic calendaring and scheduling system for individuals, groups and shared resources such as conference rooms and audiovisual equipment.[28] Users can schedule appointments for themselves or other group members, or ask the system to search for free time periods in which to schedule appointments.

TeamWARE Library is an electronic information organizer that allows documents to be organized into folders for access by a workgroup.[29] Folders can contain files of many types such as word processing documents, spreadsheets, graphics, or other data files produced by Windows applications. A search feature allows folders to be searched by keyword, text strings, author, owner, creation date, or version. Version control is supported with the most current as well as previous versions available for access.

TeamWARE Forum is an electronic bulletin board and conferencing system.[30] It is used to distribute information to a large group for their review and comments. Information distributed by Forum

25 TeamWARE Messaging, Information Backbone for Connecting Organizations (Santa Clara, California: International Computers Limited), 1995, p. 9.

26 TeamWARE Messaging, p. 10.

27 TeamWARE Office Product Overview (Santa Clara, California: International Computers Limited), April 1995, p. 5.

28 Ibid., p. 23.

29 Ibid., p. 19

30 Ibid., p. 27.

can take a number of forms, such as text files, documents, spreadsheets, graphics, or other application program data files. Members of a particular forum can comment on documents and their replies become part of a discussion chain that contains messages, replies, and attachments.

TeamWARE Flow is a workflow design and application development tool.[31] It contains a graphical planner, an application development tool, and an application management tool. The graphical development tool is used to graphically depict, model, and analyze a workflow. A workflow application is developed from the design and managed by the workflow management tool, which is used to monitor, interrupt, modify, and report on workflow. Application programming interfaces can be used to integrate TeamWARE products such as Flow with other business applications.

While TeamWARE is a relatively new product to the U.S. market, it has many features that position it to be in competition with Notes and other groupware products. The TeamWARE Office suite provides the same basic functionality of other e-mail and scheduling products mentioned previously in the text. The other components of the suite that are of particular interest in a workgroup computing environment are TeamWARE Library and TeamWare Forum. The Library product provides a functionality similar to that of Notes and Exchange, while Forum functions much like Collabra Share. The combination of these two features in addition to the base mail and scheduling products provide an integrated workgroup computing environment within a single product line.

While the TeamWARE Office suite of products addresses workgroup computing needs, the TeamWARE Flow product provides a way to implement integrated workflow systems. This product provides many of the features and functionality described earlier in the chapters on workflow application and workflow design and analysis tools. The product information on TeamWARE Flow presents a workflow modeling methodology that stresses continuous improvement, a theme common in process reengineering and total quality management.

When viewed in total, the TeamWARE product line offers many features and capabilities that would otherwise require the integration of products from several vendors. The integration of workgroup and workflow functions may be particularly attractive. While not a major player in the market at the moment, TeamWARE may prove to be contender in the groupware and workflow market of the future.

31 TeamWARE Flow Collaborative Workflow System for the Way People Work (Santa Clara, California: International Computers Limited), April 1995, p. 7.

Conclusion

Given the recent developments in the workflow and groupware markets, it is clear that these are emerging markets with a great deal of potential growth. Spending on workflow products alone is projected to reach $1 billion in 1996.[32] The groupware market is equally as active. Much of the interest in these products is fueled by the current trends in business to reengineer business processes and workflows. Downsizing, rightsizing, and total quality management have all given rise to a business environment that demands more efficient, more productive, and higher quality processes.

Workflow and workgroup software provide the technology needed to implement and manage modern business processes. Workflow can be expected to be incorporated into most applications packages, and groupware will most likely become a common feature of office automation products. As with any technology in its infancy, there will most likely be a number of products introduced, some successful and others not. As volatile as the computing industry is, the de facto standard may change several times. While software vendors will attempt to differentiate their products with specific features, a key point of any groupware product will be its ability to operate with other products and systems. The growth of the Internet and its associated products will have a major impact on groupware products in the future and may fuel the requirement for interoperability.

One might ask, If the market is this new, is it safe to invest in workflow or workgroup software? Clearly the figures for sales and market growth indicate otherwise. Firms in all segments of the economy and of all sizes are moving to workgroup computing. Advances in data communications, mobile computing, and multimedia are providing new avenues for workgroup computing solutions. Organizations are realizing the benefits of collaborative computing and are using technology to maximize the potential of their most valuable assets, their employees.

32 A Better Way to Work, *Information Week*, September 11, 1995, p. 34.

13

Using workgroup technology

Concept & vision

In this final chapter we'll look at how workgroup technology might be used to develop and use a data warehousing environment in a representative Fortune 500-class company—the XYZ Corporation. We'll look at workgroup technology throughout the entire life cycle of this sample effort, from the initial concept through development and deployment, and also in the operations of the data warehouse itself (i.e., a workflow and groupware infrastructure as part of the warehouse environment).

For each of the representative items we'll examine, we will

- Discuss what aspects of workgroup technology (i.e., workflow, conferencing, e-mail and messaging, etc.) are being used and why
- Discuss what the advantages and expected benefits are with respect to each workgroup-enabled process or component and why
- Examine why some other workgroup computing technology was *not* selected as the enabling mechanism for that particular process
- Discuss any risks or concerns that should be watched with respect to the workgroup usage.

Incidentally, it's no coincidence that our sample case study in this chapter deals with the development of a data warehouse environment. Data warehousing is, at the time of this writing, going head to head with workgroup technology—workflow and groupware together—in the race for the 1990s "overhyped technology" championship. Just as we have emphasized throughout this book that, without a supporting organizational culture built around collaborative work processes, workgroup computing may likely fail within an organization, despite its technological merits, so too can a similar argument be made for data warehousing. Though that subject is beyond the scope of this book, it is interesting to note the parallels between the workgroup computing craze and that of data warehousing. Neither area is entirely new, but rather is an outgrowth of older approaches and products that have been enhanced, thanks primarily to more robust underlying technologies (middleware, powerful desktop client machines, higher throughput networking environments, etc.), neither technology area is formally defined, and just as workgroup computing may mean different things to different organizations, the same is true for data warehousing, and the parallels go on.

Part of the reason we build our sample case study around a data warehouse implementation is that both technology areas—warehousing and workgroup computing—can, when architected, designed, and deployed in a *sensible* manner, yield tremendous productivity gains to an organization's user community, particularly when the two technology areas are architected in concert with one another, as is demonstrated in the final stages of this chapter's case study. At the same time, however, missteps are common in both of these areas, and even successful system rollout does not automatically result in successful utilization of these technologies.

Phase I—Deciding to implement a data warehouse

1. Initially floating the concept

11/5/95 11:51:18

FROM: JEFF MARTIN, CORPORATE DATABASE OPERATIONS

TO: MILLIE VANGUARD, EASTERN REGION PRODUCT MARKETING DIRECTOR

TRIXIE KRAMER, SOUTHEAST REGION PRODUCT MARKETING DIRECTOR

JULES HEYWARD, WESTERN REGION PRODUCT MARKETING DIRECTOR

. . . . *{rest of the distribution list of 25 region and district marketing executives}*

SUBJECT: DATA WAREHOUSING INITIATIVE

THE CORPORATE DATABASE CENTER WILL BE PURSUING A DATA WAREHOUSE INITIATIVE FOR FISCAL 1996. IT IS EXPECTED THAT

THIS EFFORT WILL OCCUR OVER 8 DEVELOPMENT QUARTERS, WITH FULL-SCALE DEPLOYMENT BY LATE 1998.

THE FOCUS OF THE EFFORT WILL BE A MARKETING DATA WAREHOUSE, WITH DATA COLLECTED AND FED FROM ALL REGIONAL PRODUCTION SYSTEMS PLUS ALL SYSTEMS FROM OVERSEAS SUBSIDIARIES. THE DATA WILL BE COLLECTED INTO A CENTRALIZED DATA WAREHOUSE, AND MARKETING MANAGERS AND ACCOUNT MANAGERS WILL BE GIVEN ON-LINE ANALYTICAL PROCESSING (OLAP) APPLICATION FRONT-ENDS TO THIS COLLECTED DATA.

A MEETING WILL TENTATIVELY BE HELD DURING THE MID-JANUARY CORPORATE-WIDE PRODUCT MARKETING CONFERENCE AT HQ; PLEASE REPLY BY 12/15/95 WITH (1) WHETHER YOU WILL PERSONALLY BE ABLE TO ATTEND, OR IF ONE OF YOUR MANAGERS WILL REPRESENT YOUR ORGANIZATION, AND (2) ANY SPECIFIC TOPICS THAT YOU WOULD LIKE TO DISCUSS RE: THIS INITIATIVE.

An e-mail message much like the one illustrated is used to establish the initial communication between those proposing the data warehouse initiative and the expected user community managers—in this case, the product marketing directors within XYZ Corp. Assuming this message is the first notification of this initiative—and, as discussed in the message, participation from the recipients is expected—even the tone of the communiqué is important; note that the request isn't "pushy" or authoritative, but rather simply states that a corporate initiative is being undertaken that will affect many users, and they are being given the opportunity to "get in on the ground floor" of the effort.

Why e-mail?

For a broad-based announcement of an initiative such as this data warehousing effort, e-mail is probably the best mechanism to accomplish the initial notice. The asynchronous nature of e-mail doesn't require that all recipients be physically present (for example, called to a meeting and having to be in the same room) at the time this initial notice is presented; the mail is read at each recipient's earliest convenience, he or she determines who will attend the meeting referenced in the memo, and responses are issued at the appropriate time. Though this seems like a rather trivial item, it's important to recognize that e-mail (1) traverses geographical boundaries with respect to the recipients' respective physical locations at the time contact is made, and (2) has a higher level of productivity on the part of the sender of the e-mail message than alternative communication mechanisms (e.g., 25 different phone calls with numerous sessions of "phone tag").

Why not an alternative workgroup computing mechanism? A groupware-enabled organization could have had the announcement of the meeting in question handled through a calendar/scheduling package. For example, Jeff Martin, the sender of the e-mail message, could have used the corporate-wide scheduling system to schedule a meeting at 1:00 P.M. on January 15, 1996, with automatic participation established for each of the 25 recipients of the e-mail message (who could then, if necessary, reassign the meeting attendance requirement to an alternative). Though technologically these two options are more or less equivalent, the e-mail approach is, from a corporate culture point of view, arguably the preferred option. Many people still bristle at having a meeting suddenly and automatically put on their electronic calendars without their prior knowledge, particularly when the schedulers of such a meeting are people who are barely known to them. Note also that the level of detail contained in the e-mail message would be unlikely to be handled within most scheduling packages (typically a few sentences at most of descriptive information are supported, although some systems permit longer descriptions).

In general, there is a sensitivity issue that transcends the underlying workgroup technology. For an initial contact about a major initiative, one that will no doubt require a tremendous amount of work over the two-year development cycle mentioned in the message, a mechanism such as e-mail is a preferred means to announce initial notice.

Risks and concerns

Even though e-mail is arguably the preferred mechanism to announce this initiative, there are some minor risks. This particular message refers to a meeting several months away, with a response time five weeks or so into the future with respect to the meeting. For a meeting with a shorter response time (the next day or even later that same day—an occurrence not uncommon in many organizations), there is a risk when e-mail is used as the communications mechanism because many people don't regularly check their e-mail or simply aren't at their desks all the time. In such quick-turnaround situations, alternative means (e.g., voicemail or a personal visit to someone's office) might be warranted for those who don't respond to an e-mail message. Typically quick-turnaround meeting announcements involve people within geographic proximity of one another, though there may be some degree of dispersal among the participants (e.g., different parts of the same city, working in different company buildings). In short, both time and geography must be taken into account when e-mail is used for announcements of meetings of any type. There is a tendency among many people to assume that once an e-mail message is sent, all the work is done, when in fact, the supporting tasks (e.g., handling responses, recontacting those who don't respond, etc.) are still ahead.

There is also a minor concern with respect to accidentally omitting one or more people from the intended list of recipients of an e-mail message. Typically distribution lists overcome this problem, but sometimes distribution lists are out-of-date or incomplete. Usually this isn't a problem—subsequent retransmission of a message to someone who should have received it will do the trick. But minor items like this can be blown out of proportion in a tense organization where organizational politics reigns ("He deliberately didn't send me a copy of that memo so I wouldn't have time to prepare for the meeting").

2. Suggestions for requirements submission

At the January 1996 corporate-wide product marketing meeting, the goals and scope of the data warehousing initiative are explained to the attendees. This effort will, as was briefly noted in the e-mail message, extract pertinent marketing-oriented data (sales information, customer profiles, information about competitors and their products, etc.) from numerous corporate transactional systems and merge that data into a single unified construct. The primary purpose of the effort is to permit a broad range of XYZ Corporation users to pursue on-line decision support and analytical processing functions to help them make more-informed decisions regarding product promotions, pricing, distribution mechanisms, and other marketing-oriented tasks.

Each attendee is informed that requirements will be collected over the next two and one-half months (until the end of March), and that the submission channel for those requirements will be by e-mail to Jeff Martin, the originator of the original e-mail message. Jeff Martin will collect the requirements and publish them for final review.

Why e-mail?

It's quick and easy, that's the primary advantage of using e-mail as the requirements submission mechanism. Anyone with a requirement can easily address an e-mail message to Jeff Martin with a "By the way, Jeff, here's some requirements for that data warehousing effort" theme. There isn't any need to gather people into a single room for a prolonged period of time, nor for someone like Jeff Martin to travel to many different corporate locations to meet with the many different managers.

Why not an alternative workgroup computing mechanism?

Actually, there *is* a better workgroup computing mechanism (or at least one that seems better, as is discussed in the next section). There are some shortcomings to using e-mail in this setting which may not be obvious at first, given the ease with which e-mail can be used. These are discussed in the next paragraph.

Risks and concerns

The major concern with respect to using e-mail for requirements collection is that while communications from the many product marketing executives to Jeff Martin are relatively easy to accomplish, sharing of information about data warehousing requirements *among* the product marketing executives is, at best, tedious and is, at worst, overlooked. Consider that Millie Vanguard and Trixie Kramer are each submitting requirements for their own organizations to Jeff Martin; there is nothing in the e-mail communications stream that requires the two of them to share information with each other, or with any of the other product marketing executives. At the same time, Jeff Martin must filter through the requirements from each person, eliminate duplicates, and ensure that a consolidated list is created.

True, all e-mail back to Jeff Martin could be copied to all other product marketing executives, but this will likely result in a tremendous load of e-mail traffic, much of which is likely to be ignored or, at best barely skimmed as other priorities occur.

As we'll see in the next section, a scenario such as this one—in which communications over a prolonged period of time from any one party are likely to be of interest to many different people rather than a single recipient (basically, a many-to-many relationship among those involved)—might be better handled through a means such as electronic conferencing.

3. Changing the requirements submission mechanism

Realizing that the requirements collection process via e-mail is getting out of hand—not only are the 25 product marketing executives submitting requirements, but many of people in their respective organizations are too, and many of the requirements coming in from different organizations conflict with one another—the decision is made to change the mechanism from e-mail to the corporate electronic conferencing system. Jeff Martin establishes a set of topics, each one relating to a different area of the proposed data warehouse (e.g., the client tools, the data contents, the timing of the data refresh cycles, etc.). All product marketing managers, people in their respective organizations, and—new for this round—those who were involved in a similar data warehousing effort in the contract management area, and who are being called up to lend their expertise with respect to lessons learned from their project, are given access to the conference. Not only are requirements to be entered in the appropriate subject area, but comments on entries are encouraged, the goal being to handle conflicts and issues in a logically centralized place instead of having those issues remain unresolved.

Why electronic conferencing?

Because of the limitations of e-mail, as discussed in the previous topic. The asynchronous, multiperson nature of electronic conferencing makes it a highly suitable medium for collaborative efforts such as requirements gathering, filtering, and prioritization, as in this sample case. People can join the discussion as needs warrant (examples: a new employee, or someone from an organization that becomes involved in the data warehousing project after it has already begun) and they can be given access to the entire history of the project without the need for someone else to extract the appropriate messages from his or her e-mail folders and forward the contents to the new person.

Risks and concerns

The major concern in electronic conferencing is getting people—particularly nontechnical managers—comfortable with using the medium as a way to communicate issues and items (such as data warehousing requirements, in this case) and to accept criticism and feedback in an asynchronous manner (e.g., people responding to their requirements with amendments and follow-on messages). Typically this is a cultural issue rather than a technical one, and there is always a risk that a "conference bully" will surface and dominate the medium of information exchange, skewing the discussion toward his or her benefit. One of the best ways to overcome such occurrences is by having a conference moderator (or more than one) who monitors all postings, making sure that issues are resolved in a satisfactory manner, and making sure that the tone of the postings isn't hostile.

4. Establishment of virtual meetings

At the in-person group meeting in January 1996, general buy-in among all participants is achieved. Many user-group managers are very enthusiastic about the data warehousing project, a few see it as little more than the latest in a long line of overhyped technology-driven efforts at XYZ Corporation that have provided little of the promised benefit, and most other people fall somewhere in between these two points on the interest and enthusiasm spectrum.

What is abundantly clear though, as the meeting participants depart corporate headquarters, is that the high-pressure, fast-paced atmosphere that has become the norm at XYZ Corporation since the recession in the early 1990s will *not* permit a "business as usual" approach to further developing and refining requirements before full-scale design and development is to begin. This means that unlike earlier 1980s-era efforts, where teams of users and business analysts would drop everything else for weeks on end and adjourn to a single location where they would do nothing else but develop and approve system and application requirements, an alternative means to accomplish this task must be found.

The decision is made by corporate management that a pilot data warehousing effort will be funded on a "proof of concept" basis, subject to the following constraints:

- The scope of the initial effort will be narrowed to the analysis of sales history data, both from XYZ Corporation and that obtained from public data sources with respect to competitors' sales
- All requirements, architectural and infrastructure decisions, and resolution of issues *must* occur by March 31, barely seven weeks after the conclusion of the meeting
- At the same time that the requirements gathering and resolution phase is occurring, there *must* be a "business as usual" approach to the work at hand; no other business functions or processes can suffer because of this effort.

Fortunately, XYZ Corporation began a pilot groupware program in which basic electronic conferencing services—like the bulletin board-like system used to capture the initial requirements and associated feedback—were enabled with a real-time messaging system, not unlike the "chat sessions" available through public on-line services.

By using these capabilities, a series of "virtual meetings" can be held in which real-time decisions can be made in the areas of system and application features, issues resolutions, and other functions.

Why real-time messaging?

Unlike the initial collection of requirements, in which the dominant paradigm tended to be "Let's put these items out there and see what the other people have to say," this phase of the development life cycle requires much faster turnaround with respect to (1) deciding what proposed features are and aren't within the scope of the pilot program, (2) resolving issues that come up during the next seven weeks, and (3) developing a final set of pilot program requirements and specifications. The asynchronous, time-delayed nature of bulletin board-style electronic conferencing *might* be usable for some of the tasks that must be accomplished (i.e., posting a document in a centralized location for others to download for their review), but the *discussion* aspect needs a communications paradigm that is more real-time, yet doesn't require all participants to be in the same physical location, thus the desire for real-time messaging.

Why not use an alternative workgroup computing mechanism?

An option with respect to the real-time messaging is to use video conferencing, and by the mid-1990s some commercial implementations are beginning to appear. The incremental costs of video conferencing are, many claim, not fully substantiated with respect to productivity enhancements over text-based, real-time messaging. Additionally, XYZ Corporation currently doesn't have an infrastructure in place to support the bandwidth requirements of interactive video conferencing, though plans are in place for a future pilot program in that area.

Risks and concerns

There are few risks with respect to real-time messaging. There is always the chance that a required participant won't be available for a given meeting and, unlike the scenario with asynchronous bulletin board-style electronic conferencing, it's harder to "catch up" following a missed meeting (though if logs of the interactive message traffic are maintained, they can be downloaded and read at a later time).

5. Research from public information sources

XYZ Corporation management has no desire to "reinvent the data warehousing wheel," but at the same time one of the things that has become readily apparent is that data warehousing not only lacks a consistent, formal definition, but there are numerous base technology options and architectural choices that need to be considered. Quickly, the participants from the IT organization are overwhelmed with items such as

- Should the data warehouse be centralized or distributed?
- What mechanisms should be used to feed data from production systems into the warehouse?
- Should the database engine be relational or multidimensional, and what are the trade-offs?
- What tools are available to aid in the design and development of the warehouse?
- What different classes of client desktop tools should be considered, both for the pilot program and for full-scale deployment if the latter is approved?

. . . and the list goes on and on. Fortunately, XYZ Corporation has access to Internet and public information service databases from which product reviews, articles, technology analysis papers, conference proceedings, and various other information can be obtained.

The problem though, is that the volume of data and documents is so overwhelming that the time frame allowed for the pilot program doesn't permit any dedicated browsing, "see what I can find" time on the part of the IT staff members.

It is decided to establish a workflow-enabled document research system in which:

- Each IT staff member is assigned one or more primary areas of responsibility across the spectrum of the data warehousing effort.
- Each IT staff member is also assigned several technology areas in which he or she will act as the reviewer/commentator/evaluator of the information obtained.
- Using keyword-based searches, automatic downloads from many different public access databases will take place in which (1) each IT staff member will receive new reports as they are posted into the databases, (2) he or she will read the report, provide annotated comments with respect to the contents (How applicable is the contents? Does this agree or disagree with earlier reports from other sources? What do we do with this?), and (3) the annotated report will be routed to all designated reviewers for that particular technology area for their comments.
- Following the complete review cycle—which will take no longer than two days, as established by the workflow-driven rules—the complete annotated report will be posted into the on-line electronic conferencing database with a recommended action based on that report (i.e., vendors mentioned should be contacted, a technology option investigated further, a reference site contacted, etc.).

Why the workflow-enabled research?

A great deal of information is available through publicly accessible sources such as Internet sites, but at the same time there is the matter of (1) remembering (or taking the time) to browse through locations in hopes of finding something of interest, and (2) doing something productive with the information that has been obtained rather than letting it sit idle on one's hard disk.

By using a workflow-enabled approach, the appropriate information *automatically* comes to the persons who most need it or who can most productively evaluate it for applicability. Automatic time-driven routing to other interested parties will ensure that even if the initial recipient becomes overburdened with his or her other tasks, other recipients will receive the pertinent information.

Why not an alternative workgroup computing mechanism? An alternative approach might be to have one dedicated researcher whose job it is to do little else but "surf the Net" and find all applicable information. He or she then posts it into the electronic conferencing system where it can be reviewed.

The major advantage of the workflow-enabled approach, as contrasted with that described in the preceding paragraph, is the automatic transmission/routing nature of the communications to the person or persons who most need the information. A hybrid approach might be used (e.g., automatic posting into the conferencing system in conjunction with the workflow-enabled routing), but one of the goals of the workflow-enabled routing approach is to avoid information overload (e.g., not posting every possible article or report or document into the conferencing system, but rather posting only those that are directly applicable to the tasks at hand).

Risks and concerns

With respect to XYZ Corporation's particular situation, the primary risk is in the company's (or, more specifically, the IT organization's) ability to implement and deploy this workflow-enabled system in a timely manner, given the end of March freeze on all aspects of the data warehousing pilot program. If this process has been used elsewhere before, then most (if not all) issues will have been resolved and usage can be enabled by adjusting the user base and establishing the new workflow rules, external data sources, and other environmental parameters.

If, however, this is a first attempt at using such an environment and the effort is a failure or, at best, only offers marginal productivity improvements in the research process, the major risk will likely come during subsequent efforts at using this environment, such as during full-scale data warehouse development and implementation. Seeing nothing but problems and barriers to their productivity, rather than enhancement, the IT staff members may strenuously object when the edict is handed down to use this workflow-driven research environment. "It didn't help at all!" "There is *no way* I'm getting involved in this again, nor is anyone in my organization!" The objections may come loudly and strenuously.

The main risk, therefore, in this particular workgroup-enabled part of our scenario might be the too-rapid deployment of an environment that is entirely new to its users. Given the tight time frame in which everyone must work, there simply is no time to attempt a pilot program in its usage. The mandate is made, the effort doesn't succeed, and from that point on, workflow-driven research (or, perhaps more seriously, workflow-driven *anything*) has a "bad rap" all across XYZ Corporation.

6. Formal conferences for requirements, scope, and architecture

March is now over; the research has been completed, the infrastructure has been chosen, the project scope has been refined in terms of specific user queries and functions; basically, everything is set to go. What lies ahead before full-scale development can begin is a final run-through of all aspects of the program, looking for holes that hadn't been previously found and, in general, making sure that everything that needed to be done has been.

It is decided that the company will use the electronic conferencing system as the main repository for *everything* that has been decided with respect to the pilot program. The contents of the system have become somewhat cluttered due to the frenzied pace since the program's inception, and Jeff Martin is assigned to reorganize the conference's topics and contents. He proceeds to combine similar topics that are currently stored under different discussion threads; he archives old information that is no longer pertinent; in effect, he gets the conferencing system in shape so the final round of review and decision-making can occur.

Why a cleaned-up electronic conferencing environment?

As was mentioned above, the frenzied pace of electronic conferencing often leads to a great deal of clutter, disorganization (e.g., multiple threads for the same topic), and general disarray. Over time it becomes harder and harder to quickly find items of interest and importance (example: "there are twelve different topics that discuss the trade-offs between relational and multidimensional engines for a data warehouse; in which one is that 20-page product comparison report from *Database and Data Warehousing Journal* stored?")

A suitable paradigm when using electronic conferencing for "real work" (as opposed to discussing hobbies, for example) is to periodically reorganize the contents at some critical phase in a project, such as (in this case) when a final approval cycle is about to begin. The older contents can be archived in their entirety and should be available (perhaps on alternative media, such as cartridge tape or optical disk) if something that is filtered out should be needed. At the same time

- Similar topic threads should be united and, if possible, sequenced (with exact duplicates, such as document attachments, eliminated); older versions of a final draft document might be removed to the archival realm, for example.
- Unification of multiple types of conferencing contents should take place. For example, the technology article/paper/report postings that result from the workflow-enabled research system might currently be in one conference file, while the requirements for the pilot program are in another. It may be more productive to combine similar subjects (for example, the requirements for the front-end client reporting tools, and downloaded research and evaluation reports regarding commercial reporting tool products) for ease of access.

Risks and concerns

Very few risks are associated with the cleanup process. There will likely be a brief period of reorientation where learned, semiautomatic actions such as "GOTO TOPIC 5 FOR REPLICATION SERVERS" may now take someone into a totally different topic because of the content reorganization, but these tend to be minor nuisances rather than severe problems.

7. Establishing an implementation plan with deadlines and dependencies

At last, the XYZ Corporation team is ready for development. The last step before this commences is to prepare an implementation plan, one that takes into account the roles and responsibilities of *everyone*—the three different development teams (database engine, data design and delivery, client desktop tools), the business analysts, the users responsible for testing, and the corporate technical support center (the people who are charged with adjusting all hardware and system software configurations).

The approach that is decided on is that all team leaders will create draft schedules for their respective teams, with internal tasks, precedences and successors, and internal and external dependencies clearly defined. The schedules will then be forwarded to Carl Smith, the program manager, who will merge the schedules, evaluate and resolve all dependencies, and look for any problems. The merged schedule will then be sent back to each team for their comments and acceptance, after which development will begin.

To accomplish this final predevelopment task, a mix of workgroup technologies will come into play. E-mail will be used for the initial assignment of making the schedules, and the schedules from each group will be e-mailed back to Carl Smith. Following Carl's work, a final schedule will be posted into the conferencing system, where real-time conversation messaging will be used to review, comment on, and adjust the schedule.

Why the selected technologies?

By this time everyone should be very comfortable with the e-mail, electronic conferencing, and real-time messaging environments, allowing schedule creation to occur very quickly.

Why not an alternative workgroup computing mechanism?

Conceivably, a draft schedule could have been created by Carl Smith and posted into the electronic conferencing system, after which discussion and adjustment would occur. This, however, might likely result in dissension if a schedule were "forced upon" one or more teams without their initial participation. The technology is in place for a real-time review of Carl's efforts, but this is a situation where collaborative processes (Chapter 2) and the organizational culture dramatically override the technology as the major concern at hand. By using selected workgroup computing technologies (e-mail) to request initial schedule drafts, an atmosphere of participation in the decision-making process is established, easing the way for any subsequent disagreement with the merged schedule or related activities.

Risks and concerns

There aren't many risks associated with the approach outlined here. In general, workgroup computing is used simply as a highly efficient communications tools to request and submit work (the schedule), and later to comment on the merged results. More manual processes, such as phone calls and hardcopy submissions, are generally less efficient, particularly when geographically distributed teams are involved.

Phase II—Full-scale development

The pilot program is over and it has been very successful. Development took place on time and within the allocated budget, the users are happy, the technology has proved to be successful. Now it's time for the real thing.

Many of the initial efforts in the full-scale development phase mirror those described in the preceding section, and we won't repeat them (example: collection of requirements). Many of the other efforts, such as the workflow-enabled research, are less important, though they should continue given that new products, approaches, and architectures for data warehousing appear nearly every day.

In this section, we focus on a different set of tasks that are representative of those that occur during full-scale development efforts and discuss how different types of workgroup computing might be used to boost the productivity of these processes.

1. Collaborative document generation and review

Full-scale development will be significantly more complex than that done during the pilot effort, and it becomes apparent that the required documents for this phase will be significantly larger and more all-encompassing than those from the earlier effort. In the pilot program, all documents had a single author, and he or she would take comments posted into the conferencing system into consideration and update the document before reposting it for final approval.

This time, however, most documents will require multiple authors, leading to the need for multiparticipant document generation tools. These include

- Document authoring tools, in which different portions of the same document can be assigned to various individuals and, once completed, easily merged together. References to portions done by another person (e.g., another chapter or section) need to be automatically maintained and updated as the document evolves.

- Reviewing and revision tools, in which on-line *real-time collaborative* document editing can take place. Each user's screen will show the same document, and edits made by one user will automatically reflect on the screens of the others.
- Workflow-enabled document routing, as required by the approval process.

Why document tools?

Most readers have used word processing software (particularly GUI products) in which the productivity gains and enhanced presentation as compared to simple text editors are dramatically improved. For documents with a single author, a high-powered word processor is often sufficient to meet any document generation needs.

When multiple authors are part of the picture, however, the usage paradigms become more complex as different sections are assigned to different team members, documents are merged together and subsequently split apart for another round of editing and other *group functions* (as contrasted with individual functions). In these situations, the standard nonworkgroup paradigm of one person creating a document, mailing it to someone else for his or her comments or additional components, and subsequently passing it on to others becomes inefficient and, worse, prone to errors. A document management tool that helps coordinate the multiple author process can help reduce errors and permits a greater degree of parallelism in work, yielding greater overall productivity.

Most readers have also been involved in document review cycles in which (1) a required recipient doesn't receive a copy due to an oversight, causing a delay in the overall schedule, or (2) having prepared a document and sending it out for comment to 20 or 30 others, receiving back 30 e-mail messages that read

- PAGE 2, 2ND PARAGRAPH, LEFT SIDE: CHANGE "ENABLED" TO "ASSISTED"?
- PAGE 2, 3RD PARAGRAPH, LAST LINE: WHAT DO YOU MEAN?
- PAGE 2, LAST LINE ON PAGE: YOU REFER TO FIGURE 1.1, BUT IT'S ON THE NEXT PAGE . . . COULD YOU PUT THE REFERENCE AND FIGURE ON THE SAME PAGE?

. . . and so on. It isn't uncommon to have the same misspelling pointed out by twelve different people, and by the time you, the document's author, are reading through the twelfth message that points out the same sequence of errors and corrections that the previous eleven did, you may likely miss something of importance that is crunched between the other repetitive comments. Or, you may have embedded a question within the body of your document, such as:

Re: the previous paragraph: should we really have a main menu, or should there be a series of desktop icons to bring up different analysis functions?

Much to your chagrin, the comments from the reviewers contain 11 votes for the main menu, five votes for the icons, and four who want to know what the trade-offs are, and you're no closer to answering your question than you were when you typed the message.

By using collaborative tools, in which changes can be made within the body of a document, either in real-time during collaborative processes or by "electronic annotation" to your original document, a higher degree of productivity can occur during the preparation, review, and approval process, yielding higher-quality documents that are less prone to errors because of information overload.

Risks and concerns

The primary concern with respect to using a suite of document management tools (composition, review, workflow-enabled review routing, etc.) is that there is likely to be a lack of familiarity with them during an organization's initial attempts and the productivity gains might not be noticeable. There is often a degree of incompatibility between tools from different vendors that fill different spaces in the document management realm, though standards and collaborative efforts among vendors have gone a long way toward filling these gaps.

2. Including new people and organizations in the process

As with most large-scale (or even smaller-scale) development projects, people will constantly rotate in and out of the effort. For example,

- New organizations become involved and their technologists and managers need to get up to speed as quickly as possible

- Developers come and go over the course of the effort
- New corporate-level managers come into the company's fold and want to find out what is going on with an organization's effort, hoping to possibly leverage work for their own group's benefit
- Reorganizations cause new lines of responsibility to occur

. . . and the reasons go on and on. Previously in this chapter, we discussed how electronic conferencing might be used for functional tasks such as sharing research results, collaboratively working on specific assignments, or sharing information during a quick-paced development effort. Most of these tasks are short-term (e.g., only lasting for a finite period of time) in duration, after which the contents of the various conferences might be used very sporadically, possibly even archived.

Electronic conferencing might also be used as an "institutionalized means of communication"—one in which the contents are expected to remain accessible for a long period of time, perhaps even in perpetuity. In this chapter's sample case, some of the topics that would be long-lasting might be

- On-line organization charts for the IT and user organizations—everyone who is involved in the data warehousing implementation effort and what their respective roles are.
- An on-line "fast start" package of documentation that can be downloaded by a newcomer to the effort. After reading the documentation, and perhaps running some program samples contained in the package, he or she will be quickly brought up to date with how to use the system, where it came from, what it is expected to provide to the organization, and so on.

There are many other topics and subjects that could also be included in such an environment. The main purpose of using such a system is to provide an easy-to-use, easy-to-navigate mechanism of on-line accessible documents (and in this context, *documents* means any machine-readable component that is of value in aiding someone's understanding of the project).

Why electronic conferencing?

In organizations where only a handful of workgroup computing facilities exist (typically e-mail), the typical mechanism to provide on-line accessibility to "the complete package" (as is the goal in this scenario) is to maintain common shared directories on a network where (1) a newcomer is pointed to the locations of documents, or (2) someone takes the responsibility to e-mail numerous documents to that newcomer.

In general, electronic conferencing is more efficient than these approaches in that as long as the conference database is maintained with respect to currency of information, there is little that anyone other than the newcomer needs to do. Browsing through the information can either be left up to the individual or, if there is a certain order in which the information should be studied to better facilitate understanding, a workflow-enabled application can be written underneath the conferencing system that governs the flow of information and documents to the user. For example, "PACKET #1"—the basic introductory package—might be automatically e-mailed by the conferencing system to the new user and once he or she electronically "signs off" as having read that information, the system will route "PACKET #2," after which the same process might continue.

Alternatively, a rules-based workflow might be set up where, for example, if the newcomer is a hands-on application developer on the data warehouse project, he or she is given a certain sequence of document packages that include detailed application documentation; a manager or user wouldn't be given material that relates to the applications code. This way, it can be enforced with a relatively high degree of certainty that newcomers are given the information they need for their jobs but not that which they don't need nor which isn't applicable at the moment.

Risks and concerns

The major concern—not really a risk—is that the organization take the maintenance of the conferencing system very seriously with respect to keeping it up to date. Very often initial enthusiasm about an environment such as that described here falters over time, and the information gets "stale" and out of date, yielding little benefit to the recipients of the various types of documents.

3. Development and quality assurance

The importance of the quality assurance (QA) function in the application and system development process is more apparent today than ever. Along with a general "push for quality" in American and global business, the distributed nature of IT environments (client/server, open systems, etc.) means that there exists a greater degree of dependency among physically disjoint components on one another, and that there are more opportunities than ever before for problems to suddenly appear in an environment that has already been deployed.

XYZ Corporation has adopted a methodology in which the QA function occurs throughout the development process, from the day the first module is compiled until the application is deployed. To support such a tight-turnaround environment, they have adapted a workflow-enabled development environment in which

- Modules that are deemed "ready to go" by a developer are automatically frozen (no updates can take place) and shipped to the assigned QA team member
- The testing and QA plans call for a certain number of modules to be available and completed (at least initially) before functional testing can commence. The workflow engine ensures that all necessary modules are released by the developers, no unit builds occur until all modules are available, and all pertinent people are notified of the status of that particular functional testing component (Is it on time or late? Are problems occurring?)
- Problems that are found during the test/QA phase are automatically assigned identifiers and routed to the person(s) responsible for resolution, and managers, users (the alpha testers, for example), and others who need to know the results from a particular test phase are notified.

The main point is that the frenzied pace of rapid application development—with its constant code-test-more, code-test-revise, code-test- (and so on) cycles—needs automation beneath the flow of data and code to ensure that the QA function is done correctly and that very little (or better yet, nothing) makes its way to a further stage in the development effort until problems have been found and corrected.

Why workflow-enabled QA?

The major advantage of using workflow-enabled QA is to permit a high degree of productivity during a rapid application development effort, particularly when a distributed team might be involved and many dependencies exist. By institutionalizing the development cycle rules within the tool base (as supported by the workflow engine), the tendency to forego functions such as testing and QA when faced with a frenzied pace of activity is not only minimized, but ideally isn't permitted. By forcing electronic "sign-offs" of various stages of the test and QA process, accountability is established, not from a punitive point of view but rather from a team-based, efficiency-driven, collaborative view ("This will help us all do our jobs better and get done much quicker than before").

Why not an alternative workgroup computing mechanism? In situations such as those described previously, workflow-enabled services are much more efficient and applicable to the process than electronic conferencing, for example. Postings of the test and QA results into a conferencing system are typically overlooked by a developer whose deadline is rapidly approaching ("You want me to look at what? When? You've got to be kidding!"). If, for example, the workflow engine contains timers that remind the developer that he or she has, say, three days to fix problem "X" and two days to fix problem "Y"—visual reminders on the developer's screen are part of the environment—then there is less of a tendency for the developer to disregard such critical assignments.

Risks and concerns

In addition to technical sophistication (trying to improve the software and system development process is difficult using *any* technology when there is still so much uncertainty about the processes themselves), there are also cultural issues that must be considered. Some developers are likely to resent the automatic transmission of problem reports (each of which contain the notice that a copy has been sent to his or her boss). This is a prime example of how the culture established along with workgroup computing becomes as important as the technology in making things work. A team that has adopted a collaborative work culture such as that described in Chapter 2 is less likely to have its members revolt against workflow-enabled processes than one in which a combative philosophy of "us against them" (for example, the developers versus the QA staff) reigns.

4. Establishing traceability and impact analysis mechanisms

One of the hallmarks of a data warehousing environment of any type or architecture, as contrasted with a transaction processing system, is that most or all of the data comes from some other source (i.e., feeds from production applications, both those newly developed or running on legacy systems, or feeds from public sources of the data, etc.). Unlike, say, an application where a telephone operator processes a phoned-in catalog sale for five sweaters and four pairs of jeans, with accompanying database entries into the sales and inventory management portions as a result of that transaction, a data warehousing environment might

- Take daily feeds from many different catalog systems owned by the headquarters corporation and reformat all of the data into structures that enable cross-business analysis of what the big sellers are
- Download new data that is available weekly on the Internet from a market research source, in which competitors' sales activity can be analyzed
- Roll up the in-store sales from all outlets across the country, helping corporate management determine what areas are ripe for new store openings

The main point is that all of the data in the environment originates in some other database, typically one internal to some portion of the corporation's environments but increasingly from a public source.

This data loading paradigm introduces a number of issues, most of which are far beyond the scope of this book, but we will focus on one of them. Unlike a given transaction processing application, in which database changes must be reflected in the application code that runs against those databases (otherwise the applications will likely fail), a data warehouse environment is typically outside the "ownership domain" of production applications. That is, very often changes to production databases are not communicated in a timely manner to the owners of the data warehousing environment, and the loading procedures might suddenly fail due to this lack of knowledge.

For example, the production environment might modify its sales database table structures to better support the users of the order-entry system. When it's time to run the software that extracts certain columns from certain tables and sends the resulting data to the data warehouse, suddenly the data is no longer where it used to be, and the loading procedures will fail.

One way of improving communications with respect to changes in structure, content, or other attributes of the data is to institute an infrastructure built around *traceability* and *impact analysis* services. By using such services, for example, it can be determined, if a given production database table were to have its structure changed, what data warehousing systems across XYZ Corporation would be affected.

One way of supporting these services is to keep a repository-based (or database-based) store of the relationships between production data and that which is part of the data warehousing environment. To support the automatic communications, a workflow-enabled mechanism could be put in place. For example, a database administrator for the billing system in the western region could trigger the impact analysis component when he or she contemplates a restructuring of the production database, and the administrators for all data warehousing systems across XYZ Corporation could be automatically notified that a change is being contemplated. With a high degree of granularity in the impact analysis component (e.g., a great deal of information is maintained at relatively low levels of detail), the particular data loading and transmission routines, the modules that restructure the data, the desktop client applications and canned queries, and all other components that would be affected by the change are instantly identified.

Why workflow-enabled impact analysis?

In general, the need for traceability and impact analysis supersedes both the data warehousing example in this chapter and the workgroup computing subject of the book. Legacy systems migration, for example, can be greatly aided by institutionalizing these classes of services (e.g., making sure that all needed data and functionality in the current environment are accounted for in the new system's design).

This particular example illustrates how the automatic trigger-based nature of workflow can be used to aid this perplexing problem.

Risks and concerns

The primary issue (not so much a risk) is the immaturity of the required *metamodels* (the "roadmaps of all components of the environment") that would be needed to support full-functioned impact analysis and traceability. Over the next few years this issue will likely be resolved, so this is an area that XYZ Corporation (in the context of this chapter) and IT planners (in general) should track; tremendous productivity benefits can be gained from utilizing services in these areas.

Phase III— The operational environment

1. Ad hoc data analysis

The date warehouse is completed! True, functionality will continue to be added, probably forever, but the full-scale version has been rolled out to the user community and its a success!

In addition to unprecedented access to a consistent view of corporate data, the facilities that have most enthralled the user base are the groupware-based services that are built into the applications and tools. For example, a user may execute a query against the data warehouse and, based on the results, highlight certain data (or groups of data) and, based on returned values, for example, cause some workgroup-enabled function to occur (example: "The store in Minneapolis has consistently had an average weekly sales volume of 25 percent less than the store in Duluth; route all pertinent data to the district manager for *IMMEDIATE* action!").

In effect, the users exclaim, "it's like we're all working together on this effort."

Why workflow-enabled queries?

Even though the data warehouse environment, and the tools deployed on client desktops, can provide a high degree of access to corporate and external data, much of that productivity gain is on a singular, "personal productivity" basis ("Tell me what *I* need to know for *my* organization"). As business processes themselves become more collaborative (again, as discussed in Chapter 2), the data sharing/routing needs become very important.

By enabling the data warehousing environment with capabilities such as those described earlier, a paradigm of "I found something interesting . . . send it to everyone who needs to know about this?" can be automatically handled by a rules-based environment. The tendency for someone who ran a report at 5:45 P.M. in Los Angeles and found something of interest to a district manager in Pittsburgh, where it's now 8:45 P.M., to say, "Ah, I'll call her tomorrow, it's late," can be overcome by little more than the push of a button (or a GUI-enabled equivalent).

In short, a higher degree of group-level productivity can be attained by enabling the environment with workflow services that support these communications paradigms than if no such services existed.

Why not an alternative workgroup computing mechanism?

Conceivably, someone could use a "COPY" GUI function and subsequently "PASTE" the results into a file, then e-mail that file to one or more recipients. But this process is more tedious than the "just push a button" approach, and in many cases, it isn't known who the district manager in Pittsburgh is (in the example). The results that have been e-mailed might be sitting in an e-mail in-basket along with 100 or so other messages.

Risks and concerns

There really aren't many risks or concerns, but perhaps some cultural issues ("Who the heck is this person in L.A., and why is he sending me this? What business is it of his?")—again, an underlying collaborative work culture will mitigate these reactions.

2. Report-driven workflow

The preceding example of workflow-enabled ad hoc data analysis works nicely in human-driven scenarios, with a certain class of users responsible for "first line data analysis" with subsequent feeding of results to managers and other employees.

Most data warehousing environments, however, also feature some degree of "production reports," or automated quasi-batch jobs that regularly access, group, filter, and analyze very large volumes of data. For example, a 25-gigabyte table of by-hour, by-store, by-product sales for all 350 retail stores in the XYZ Corporation's consumer clothing division might be analyzed weekly, looking for trends that could either be capitalized on or that might foretell slowdowns, either across the board, by region, by product, or in accordance with some combination of factors.

In such cases, the same workflow-enabled "look what I found" paradigm, as described in the scenario, could be part of the environment, with one major difference: instead of a human action being the deciding factor to instantiate a particular workflow, it might be now done in an automated, rule-based manner. In effect, this particular analysis paradigm would *not* alert any users if results were within some predetermined threshold of normalcy, but rather only if variances outside those thresholds should occur ("reporting by exception").

By equipping the reporting environment with these capabilities—and others such as extracting portions from a larger report and routing each one to one or more pertinent individuals (example: the monthly sales report for the entire corporation will be run against the data warehouse, but regional managers will only receive results for their respective regions)—a high degree of timely transfer of pertinent information can occur.

Why workflow-enabled reporting?

Basically, the same rationale as for ad hoc reporting applies, with the additional aspect of not requiring human intervention in the analysis of huge amounts of data.

Risks and concerns

Not many; ideally, production reporting systems should be equipped with capabilities such as those described in this section.

3. Report-driven conferencing

An enhancement to the workflow-driven paradigms described in the previous two sections might be as follows: XYZ Corporation's district managers have all been alerted to slowdowns in sales volume in the past three months in each part of the country, so *something* is going on. Is it the economy? Is it the inventory management process? Is stock not being replenished in a timely enough manner? Is a new competitor taking business away?

Everyone has seen their sales numbers, now it's time to do something about it. By integrating the data warehousing environment with facilities such as electronic conferencing, the managers would be able to

- Engage in real-time, on-line discussions regarding the problems they're encountering
- Send a video image of the one store in the Arizona region that did a test remodeling, and whose sales *increased* instead of decreasing. Everyone can then see what the Arizona district manager is pointing out as the key winning points, so they can quickly adjust their own store's layout

In general, the primary focus is enabling the user base to not only receive data and information about their performance, but to *efficiently* take action to exploit opportunities or overcome any deficiencies.

Why conferencing?

As with the examples earlier in this chapter, a variety of conferencing mechanisms (real-time, bulletin board-style, video, or still image) can greatly boost group productivity and, in the spirit of collaborative work processes, benefit the user community as a whole.

Risks and concerns

Very few, if any.

4. Feedback on usage—suggestions for modifications and enhancements

And finally, our last example: an ongoing electronic conference in which suggestions can be made for modifications and enhancements to the data warehousing and reporting environment. We will skip the details, as we've examined the conferencing paradigm several times in this chapter, but we wish to emphasize that even after an environment has been deployed (in contrast to the planning or development stages, as discussed earlier), it is desirable to provide easy-to-use feedback mechanisms for the user community.

Why electronic conferencing?

The asynchronous nature of the medium is particularly suitable for postings of suggestions, getting feedback from others, and driving each topic to some conclusion.

Risks and concerns

The only risk is *not* including such a mechanism in this environment.

Summary

This chapter wraps up our workgroup discussion with an inclusive look at one particular thread in the life of a fictional XYZ Corporation—the planning, development, deployment, and usage of a data warehousing environment—and how many different workgroup computing services can be used throughout the entire life cycle. You could take any other business process, not only IT-driven ones such as development of an application or a system, but ones such as a large-scale business process reengineering (BPR) effort, the decision to build a new business unit, or nearly anything else, and map the workflow and groupware services we've discussed in this book and in this chapter to the various functions of the task.

Once again, we wish to emphasize that while workgroup technology is maturing and becoming far more widespread than in years past, a key part of it successful usage lies in the underlying business culture. An organization may not follow the particular collaborative processes we discussed in Chapter 2—there are many other instantiations of the basic principles of finding new ways to work better and more efficiently—but the main point is that technology by itself is *not* a solution. This not only applies to workgroup technology but to data warehousing, client/server applications, and Internet-based applications; you name it, and culture is equally as important as the technology.

A

Workgroup computing products

Electronic mail and scheduling

Beyond Mail
Banyan Systems, Inc.
120 Flanders Rd.
Westboro, MA 01581

cc:Mail
Lotus Development Corp.
55 Cambridge Pkwy.
Cambridge, MA 02142

Emc2/TAO
Fischer International Systems Corp.
4073 Merchantile Ave.
Naples, FL 33942

GroupWise
WordPerfect Corp.
1555 North Technology Way
Orem, UT 84057-2399

Microsoft Mail
Microsoft Corp.
One Microsoft Way
Redmond, WA 98052

TeamWARE, ICL, Inc.
800 Central Expressway
Santa Clara, CA 95052

Electronic forms routing

FormFlow
Delrina Corp.
6830 Via Del Oro, Suite 240
San Jose, CA 95119

JetForms
JetForm Corp.
800 South St.
Waltham, MA 02154

Microsoft Electronic Forms
Microsoft Corp.
One Microsoft Way
Redmond, WA 98052

WordPerfect InForms
WordPerfect Corp.
1555 North Technology Way
Orem, UT 84057-2399

Workflow.2000/ Workflow.2020
Fischer International Systems Corp.
4073 Merchantile Ave.
Naples, FL 33942

Image processing

FileNet
FileNet Corp.
3565 Harbor Blvd.
Costa Mesa, CA 92626

IMAGEWorks
Bull HN Information Systems, Inc.
300 Concord Rd.
Billerica, MA 01821

KeyFile
KeyFile Corp.
22 Cotton Rd.
Nashua, NH 03063

OPEN/Image
Wang Laboratories, Inc.
One Industrial Ave.
Lowell, MA 01851

ViewStar
ViewStar Corp.
1101 Marina Village Pkwy.
Alameda, CA 94501

Document management

Documentum
Documentum, Inc.
4683 Chabot Dr., Suite 102
Pleasanton, CA 94588-2748

FileNet
FileNet Corp.
3565 Harbor Blvd.
Costa Mesa, CA 92626

Mezzanine/Document Manager
Saros Corp.
700 Plaza Center
10900 NE Eight St.
Bellevue, WA 98004

PC DOCS OPEN
PC DOCS, Inc.
124 Marriot Dr.
Tallahassee, FL 32301

SoftSolutions
WordPerfect Corp.
1555 North Technology Way
Orem, UT 84057-2399

WorkManager
Hewlett-Packard Company
Work Management Operation
3404 East Harmony Rd.
Fort Collins, CO 80525

Business process automation

ActionWorkflow Management System
Action Technologies, Inc.
1301 Marina Village Pkwy., Suite 100
Alameda, CA 94501

ProcessIT
AT&T Global Information Solutions
3245 Platt Springs Rd.
West Columbia, SC 29170

Lotus Notes
Lotus Development Corp.
55 Cambridge Pkwy.
Cambridge, MA 02142

OPEN/Workflow
Wang Laboratories, Inc.
One Industrial Ave.
Lowell, MA 01851

Quality At Work
Quality Decision Management
200 Sutton St., Suite 225
North Andover, MA 01845

Staffware(R)
Staffware Place
70 Walnut St.
Wellesley, MA 02181

FlowMaker
Workflow, Inc.
P.O. Box 896
Concordville, PA 19331

TeamWARE, ICL, Inc.
800 Central Expressway
Santa Clara, CA 95052

Business process analysis

ActionWorkflow Analyst
Action Technologies, Inc.
1301 Marina Village Pkwy.,
Suite 100
Alameda, CA 94501

BPwin
Logic Works, Inc.
1060 Route 206
Princeton, NJ 08540

Extend+BPR
Imagine That, Inc.
6830 Via Del Oro, Suite 230
San Jose, CA 95119

ProcessIT
AT&T Global Information Solutions
3245 Platt Springs Rd.
West Columbia, SC 29170

Process Vision
Antares Alliance Group
17304 Preston Rd., Suite 1200
Dallas, TX 75252

B

Lotus Notes products

Lotus Notes calendaring/scheduling products

@ScheduleBase
WorkFlow Designs, Inc.
14901 Quorum Dr., Suite 300
Dallas, TX 75240

Employee Locator
GroupQuest Software, Inc.
6709 La Tijera Blvd., Suite 221
Los Angeles, CA 90045

Express Schedule Link
Corporate Software, Inc.
1700 N Moore St., Suite 1705
Arlington, VA 22209

Group Scheduling Starter Kit
Synectic Systems Limited
411 Western Ave.
Brattlebro, VT 05301

Resonance
Ergo Training, Inc.
261 W 7 St.
New York, NY 10023

Resource Scheduler
McClurg Business Systems
6880 Corrine Dr., NW
Canton, OH 44718

W-6 Workflow Manager
IET Intelligent Electronics Ltd.
67 S Bedford St., Suite 400W
Burlington, MA 01803

Lotus Notes database access products

Enterprise Wide
TechSmith Corp.
3451 Dunckel Rd., Suite 200
Lansing, MI 48911

Foreign Exchange for Lotus Notes
Groupware Concepts, Inc.
4308 Village Green Dr.
Irving, TX 75038

HCS Exporter
Hayes Computer Systems, Inc.
1311-A Paul Russel Rd.
Tallahassee, FL 32301

InfoPump
Trinzic Corp.
One Harbour Place, Suite 500
Portsmouth, NH 03801

IntellAgents
Veritas Technologies, Inc.
12750 Merit Dr., Suite 830
Dallas, TX 75251-1241

Notrix
Percussion Software
222 Berkeley St., Suite 1620
Boston, MA 02116

Notrix Composer for EDA/SQL Version 1.0
Percussion Software
222 Berkeley St., Suite 1620
Boston, MA 02116

PW/Wire
Price Waterhouse
55 E Monroe, 30th Floor
Chicago, IL 60603

SMARTLINK 2000
VELOX Systems Corp.
555 Van Reed Rd.
Wyomissing, PA 19610

SQLWindows
Gupta Corp.
1060 Marsh Rd.
Menlo Park, CA 94025

Tandem Database Exchange for Lotus Notes
Transaction Innovation Corp.
60 Cuttermill Rd., Suite 614
Great Neck, NY 11021

VB/Link for Lotus Notes
Brainstorm Technologies, Inc.
24 Thorndike St., 4th Floor
Cambridge, MA 02141

ZMERGE Power Tool for Lotus Notes
Granite Software, Inc.
300 E Main St., Suite 207
Milford, MA 01757

Lotus Notes database administration products

Automated Test Facility
Softbridge, Inc.
ATF Sales & Marketing
125 Cambridge Park Dr.
Cambridge, MA 02140

DataFlow Replicator
Brainstorm Technologies, Inc.
24 Thorndike St., 4th Floor
Cambridge, MA 02141

Essential Tools for Lotus Notes
GroupQuest Software, Inc.
6709 La Tijera Blvd., Suite 221
Los Angeles, CA 90045

j&t Advanced Information Agent
J & T Associates, Inc.
571 Birkshire Dr., Suite 302
Saline, MI 48176

j&t Shell
J & T Associates, Inc.
571 Bircher Dr., Suite 302
Saline, MI 48176

Notrix/EDA Copy Manager for Lotus Notes
Information Builders
1250 Broadway
New York, NY 10001

Patient Tracking System
Management Directions, Inc.
6055 Primacy Pkwy., Suite 401
Memphis, TN 38119

Physician Electronic Record Clinical System (PERCS)
Management Directions, Inc.
6055 Primacy Pkwy., Suite 401
Memphis, TN 38119

Rapid Application Deployment and Development for Lotus Notes
Workgroup Productivity Corp.
2021 Midwest Rd.
Oak Brook, IL 60521-1342

Lotus Notes desktop accessory products

The Application Outliner for use with Lotus Notes
Cambridge Software Group, Inc.
101 Rodgers St., Suite 406
Cambridge, MA 02142

First Aid for Windows Users
CyberMedia Corp.
1800 Century Park E, Suite 1145
Los Angeles, CA 90067

The Interface Library for use with Lotus Notes
Cambridge Software Group, Inc.
101 Rodgers St., Suite 406
Cambridge, MA 02142

Lotus Notes dictionaries/ language products

3-D Keyboard
Exceller Software Corp.
2 Graham Rd. W
Ithaca, NY 14850

Key Into French
Exceller Software Corp.
2 Graham Rd. W
Ithaca, NY 14850

Key Into German
Exceller Software Corp.
2 Graham Rd. W
Ithaca, NY 14850

Key Into Italian
Exceller Software Corp.
2 Graham Rd. W
Ithaca, NY 14850

Key Into Spanish
Exceller Software Corp.
2 Graham Rd. W
Ithaca, NY 14850

Longman Dictionary of American English
Exceller Software Corp.
2 Graham Rd. W
Ithaca, NY 14850

Lotus Notes document management products

Access Disclosure
Disclosure, Inc.
888 Seventh Ave., 44th Floor
New York, NY 10106

Audience
Intermation
P.O. Box 2107
Redmond, WA 98073-2107

CADE Groupware
Microstar Software Limited
34 Colonade Rd. N
Nepean, Ontario
K2E 7J6 CANADA

Consulting, Training, and Custom Applications
Data Solutions Corp.
8930 State Rd. 84, Suite 790
Fort Lauderdale, LA 33324

CypherScan 1000
Cyphertech, Inc.
250 Caribbean Dr.
Sunnyvale, CA 94089

ILT Computer Output Management System
ILT Systems, Inc.
Two Penn Plaza
New York, NY 10121

KeyFile
KeyFile Corp.
22 Cotton Rd.
Nashua, NH 03063

Literature & Presentation Library Starter Kit
Synectic Systems Limited
411 Western Ave.
Brattleboro, VT 05301

MTR for Notes
NetConnect Systems
4200 Montrose, Suite 340
Houston, TX 77006

PaperFree
NotesBook
12 Blossom Rd., Suite 2
Rumson, NJ 07760

Patient Knowledge System
Digital AV
9715 Truckers Ln.
Knoxville, TN 37922

PC DOCS OPEN
PC DOCS, Inc.
124 Marriot Dr.
Tallahassee, FL 32301

Policies and Procedures Manual Starter Kit
Synectic Systems Limited
411 Western Ave.
Brattleboro, VT 05301

Real Estate Manager
InterPersonal Computing
20 Plymouth Rd., Suite 210
Darien, CT 06820-5721

Seqret
Docutech, Inc.
21519 NE 29th
Redmond, WA 98053

Technical Information/Solutions Library Starter Kit
Synectic Systems Limited
411 Western Ave.
Brattleboro, VT 05301

TRADECOM
21st Century Systems, Inc.
2393 N Allen Ave.
Altadena, CA 91001-2755

Virtual Forms
Computer Information Technology, Inc.
2136 Gallows Rd., Suite C
Dunn Loring, VA 22037

WIT—The API Library
Application Partners
120 Wood Ave. S
Iselin, NJ 08830

Lotus Notes application products

AdminQuest
GroupQuest Software, Inc.
6709 La Tijera Blvd., Suite 221
Los Angeles, CA 90045

ATTACK Real Estate Management System
Attack Systems, Inc.
111 Pine St., #950
San Francisco, CA 94111

BookQuest—The Online Book
GroupQuest Software, Inc.
6709 La Tijera Blvd., Suite 221
Los Angeles, CA 90045

BookQuest Review—The Group Review System
GroupQuest Software, Inc.
6709 La Tijera Blvd., Suite 221
Los Angeles, CA 90045

Call Center/Help Desk Software
D&G Infosystems, Inc.
148 Patterson Ave.
Hempstead, NY 11550

CamBridge CAD & Image Viewer
Teamwork Solutions
242 Reinhard Ave.
Columbus, OH 43206

CARTHAGE TODAY
Carthage International, Inc.
2501 Oak Lawn Ave., Suite 275
Dallas, TX 75219

Commerce 2.1
Jensen-Jones, Inc
Parkway 109 Office Center
328 Newman Springs Rd.
Red Bank, NJ 07701

Customer Service & Incident Tracking System
Concept Information Systems
2701 Summer St., Suite 200
Stamford, CT 06905

DOCMAN
ECS Associates, Inc.
20725 Western Ave, #113
Torrance, CA 90501

EKS—The Enterprise Knowledge Server
Metapraxis
900 Third Ave., 36th Floor
New York, NY 10022

EKS+ for Lotus Notes
Metapraxis
900 Third Ave., 36th Floor
New York, NY 10022

Forest & Trees
Trinzic Corp.
One Harbour Place, Suite 500
Portsmouth, NH 03801

GroupSystems for Windows
Ventana Corp.
1430 E Fort Lowell, Suite 301
Tucson, AZ 85719

Hotel Management Tools
Inn-formation Systems, Inc.
2481 Route 9
Fishkill, NY 12524

HRQuest* Human Resources Manager
GroupQuest Software, Inc.
6709 La Tijera Blvd., Suite 221
Los Angeles, CA 90045

SkillQuest—The Personnel Inventory
GroupQuest Software, Inc.
6709 La Tijera Blvd., Suite 221
Los Angeles, CA 90045

Student Attendance
Workgroup Technologies, Inc.
106 Hill Pkwy.
Middlebury, CT 06762

SupportQuest
GroupQuest Software, Inc.
6709 La Tijera Blvd., Suite 221
Los Angeles, CA 90045

Lotus Notes imaging products

CAD and Image Viewer
Cambridge Publishing Group, Inc.
1650 Lake Shore Dr., Suite 210
Columbus, OH 43204

ImageBasic for Lotus Notes
Edge Research, Inc.
One Harbour Place, Suite 455
Portsmouth, NH 03833

Imaging for Notes
Micronet Software Corp.
12520 Prosperity Dr., Suite 350
Silver Spring, MD 20904

Intelliscan
Pictronics Corp.
1475 Saratoga Ave., #160
San Jose, CA 95129

Liberty Information Management System
Alliance INFONET
1201 Dove St., Suite 410
Newport Beach, CA 92660

Lotus Notes mail products

cc:Pager
RJT Advanced Technologies
P.O. Box 10182
Burbank, CA 91510

Enterprise Messaging Audit
New England Systems
60 First Ave.
Waltham, MA 02154

j&t Mail Monitor
J & T Associates, Inc.
571 Bircher Dr., Suite 302
Saline, MI 48176

MailCheck
Baranof Software, Inc.
479 Washington St.
Brighton, MA 02135

MailWatch
Uniplex Integration Systems
Greenwich Office Park #1
Greenwich, CT 06831

The Meeting Room
Eden Systems Corp.
9402 N Meridian St.
Suite 350
Indianapolis, IN 46260

Nform
Q-M Consulting Group
141 Fifth Ave.
New York, NY 10010

Outside In
System Compatibility Corp.
410 N Wabash, #600
Chicago, IL 60611

PostalUnion for Lotus Notes
Information Electronics
520 West Lake Rd.
Hammondsport, NY 14840

Lotus Notes workflow products

Action_!
NotesBook
12 Blossom Rd., Suite 2
Rumson, NJ 07760

Action Workflow System
Action Technologies, Inc.
1301 Marina Village Pkwy.
Alameda, CA 94501

allClear for Windows
CLEAR Software, Inc.
385 Elliot St.
Newton, MA 02164

CM/1
Corporate Memory Systems, Inc.
8920 Business Park Dr.
Austin, TX 78759

Delrina FormFlow
Delrina Corp.
6830 Via Del Oro, Suite 240
San Jose, CA 95119

flowMAKER
Workflow, Inc.
135 Commons Ct.
Chadds Ford, PA 19317

JetForm Filler
JetForm
800 South St.
Waltham, MA 02154

Quality At Work
Quality Decision Management
200 Sutton St., Suite 225
North Andover, MA 01845

ViewStar Business Process
Automation Software
ViewStar Corp.
1101 Marina Village Pkwy.
Alameda, CA 94501

WorkMAN for Lotus Notes
Reach Software Corp.
872 Hermosa Dr.
Sunnyvale, CA 94086

Lotus Notes audio and video training materials

Personal Training for Lotus Notes
Personal Training Systems
173 Jefferson Dr.
Menlo Park, CA 94025

Lotus Notes Application Development:
Solving Business Problems and Increasing Competitiveness
The Knowledge Partnership, Inc.
708 N 1st St., Suite 237
Minneapolis, MN

Technology for Teams:
Enhancing Productivity in Networked Organizations
Susanna Opper & Associates
388 West Rd.
Alford, MA 01266-9756

Lotus Notes training resources

Advanced End User Computer Based Training
for Lotus Notes Release 3.0
Global Training Technologies, Inc.
1223 Wilshire Blvd., MS-196
Santa Monica, CA 90403

Lotus Notes 3.0 Modules I & II
ComputerPREP, Inc.
410 N 44th St., Suite 600
Phoenix, AZ 85008

NBT for Lotus Notes 3.0
ReCor
906 University Pl.
Evanston, IL 60201

End User Basics Computer Based Training Module for Lotus Notes Release 3.0
Global Training Technologies, Inc.
1223 Wilshire Blvd., MS-196
Santa Monica, CA 90403

Lotus Notes Basics
Comsell Training
3060 Peachtree Rd. NW, Suite 1500
Atlanta, GA 30305

QuickCards
Usability Sciences Corp.
5525 MacArthur Blvd., Suite 575
Irving, TX 75038

Regulatory Requirements Application
The Productivity Center, Inc.
5450 Northwest Central Dr., Suite 300
Houston, TX 77092

STEP Master
Software Quality Engineering
3000-2 Hartley Rd.
Jacksonville, FL 32257

Training for Lotus Note, AmiPro, 1-2-3, and Freelance
Atlanta Desktop
75 14th St., Suite 2500
Atlanta, GA 30309

TrainingTrax
Productivity Software Resources, Inc.
800 North Magnolia Ave, Suite 1305
Orlando, FL 32803

The Virtual College
New York University
48 Cooper Square
New York, NY 10003

Lotus Notes books

Developing Lotus Notes Applications
Carolyn Kraut
John Wiley & Sons, Inc.
605 Third Ave.
New York, NY 10158-0012

Lotus Notes Developer's Guide
Eric Rayl
Sams Publishing
201 West 103rd St.
Indianapolis, IN 46290

Quick Reference Guides for Lotus Notes, 1-2-3, AmiPro, and cc:Mail
DDC Publishing
14 East 38 St.
New York, NY 10016

Using Lotus SmartSuite
Que Corp.
201 West 103rd St.
Indianapolis, IN 4629

C

Workgroup computing resources

Note: Many of the resources listed below are available on the Internet from various universities and private companies. A Net search on groupware will provide a listing of information currently available.

Journals and professional publications

Applegate, L. M. "Technology support for cooperative work: A framework for studying introduction and assimilation in organizations." *Journal of Organizational Computing* 1 (1991): 11–39.

Benbasat, I., and L. Lim. "The effects of group, task, context and technology variables on the usefulness of group support systems: A meta-analysis of experimental studies." *Small Group Research* 24, no. 4 (1993): 430–462.

Benbasat, I., and B. R. Nault. "An evaluation of empirical research in managerial support systems." *Decision Support Systems,* Vol. 1 (1990): 203–226.

Chidambaram, L., R. Bostrom, and B. Wynne. "A longitudinal study of the impact of group decision support systems on group development." *Journal of Management Information Systems* 7, no. 3 (1990): 7–25.

Connolly, T., L. M. Jessup, and J. S. Valacich. "Effects of anonymity and evaluative tone on idea generation in computer mediated groups." *Management Science* 36, no. 6 (1990): 689–703.

Dennis, A., J. George, L. Jessup, J. Nunamaker, Jr., and D. Vogel. "Information technology to support electronic meetings." *MIS Quarterly* 12, no. 4 (1988): 591–624.

Dennis, A. R., J. F. Nunamaker, Jr., and D. Paranka. "Supporting the search for competitive advantage." *Journal of Management Information Systems* 8, no. 1 (1991): 5–36.

Dennis, A. R., J. F. Nunamaker, Jr., and D. R. Vogel. "A comparison of laboratory and field research in the study of electronic meeting systems." *Journal of Management Information Systems* 7, no. 3 (1990): 107–135.

Dennis, A. R., D. Vogel, J. Nunamaker, Jr., and A. Heminger. "Bringing automated support to large groups: The Burr Brown experience." *Information Management* Vol. 1 (1990): 111–121.

DeSanctis, G., and R. Gallupe. "A foundation for the study of group decision support systems." *Management Science* 33, no. 5 (1987): 589–609.

DeSanctis, G., and M. S. Poole. "Capturing the complexity in advanced technology use: Adaptive structuration theory." *Organization Science* 5, no. 2 (1994): 121–147.

DeSanctis, G., M. S. Poole, H. Lewis, and G. Desharnais. "Using computing in quality team meetings: Initial observations from the IRS-Minnesota project." *Journal of Management Information Systems* 8, no. 3 (1991), 7–26.

Dickson, G. W., J. L. Partridge, and L. H. Robinson. "Exploring modes of facilitative support for GDSS technology." *MIS Quarterly* 17, no. 2 (1993): 173–194.

Gallupe, R. B., A. R. Dennis, W. H. Cooper, J. S. Valacich, L. M. Bastianutti, and J. F. Nunamaker, Jr. "Electronic brainstorming and group size." *Academy of Management Journal* 35 (1992): 350–369.

Gallupe, R. B., and G. DeSanctis. "Computer-based support for group problem-finding: An experimental investigation." *MIS Quarterly* 12, no. 2 (1988): 276–296.

George, J., G. Easton, J. Nunamaker, Jr., and G. Northcraft. "A study of collaborative group work with and without computer-based support." *Information Systems Research* 1, no. 4 (1990): 394–415.

Gray, P., D. Vogel, and R. Beauclair. "Assessing GDSS empirical research." *European Journal of Operations Research* 46, no. 2 (1990): 163–176.

Grohowski, R., C. McGoff, D. Vogel, B. Martz, and J. F. Nunamaker, Jr. "Implementing electronic meeting systems at IBM: Lessons learned and success factors." *MIS Quarterly* 14 (1990): 369–383.

Hollingshead, A. B., J. E. McGrath, and K. M. O'Conner. "Group task performance and communication technology: A longitudinal study of computer-mediated versus face-to-face work groups." *Small Group Research* 24, no. 3 (1993): 307–333.

Huber, G. "Issues in the design of group decision support systems." *MIS Quarterly* 8, no. 3 (1984): 195–204.

Jessup, L., T. Connolly, and J. Galegher. "The effects on anonymity on GDSS group process with an idea generating task." *MIS Quarterly* 14 (1990): 313–321.

Kraemer, K., and J. King. "Computer-based systems for cooperative work and decision making." *ACM Computing Surveys* 20, no. 2 (1988): 115–146.

Lewis, L. F. "A decision support system for face to face groups." *Journal of Information Science* 13 (1987): 211–219.

McLeod, P. L., and J. K. Liker. "Electronic meeting systems: Evidence from a low structure environment." *Information Systems Research* 3, no. 3 (1992): 195–223.

Pinsonneault, A., and K. Kraemer. "The impact of technological support on groups: An assessment of the empirical research." *Decision Support Systems*, 5, no. 2 (1989): 197–216.

Poole, M. S., and G. DeSanctis. "Micro-level structuration in computer-supported group decision making." *Human Communication Research* 19, no. 1 (1992): 5–49.

Post, B. Q. "A business case framework for group support technology." *Journal of Management Information Systems* 9, no. 3 (1992): 7–26.

Sambamurthy, V., and M. S. Poole. "The effects of variations in capabilities of GDSS designs on management of cognitive conflict in groups." *Information Systems Research* 3, no. 3 (1992): 224–251.

Srinivasan Rao, V., and S. L. Jarvenpaa. "Computer support of groups: Theory-based models for GDSS research." *Management Science* 37, no. 10 (1991): 1347–1362.

Turoff, M., and S. Hiltz. "Computer support for group versus individual decisions." *IEEE Transactions on Communications* 39, no. 1 (1982): 82–90.

Valacich, J. S., A. R. Dennis, and T. Connolly. "Idea generation in computer-based groups: A new ending to an old story." *Organizational Behavior and Human Decision Processes* 57, no. 3 (1994): 448.

Watson, R. T., G. DeSanctis, and M. S. Poole. "Using a GDSS to facilitate group consensus: Some intended and unintended consequences." *MIS Quarterly* 12, no. 3 (1988): 463–478.

Zigurs, I., G. DeSanctis, and J. Billingsley. "Adoption patterns and attitudinal development in computer supported meetings: An exploratory study with SAMM." *Journal of Management Information Systems* 7, no. 4 (1991): 51–70.

Zigurs, I., and K. Kozar. "An exploratory study of roles in computer-supported groups." *MIS Quarterly* 4, no. 1 (1994): 277–297.

Zigurs, I., M. S. Poole, and G. DeSanctis. "A study of influence in computer-mediated group decision making." *MIS Quarterly* 12, no. 4 (1988): 625–644.

Books

Bostrom, R. P., R. Watson, and S. T. Kinney, eds. *Computer Augmented Teamwork: A Guided Tour.* Florence, Ky.: Van Nostrand Reinhold, 1993.

Dennis, A. R., and R. B. Gallupe. "A history of group systems empirical research: Lessons learned and future directions" in *Group Support Systems: New Perspectives*, L. M. Jessup and J. S. Valacich, eds., 59–77. New York: Macmillan Publishing Company, 1993 .

Jessup, L., and J. Valacich, eds. *Group Support Systems: New Perspectives.* New York: Macmillan, 1993.

Johansen, R. *Groupware: Computer Support for Business Teams.* New York: Free Press, 1988.

McGrath, J. E., and A. B. Hollingshead. *Groups Interacting With Technology: Ideas, Evidence, Issues, and an Agenda.* Thousand Oaks, Calif.: Sage Publications, 1994.

Glossary

AIX An IBM UNIX operating system.

American National Standard Code for Information Interchange (ASCII) The code developed by the American National Standards Institute for information exchange among data processing systems, data communications systems, and associated equipment.

American National Standards Institute (ANSI) The principle standards development body supported by over 1000 trade organizations, professional societies, and companies. The United States' member body to the ISO (International Standards Organization).

application programming interface (API) A set of interfaces through which applications programs can communicate with various types of services. APIs are used primarily in client/server computing to allow applications to interact with each other.

AS/400 An IBM midrange computer system.

asynchronous transmission Transmission in which the time of occurrence of the start of each character, or block of characters, is arbitrary. Also known as start-stop transmission.

binary large object (BLOB) A data object used to store large amounts (up to several megabytes) of binary information. Typically used to store images in databases.

BPS Bits per second.

bridge Hardware and software used to interconnect local area networks.

business process A series of steps or operations that support a key business function.

business process reengineering (BPR) A methodology by which business processes are analyzed and redesigned to become more efficient, less costly, or more responsive.

byte A binary element string functioning as a unit. Eight-bit bytes are most common. Also called a "character."

CASE (computer-aided software engineering) Automated tools used to aid in the software development process.

CCITT The International Consultative Committee for Telephone and Telegraph, the committee responsible for establishing e-mail and directory standards.

central processing unit (CPU) The main processor used to execute instructions in a computer.

client/server computing A computing architecture in which the computing process is divided between a client platform and a server platform.

COBOL (common business oriented language) A high-level programming language, based on English, that is used primarily for commercial data processing.

common user access (CUA) The user interface portion of IBM's SAA enterprise architecture.

communication protocol The rules governing the exchange of information between devices on a data link.

compound document A document that contains information created by using more than one application.

customer information control system for virtual storage (CICS/VS) A licensed program that operates on a host system, such as System/370, 30xx, or 43xx, which can be used in a communications network.

database A collection of interrelated or independent data items to serve one or more applications.

database management system (DBMS) A structured software component designed to coordinate and facilitate management of data for multiple applications. DBMS products usually conform to one of several models (hierarchical, network, relational, or object-oriented).

DB2 An IBM relational database management system.

DOS See MS-DOS.

downloading The process of sending software or data from a central source to remote stations.

dumb terminal Terminals that are connected to a central processor and do not possess any processing capability.

dynamic data exchange (DDE) A Windows feature that provides a way to transfer data between Windows applications.

dynamic-link libraries (DLL) A Windows feature that enables code modules to be loaded on demand and linked when run.

emulation The imitation of a computer system, performed by a combination of hardware and software, that allows a workstation to act as a terminal or other device attached to a host system.

enterprise computing The goal of seamless integration of applications, data, user interfaces, and other computing resources among distributed heterogeneous systems of all sizes.

Ethernet A bus local area network developed by Digital Equipment Corporation, Intel, and Xerox. Ethernet formed the basis for the IEEE 802.3 standard.

extended binary-coded decimal interchange code (EBCDIC) A coded character set of 256 eight-bit characters used primarily in IBM environments.

gateway Hardware and software used to interconnect local area networks to other systems, usually midrange or mainframe computers.

giga Ten to the ninth power (109) or 1,000,000,000 in decimal notation.

graphical user interface (GUI) A user interface for a terminal or PC built around menus, windows, and pointing devices. Microsoft Windows, OSF Motif, Sun Open Look, and OS/2 Presentation Manger are examples of GUIs.

hierarchical network A network in which processing and control functions are performed at several levels by computers specially suited for the functions performed.

high-level language (HHL) A programming language, such as RPG, CL, BASIC, PL/I, Pascal, and COBOL, that translates computer programs in that language into several different machine codes.

IEEE (Institute of Electrical and Electronic Engineers) An international professional society that issues its own standards and is a member of ANSI and ISO.

information warehouse An IBM-distributed database management architecture under SAA.

input/output (I/O) Pertaining to a device or to a channel that is involved in an input process and, at a different time, in an output process.

International Standards Organization (ISO) An organization established to promote the development of standards to facilitate the international exchange of goods and services, and to develop mutual cooperation in areas of intellectual, scientific, technological, and economic activity.

kilo (K) Thousand.

local area network (LAN) A data communications system confined to a limited geographic area with moderate to high data rates (100 Kbps to 100 Mbps). The area served may consist of a single building, a cluster of buildings, or a campus-type arrangement. The network uses some type of switching technology and does not use common carrier circuits, although it may have gateways or bridges to other public or private networks.

log-off The procedure by which a user ends a terminal session.

log-on The procedure by which a user begins a terminal session.

mail gateway Hardware and/or software that interconnects two or more dissimilar mail systems. This usually involves reformatting the mail message to the required format of the destination system.

mainframe A large-scale, centralized, computer system.

mega Ten to the sixth power (106), or 1,000,000 in decimal notation.

megahertz (MHz) A unit of measure of frequency. 1 MHz = 1,000,000 hertz.

message handling system A messaging protocol promoted by Novell Inc.

message transfer agents The X.400 components that store and forward e-mail in an enterprise environment.

message transfer system A collection of message transfer agents.

MIPS Million instructions per second.

modem A functional unit that modulates and demodulates signals. One of the functions of a modem is to enable digital data to be transmitted over analog transmission facilities, or common telephone lines.

MOTIF A GUI environment from OSF.

MS-DOS An operating system from Microsoft that has been the dominant operating system of IBM personal computers and compatibles.

MS Windows Microsoft Windows, a GUI environment for desktop PCs.

MVS An IBM operating system.

network file system (NFS) A standardized file sharing and transfer facility used in UNIX environments.

Office Vision An IBM office information system that operates under SAA.

Open Software Foundation A consortium of vendors founded with the goal of promoting open systems and standardized UNIX facilities for information systems.

open systems Environments that adhere to a set of commonly accepted standards rather than a proprietary architecture.

open systems interconnection (OSI) The use of standardized procedures to enable the interconnection of data processing systems in networks.

operating system Software that controls the execution of programs. An operating system can provide services such as resource allocation, scheduling, input/output control, and data management.

ORACLE A relational database management system from Oracle Corp.

OS/2 An IBM PC operating system and graphical user interface.

OS/400 An IBM operating system for the AS/400 computer.

OSF/1 The UNIX offering from the Open Software Foundation.

password A unique string of characters that a program, computer operator, or user must supply to meet security requirements before gaining access to data.

peer-to-peer networking A network in which nodes communicate with each other as peers rather than in a hierarchical relationship.

PROFS (professional office system) An IBM office information system product.

protocol A specification for the format and relative timing of information exchanged between communicating parties.

RISC (reduced instruction set computing/computer) RISC is an architecture style under which various processors have been developed.

server One of the components in client/server computing. Generally the server runs the database management system or other shared applications.

simple mail transfer protocol (SMTP) The TCP/IP standard protocol for transferring e-mail between platforms.

structured query language (SQL) The standard, widely accepted relational database management language, developed by IBM, that is used in varying forms by most vendors of relational database management system products.

systems network architecture (SNA) An IBM architecture that describes the logical structure, formats, protocols, and operational sequences for transmitting information units through and controlling the configuration and operation of networks.

TCP/IP (transmission control protocol/Internet protocol) A protocol set, originally developed for U.S. Department of Defense environments, used for specific layers of a multilayer communication protocol suite.

terminal A device in a system or network at which data can either be entered or displayed.

time sharing A method that allows several interactive terminals to use one computer.

token-ring network A local area network that sends data in one direction throughout a specified number of locations by using the symbol of authority for control of the transmission line, called a token, to allow any sending station in the network (ring) to send data when the token arrives at that location.

transaction In systems with time sharing, an exchange between a terminal and another device that accomplishes a particular action or result; for example, the entry of a customer's deposit and the updating of the customer's balance.

UNIX An operating system developed by AT&T that has become a de facto standard in the computer industry. Multiple variants are available from various consortia and vendors.

user Anyone who requires the services of a computer system.

user identification (user ID) The name used to associate the user profile with a user when he or she signs on the system.

user password A unique string of characters that a system user must enter to identify him- or herself to the system, if the system resources are secured.

X.25 A CCITT standard protocol for network communications.

X.400 A CCITT standard that provides a set of protocols for e-mail.

X.500 A CCITT standard for directory services.

X/Open An open systems consortium.

X Windows A GUI environment that is the basis of MOTIF.

wide area network (WAN) A communications network similar to a local area network, covering a larger geographical area.

Windows See MS Windows.

Windows NT A 32-bit operating system and graphical user interface.

workgroup computing A computing environment is which a group works collaboratively on a project or business process.

workstation A device used to transmit information to or receive information from a computer; for example, a display station or printer.

write once read many (WORM) An optical storage medium in which data is written in an unalterable form.

3GL Third-generation language. COBOL, FORTRAN, C, or any one of a number of other procedural languages.

4GL Fourth-generation language. An "advanced" language usually found in vendor-specific environments. 4GLs usually feature reporting and querying facilities, advanced file and data management, and other capabilities that traditionally must be created by developers in 3GL environments.

Index

Boldface numbers indicate illustrations.

About the authors

Alan R. Simon is the author of *How to Be a Successful Computer Consultant*, 3rd edition (McGraw-Hill), and many other professional computing titles. He is a consultant who specializes in emerging technology areas. Simon works in New Jersey.

William Marion is on the faculty of the information systems department of Golden Gate University in San Francisco. He has more than 16 years of experience in information systems. The author of *Client/Server Strategies* (McGraw-Hill), Marion holds a B.S. in computer information systems from Arizona State University and a master's in information systems from City University.